Guide to the Recom

COUNTRY INNS
of the Midwest

"With an eye for detail and a talent for description, Bob Puhala has searched out and chosen some of the best in the Midwest. . . . A reference you will want to add to your travel library."
—Norman Strasma, *Inn Review*

"Reading Bob Puhala's *Guide to the Recommended Country Inns of the Midwest* is like asking a good friend for vacation advice. He gets right to the heart of the matter and tells you exactly what you want to know. The book is comprehensive, well researched, and written in a warm, chatty, and highly readable style."
—M. Eileen Brown, travel editor, *The Daily Herald*, Arlington Heights, Illinois

"This guide certainly conveys the warmth and friendliness of Minnesota's country inns, providing detailed, accurate descriptions that tempt the traveler in search of personal, unique country visits."
—Joan Hummel, Minnesota Office of Tourism

The "Guide to the Recommended Country Inns" Series

"The guidebooks in this new series of recommended country inns are sure winners. Personal visits have ensured accurate and scene-setting descriptions. These beckon the discriminating traveler to a variety of interesting lodgings."
—*Norman Strasma, publisher of* Inn Review *newsletter*

The "Guide to the Recommended Country Inns" series is designed for the discriminating traveler who seeks the best in unique accommodations away from home.

From hundreds of inns personally visited and evaluated by the author, only the finest are described here. The inclusion of an inn is purely a personal decision on the part of the author; no one can pay or be paid to be in a Globe Pequot inn guide.

Organized for easy reference, these guides point you to just the kind of accommodations you are looking for: Comprehensive indexes by category provide listings of inns for romantic getaways, inns for the sports-minded, inns that serve gourmet meals . . . and more. State maps help you pinpoint the location of each inn, and detailed driving directions tell you how to get there.

Use these guidebooks with confidence. Allow each author to share his or her selections with you and then discover for yourself the country inn experience.

Editions available:
Guide to the Recommended Country Inns of
New England • Mid-Atlantic States and Chesapeake Region
West Coast • South • Midwest
Rocky Mountain Region • Texas and the Southwest

Guide to the Recommended
COUNTRY INNS
of the Midwest

Illinois • Indiana • Iowa
Michigan • Minnesota • Missouri
Ohio • Wisconsin

by Bob Puhala
illustrated by Bill Taylor Jr.

A Voyager Book

The Globe Pequot Press

Chester, Connecticut 06412

Library of Congress Cataloging in Publication Data

Puhala, Bob.
    Guide to the recommended country inns of the Midwest.

    (The "Guide to the recommended country inns" series)
    Includes index.
        1. Hotels, taverns, etc.—Middle West—Directories.
2. Bed and breakfast accommodations—Middle West—
Directories. I. Title. II. Series.
TX907.P86 1987   647'.957701   86-31954
ISBN 0-87106-814-1 (pbk.)

Manufactured in the United States of America
First Edition/First Printing

Contents

Indexes

For my wife, Debbie, who lovingly shared late nights working on the manuscript, grueling long-distance road trips, and lots of inn-credible fun; for Baby Kate, three months old and already a veteran Midwest inn hopper; my Pa, for packing his bags and traveling with me for more than 4,100 miles' worth of inn wanderings—and making the research infinitely more fun just by his presence; my Ma, for her love, unending encouragement, and frequent baby-sitting sessions with her new granddaughter.

I love all you guys.

How This Guide Is Arranged

Country inns, historic hotels, and outstanding B&Bs are listed state by state, and alphabetically by city, town, and village within each state. You'll find them in the following order: Illinois, Indiana, Iowa, Michigan, Minnesota, Missouri, Ohio, and Wisconsin. Preceding each state grouping is a map guide and handy index. There's also a complete index at the end of the book.

Helpful guidebook features are the special inn indexes. These list particularly noteworthy inn activities and features. They will help you select the inn that's right for you.

The ☞ ☞ in the text indicate special inn features, interesting details, and not-to-miss inn highlights. They do *not* suggest any kind of rating system. They've been thoughtfully inserted into the text to ensure that you do not miss those extra touches that make inn-hopping so special.

When you see a "B" (it stands for Bob) at the end of an inn selection, it means that I felt compelled to add one last personal comment before moving on.

There is no charge of any kind for an inn to be included in this guidebook. I have chosen inns based on my professional and personal standards to give readers a choice among the finest, most interesting, and historic accommodations available in the Midwest. I welcome comments, questions, and information about your favorite inn—whether or not it's included in my selections—or newly opened and soon-to-be-opened inns. Please address all correspondence to Bob Puhala, *Guide to the Recommended Country Inns of the Midwest*, The Globe Pequot Press, Box Q, Chester, Connecticut 06412.

Things You Should Know Before Choosing an Inn

Rates: Inns often change their rates without notice. The range of prices I have quoted is meant to be used only as a guideline to give you a reasonable idea of what a room might cost. Also, I haven't included tax rates or service charges, which add to your bill; neither have I described tipping suggestions. Inquire upon making reservations.

Menus: As quickly as prices change, menus change even faster. An inn that offers a particular specialty may change chefs, and thus, its entire entrée list. More inns are constantly adjusting their breakfast policies, some offering full breakfasts one season, then continental or buffet-style breakfasts the next. Ask so you know what to expect.

Innkeepers: Some inns remain in the same family for decades. More often, they change ownership on a frequent basis. This might result in entire revisions of previous inn policies. Or inns might completely close their doors to the public as they convert to private residences. Be sure to call ahead.

Reservations and Deposits: Many inns maintain such a sterling reputation of excellence and service that they require reservations made long in advance. A northern Wisconsin inn once suggested that people call at least eight months in advance! Of course, that's an exception rather than the rule, but it is advisable to call at least one month in advance at most inns, especially if you're planning to visit during the high-volume travel season (usually summer). Smaller establishments may require even more advance notice. And if you wish to stay at an inn during annual town festivals, no time can be too soon.

On the other hand, it's always possible to make reservations with short notice—possible, but not very likely.

As for deposits, this is such a common requirement that I do not mention specific inn policies. Assume that with few exceptions, you'll be required to pay a deposit to reserve a room, using a personal check or credit card. Be sure to inquire about refund policies.

Credit Cards: Visa and MasterCard are accepted unless otherwise stated. Many inns accept additional credit cards, too. Others accept only cash or personal checks. Call ahead to be sure.

Children: If I've spotted a trend in the Midwest, it's that an increasing number of inns do not allow children. In each inn selection, I've noted the policy.

Pets: Spot usually won't be allowed inside. The rule: No pets unless otherwise stated.

Minimum Stay: Two-night minimums on weekends and even three nights during holidays are requirements at some inns, as noted. This is a frequently changing policy.

Bed Size: Inns may use three-quarter beds, twins, doubles, queens, or kings. While a few historic selections may offer antique rope beds or other fanciful contraptions, exotica is usually not a worry. If you have a preference, make it known in advance.

Television and Air Conditioning: Are you the type of person who loves to travel into the heart of the wilderness but still must get a nightly fix of David Letterman? Were you born to live in air-conditioned rooms? If so, make sure you ask ahead.

Food for Thought: A number of B&Bs are included in my selections. Oftentimes, innkeepers will keep on hand dinner menus from area restaurants for guests to look over. At the least, the innkeeper will inquire about your food preferences and suggest an appropriate eatery. Most of the time, choices range from the casual to fine dining.

If you have any special dietary requirements, you should realize that special requests often are considered by inn restaurants. Vegetarians will usually be able to find seafood and fowl entrée selections.

Therefore, if I don't mention restaurants as part of my inn descriptions, be assured that your hosts will advise you.

Wheelchair Access: Inns do not have wheelchair access or facilities for the disabled unless noted.

Bad Habits: More inns than ever prohibit smoking in guest rooms or common areas. I've noted when that's the case.

A Special Inn-vitation to You

Searching for the perfect country inn is my personal "Holy Grail" quest. That's because I love inns, and it's not just because I met my wife while we were staying in different inns on the rugged Door County peninsula of northeastern Wisconsin. Well, maybe a little bit.

I love inns because of all the people I meet. Innkeepers are friendly hosts and everyday people—teachers, lawyers, fishermen, professional chefs, farmers, ex-soldiers, homemakers, armchair philosophers—who tackle the day-to-day hassles of running an historic hostelry mostly for the pleasure of making travelers feel as though there's a little bit of home awaiting them no matter where they go. They have to love their innkeeping role; the work's too hard for any other reason to make sense.

And then there are the fellow guests, who are infinitely more friendly at inns. They talk to one another; yes, they really do! They express a genuine interest in the world around them: a special drive to experience new things, explore the past, or relive a little part of history.

My search for the best Midwestern country inns, historic hotels, and outstanding B&Bs was exhaustive. I repeatedly criss-crossed the interstates, country highways, and back roads of eight states, traveling almost 12,250 miles by car, and several thousand more by plane, to offer you the very best that America's heartland has to offer.

I personally visited nearly 300 inns, comparing guest rooms, talking with innkeepers, probing guests for honest impressions, sampling food, sleeping in the beds, walking the grounds, and exploring the towns.

Finally, I'm recommending 152 of them to you.

The rewards of my journeys are many: an elegant Victorian mansion in an historic rough-and-tumble river town; inns where magnificent Great Lakes sunsets bathe rooms in a fiery glow and where bass are caught just off your patio; heavy-beamed log lodges that overlook Canadian wilderness, nestle on a world-class white-water rapids river, or are tucked deep into the Ozark Mountain foothills; places where eagle and osprey soar overhead, or where you can help tap sap from a grove of maple trees; even an inn that rents pussycats to make guests feel more at home.

So many choices. That's why I find it impossible to come up with an acceptable definition of a country inn. It's an elastic concept, especially here in the Midwest.

I do believe that an inn is an inn if it has a certain . . . something—atmosphere, inherent charm, historical significance, interesting architectural style, spectacular location, feeling . . . soul.

Some inns have always served the traveler. Many relied on stagecoach or steamboat passengers to fill up their rooms; others called the railroad their best friend.

Some were magnificent private homes, playgrounds for local notables now almost forgotten; others were spacious summer retreats, used to escape scorching Midwest sunshine by perching on lakes and coaxing cool breezes to the shore. Still more were merchant buildings, grist mills, once-grand hotels, modest frontier homes. . . .

Whatever, they're all country inns, and they all have something special and exciting to offer the traveler.

I wouldn't be surprised if someday we bumped into each other at your favorite country inn. See you then.

Bob

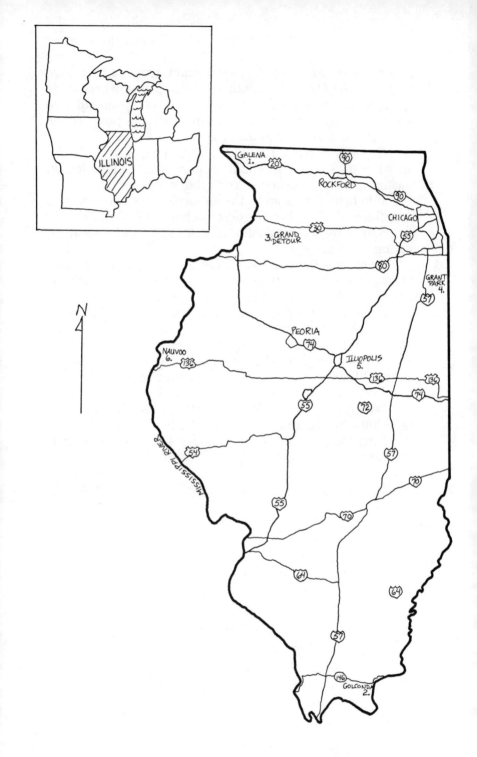

Illinois

Numbers on map refer to towns numbered below.

Aldrich Guest House
Galena, Illinois
61036

Innkeeper: Judy Green
Address/Telephone: 900 Third Street; (815) 777–3323
Rooms: 4; 3 with private bath.
Rates: $50 to $60; singles, seniors, subtract $5. Full breakfast included with room. Children over 6 OK.
Open: All year.
Facilities & Activities: All the historic attractions of the old lead-mining town of Galena, including the U.S. Grant home and scores of antique, specialty, and art shops.

I never expected innkeeper Judy Green to greet me at the door of the Aldrich Guest House and then come out to my car and help me inside with my bags. But that's just the start of all the pampering guests receive here.

The Aldrich Guest House, an elegant 1853 Greek Revival mansion with Italianate touches, is part of the Galena legend of hometown-boy-made-good U.S. Grant. Tales say that Grant mustered his Civil War troopers on the "green" next to the home. So I sat on the inn's screened porch, gazing at the expansive yard, trying hard to imagine the stoical

2

figure of the bearded general drilling his ragtag army collection of Illinois farmboys, readying them for furious battle.

Judy uses Victorian hues—green, mauve, and white—to brighten her delightful guest house. I especially like the parlor's tall, wide windows that wash the room in sunny daylight. There's a baby grand piano in the corner; I tested it by playing three chords of a Billy Joel love song.

A broad fluted oak banister heads the stairway leading to the second-floor guest rooms. Judy led me to mine, and I immediately felt like the proverbial bull in the china shop. It was quite beautiful—soft pastel colors offset by white wicker furniture and an antique lace quilt gracing my bed. Old-fashioned pull-chain commodes in some of the bathrooms add to the feeling of historic authenticity.

However, my favorite is the Cyrus Aldrich Room, the oldest part of the house. Judy said that it was the home's sleeping loft, now charmingly decorated but still with its original plank floor, slanting roof, and tiny sliding window intact.

Breakfast here is a treat. There was lots of chatter among couples from the Chicago area, Brooklynites, and even a doctor and his family from Rhode Island, all gathered around a long dining-room table. Fresh flowers, balloon-style draperies, and fancy china place settings all harkened back to a more elegant era.

Then came the food: delicious quiche, hot homemade bread, fresh fruit, eggs, and sausage. And Judy's home-baked coffeecake makes you forget about your waistline. She also will recommend restaurants to suit your dinner tastes; I found the Kingston Inn to be just about everybody's Galena favorite.

How to get there: Take U.S. 20 (across the bridge toward U.S. Grant's house) to Third Street. Turn left and go to the end of the block to the inn.

🌾

B: *After a night of fun conversation, I found that my bedcovers had been turned down and a chocolate mint placed on my pillow. Just some more pampering.*

3

The Bedford House
Galena, Illinois
61036

Innkeeper: Linda K. Pluym
Address/Telephone: Route 20 West; (815) 777–2043
Rooms: 4; all with private bath.
Rates: $48 to $61. Includes continental breakfast. Children welcome. No credit cards.
Open: All year.
Facilities & Activities: All historic Galena attractions nearby: U.S. Grant home, the Galena National Historic District, special fall and winter tours of historic houses. Scores of antique and specialty shops, numerous city festivals, acres of parkland, and countryside featuring hills and limestone bluffs.

Linda is one sharp businesswoman. She owns The Bedford House, The Ryan Mansion, and a small motel that sits unobtrusively on property between the two. But she's also a dedicated country-inn lover who's immersed herself in the task of restoring the historic properties that are so much a part of Galena's legacy.

The Bedford House is a small 1850 clapboard home that sits on the crest of a hill surrounded by majestic pine trees on what once was the estate of a prominent local attorney.

I liked it right away. I walked through 🖙 original double entryway doors, made with heavy leaded glass, into a hallway adorned with a fine chandelier and dominated by a gold Victorian dressing mirror. Straight ahead was a beautiful walnut staircase with clean, simple lines leading to the second-floor guest rooms.

I climbed the stairs and found charming antique furnishings in bright, airy rooms with many windows. The blue-and-white floral wall coverings gave me more of that cheery feeling I had as soon as I'd seen the house from the side of the road. Ceiling fans turn overhead to provide welcome breezes on hot Midwestern days (although all rooms are air-conditioned).

🖙 Queen-sized four-poster brass beds, rocking chairs, and brass lamps add to the "country gentleman" charm. And I discovered my favorite spot. There's a little sun room up here, with 🖙 French doors that open onto a small balcony. Even on a sassy spring day, I stood outside and let the sun warm me over. This is a great spot for lazy summer sunlovers.

Linda serves guests a continental breakfast—rolls, juice, and coffee. For heartier choices, you have a wide selection of eateries downtown. She'll be happy to make dinner suggestions, as well.

How to get there: Take U.S. 20 west into Galena. The inn is just on the edge of town off the highway.

B: *A touch of elegance in a small historic country home.*

Belle-Aire Mansion
Galena, Illinois
61036

Innkeepers: Evelyn and James Nemecek
Address/Telephone: 11410 Route 20 West; (815) 777–0893
Rooms: 4; 1 with private bath.
Rates: $40 to $50. Includes full breakfast. Well-behaved children only; small pets OK. No credit cards.
Open: All year.
Facilities & Activities: Expansive lawn and back yard. Near all the historic attractions of Galena, including the home of U.S. Grant.

Up a long, stately driveway lined with towering pine trees is a sparkling white home that's a fine example of nineteenth-century Federal architecture. Its graceful white pillars, clean lines, and generous second-story porch suggest antebellum influences.

But inside, the mood is less formal. You're likely to find Evelyn baking goodies in her kitchen and calling out to her husband, Jim (doing endless yard work to maintain the finely manicured look of a country estate), that "company's just arrived."

6

That's how Evelyn greeted me on my recent visit. She'd just finished baking some nut bread and offered me a hot slice. "If you're on the lean side, I try to fatten you up during your stay," Evelyn joked. And that's just what she did to me.

Evelyn's quite proud of her home, and she showed me the elegant sitting and dining rooms appointed with ornate furniture. The guest rooms include more subdued Victorian pieces: marble-topped dressers and even an 8-foot-high walnut headboard on the bed.

Evelyn made the hand-crocheted bedspreads, and she sees to it that guests feel like part of the family during their stay. You can even raid the refrigerator or dip your hand into a "bottomless" cookie jar.

If it's a home-cooked breakfast you want, Evelyn will whip up a dandy. Eggs, bacon, and some of her sweet-tooth treats will give you the energy to explore this historic town with its winding, tiered streets and antique shops. She'll be happy to recommend dinner spots, with the Kingston Inn rated tops.

How to get there: The home is on the outskirts of Galena, right off U.S. 20 west.

⌛

B: *The back yard overlooks farmlands that stretch on and on.*

Colonial Guest House
Galena, Illinois
61036

Innkeeper: Mary C. Keller
Address/Telephone: 1004 Park Avenue; (815) 777–0336
Rooms: 4, with 1 penthouse; all with private bath.
Rates: $35 single, $40 double. Breakfast sometimes included with
    room. Children OK. Wheelchair access. No credit cards.
Open: All year.
Facilities & Activities: Just a short walk from all the historic attrac-
    tions, antique and specialty shops, and art galleries of this
    well-preserved mid-1800s town.

If I'd been here just a few weeks earlier, I'd have seen
beautiful models, bearded directors, and an entire crew of
video technicians filming a blue-jeans commercial right on
the porch of this 1826, twenty-one-room mansion. But that's
nothing unusual, Mary told me. It seems the Colonial Guest
House is a favorite of inn hoppers and the media alike. Its
roster of guests includes many newspaper and local TV-news
notables, and it was even featured on a "P.M. Magazine"
television segment.

It's easy to see why. Mary has successfully established a

true Victorian atmosphere at her inn. (Don't be put off by the small antique shop at the entrance. The upstairs guest rooms are a world away from the collectibles-jammed store, and they provide a quiet retreat from the bustle of busy Galena.)

Besides guest rooms that are furnished with authentic period furniture like high walnut headboards and delicate lace bedcovers, the second-floor sitting rooms are exquisite. Mary proudly pointed out her elaborate silver service that she sometimes uses to serve winter guests warming cups of coffee and tea.

And the parlor looks just like my grandma's big parlor in my old neighborhood: rich red Oriental rugs, crystal chandeliers, curvy Victorian sofas and chairs, period print wallpaper, and a marble fireplace.

Mary has lived here for more than forty years and has been running the house as an inn for nearly three decades. She still marvels at some of the crazy architectural designs.

"I've got eleven outside doors, eight staircases, a long outside porch, and little ones upstairs for the guest rooms," she told me. "My ceilings are 9 feet high downstairs, and 11 feet high on the second and third floors."

Why's that?

"In 1846, they jacked up the building and built another floor underneath the second and third. Can you beat that?"

Mary doesn't get around as well as she used to, so she is not always able to serve the breakfast of juice, coffee, and rolls. But she is happy to recommend food spots. She likes the Farmers' Home Hotel for hearty, inexpensive breakfasts, and she recommends the Kingston Inn for elegant dinners.

I noticed that the only inn items out of character with the rest of the décor are what Mary calls "just comfortable chairs" in the guest rooms. "People tramp around Galena all day; they want to come to a room with a good davenport and lounge chair."

That's plain talk, but it's also the plain truth.

How to get there: From Chicago, take the Northwest Tollway (I–90) to U.S. 20 and continue west into Galena. Just before the bridge, turn left on Park Avenue. The inn is on the left side of the street.

The Comfort Guest House
Galena, Illinois
61036

Innkeepers: Tom and Connie Sola
Address/Telephone: 1000 Third Street; (815) 777–3062
Rooms: 3, sharing 2 full baths.
Rates: $40 first night, $30 second night. Includes hearty country breakfast. No children. No credit cards.
Open: All year.
Facilities & Activities: Drive or walk across bridge over Galena River to historic sites, antique and specialty shops, and art galleries in a architecturally preserved Civil War–era town.

Tom and Connie have owned the 1856 Comfort Guest House for only a short time, but already this inn near the Fever (Galena) River has established itself as a comfortable place to stay while exploring historic Galena.

The young couple have named guest rooms for spirits—the alcoholic kind, that is. "When we first moved in here, Connie constantly would tell me to move cartons upstairs to the bedroom," Tom told me. "I always said, 'Which one? We have three, you know.' Finally, I just decided that they needed names. Saved me lots of extra walking."

The Wine Room is Tom's favorite, decorated in deep burgundy colors and graced with antique furnishings, including a ☞ red-and-white striped hand-tied bed quilt that was so beautiful I wanted to take it home with me. Connie is thoroughly knowledgeable about all the antique furnishings, and she told me that the design became popular in England during the mid-1800s.

She's something of a quilting expert and has personally designed and made by hand the attractive quilts that brighten each guest room.

The Champagne Room is done is soothing beiges and has an iron-rail bed, long blue drapes, and a tall bay window looking out onto the tree-lined street. I found it airy and inviting.

In the Ale Room, a ☞ huge brass bed seems to invite you to jump right on it. Lace curtains on two big windows, charming wall borders, and an unusual basket-weave quilt add to the lighthearted atmosphere.

Hearty, healthful breakfasts of granola, seasonal fruit platters, muffins, breads, juices, and other beverages are served in the dining room, decorated with crown ceiling moldings, a brass chandelier, and with the inn's only fireplace, made of fine marble.

"That fireplace is another story," Tom said as he ran his hand along the marble mantel. "This home belonged to a local banker who insured riverboats that ran the Fever River and the Mississippi. The captains reciprocated by presenting him with marble carried as freight on their ships. And that's how our home got its marvelous hearth."

Tom and Connie, gourmets of some note, will recommend the town's best restaurants for discriminating tastes. They both agree that the Kingston Inn offers Galena's finest dining experience. Specialties include *cioppino*, seafood served in a spicy tomato-based sauce; redfish and fettuccine; with French silk chocolate pie and homemade strawberry cheesecake for dessert.

How to get there: From Chicago, take the Northwest Tollway (I-90) to U.S. 20 and continue west into Galena. Before you cross the bridge, turn left on third Street. The inn is on the corner.

DeSoto House
Galena, Illinois
61036

Innkeeper: Lev Blaha
Address/Telephone: 230 South Main Street; (815) 777–0090
Rooms: 55, with 2 suites; all with private bath.
Rates: Rooms: $65 to $85 single, $75 to $95 double. Suites: $100 to $180 single, $110 to $190 double. Special weekend packages. Children OK. Wheelchair access.
Open: All year.
Facilities & Activities: Two full-service restaurants, bar, indoor courtyard, courtyard specialty shops. Right on Main Street in historic Galena. Tour home of U.S. Grant; see preserved Civil War architecture; visit specialty shops and museums.

General U.S. Grant stood in front of the grand DeSoto House. He was unmistakable in his heavy navy-blue Union Army greatcoat, wide-brimmed hat, full beard, and ever-present cigar.

I walked up to him, aimed my camera, said, "Smile," and clicked the shutter. The General wasn't even startled. In fact, he said, "You need another shot? I'll strike my presidential pose for ya." Now I was the one who was quite surprised.

I didn't expect to find Grant at the DeSoto House, even

though he made it headquarters for his 1868 presidential bid. But Galena is full of surprises.

Of Course, "Grant" turned out to be a local actor who portrays the General at special functions. The likeness is striking. And it's a stroke of advertising genius for the hotel.

Not that the massive 1855 structure—opened during the period when unprecedented lead-mining profits transformed Galena into a trade and commerce center rivaling Chicago—needs any gimmicks. Innkeeper Lev Blaha told me that more than eight million dollars was poured into the restoration project. That kind of money is reflected in the elegance evident throughout the building, which was once billed as "the largest hotel in the West."

On my way to the guest rooms, I passed through an enclosed courtyard with high skylight windows that sent a rush of sun toward diners enjoying an elegant al fresco buffet in its open space. The guest rooms are decorated in various shades of soothing blues and beiges. Some of the furnishings include high-back chairs, dressers, and writing desks. Lev is proud that even the inside rooms have views, with windows overlooking the Grand Court.

For dining, Truffles is the elegant formal dining room located in the basement, a romantic showplace with exposed brick walls and original ceiling beams. Menu choices include the finest steaks and seafood. More informal treats can be sampled at The Bakery, which features old-fashioned deli sandwiches and scrumptious pastries guaranteed to tickle your taste buds.

And how can you pass up a chance to relax in the Einsweiler Library with a cognac nightcap in front of a roaring fireplace—an elegant way to end a day.

How to get there: Take U.S. 20 to Galena. Turn north on South Main Street. The DeSoto House is halfway up the block, at the corner of Main and Grand.

B: *Nine presidents have stayed at the DeSoto House, as well as the likes of Mark Twain, Ralph Waldo Emerson, Susan B. Anthony, and Horace Greeley.*

Farmers' Home Hotel
Galena, Illinois
61036

Innkeepers: Floyd Mansberger and Tom Kristianson
Address/Telephone: 334 Spring Street; (815) 777–3456
Rooms: 8, with 1 suite; all with private bath.
Rates: $59 single, $65 double. Includes full breakfast off dining
  room menu. Children 12 and over only.
Open: All year.
Facilities & Activities: Near all the historic attractions of Galena, a
  mid-1800s lead-mining boom town and home of U.S. Grant.

The first thing I noticed about the Farmers' Home Hotel
was a real "frontier" atmosphere established by the high
ceilings and long corridors. That's easy to understand, because this long brick building was built in the fall of 1867,
housing a bakery and a boarding house for area farmers
bringing their produce to the town market.

Innkeepers Floyd and Tom have restored the Farmers'
Home Hotel, updating plumbing and heating systems while
retaining its nineteenth-century charm. They proudly
pointed out the original pinewood plank floors—a throwback
to the hotel's old commercial days. I could even see the origi-

nal hand-painted numbers faintly visible on the doors of the guest rooms.

Floyd and Tom have worked hard to find the period antique furnishings. I saw high walnut, iron-rail, and four-poster beds adorned with handmade quilts, rich armoires, dressing tables, and period-print wallpaper. The original window glass was retained when the frames were restored; I could still see the wavy lines in the old lead glass.

Round tables (covered with red-checkered tablecloths) and bentwood-style chairs bring home the rough-hewn country atmosphere in the breakfast dining room. Hobo hash, eggs and toast, or pancakes with fruit will get you started right. The restaurant also offers lunch to both overnight guests and the public. The innkeepers are happy to offer dinner suggestions; of course, you can't go wrong at the popular Kingston Inn.

Finally, notice the extremely tall front door of the hotel. Its panels are carved to resemble a cross with an open Bible at the foot. Floyd and Tom told me that this represents an old German folk custom used to bless a house.

How to get there: Drive into Galena heading east on U.S. 20 west and follow the road as it turns into Spring Street, where the hotel is located.

Felt Manor Guest House
Galena, Illinois
61036

Innkeeper: Linda Hilliard
Address / Telephone: 125 South Prospect Street; (815) 777–9093
Rooms: 4; all with shared bath.
Rates: $50. Includes breakfast. No children under 12.
Open: All year.
Facilities & Activities: Front porch with swing, pool table in billiard
   room. Just a short walk to all of Galena's historic attractions
   and near to home of U.S. Grant.

Linda and I stood on the front porch of her inn as she
told me that her guests have one of the best views of Galena.
That's certainly no exaggeration; Felt Manor Guest House is
☛ located on a high, steep bluff that overlooks the entire
town, the winding Galena River, and the rolling green of
Grant Park.

The mid-1800s home, with its distinctively broad, flat
mansard roof, has all the right touches. ☛ Rich rosewood
and mahogany add luster to the high-ceilinged sitting and
dining rooms that sport tall bookcases and Italian marble
fireplaces. Linda still marvels that there are ☛ *seven* fire-

places throughout the historic house. Add to that Victorian pocket doors that slide unobtrusively into walls, oak floors, and crowned ceilings with dangling chandliers, and you have something special.

Linda lives here with her sons and with the inn's friendly (and quiet) pups, Murphy and Bogart. They've fashioned a home rife with period antiques, yet still as warm and comfortable as your favorite easy chair. The guest rooms have captured the charm of the past with their antique beds, quilts, dressers, and other Victorian finery. Before turning in at night, I suggest that you go outside to the long front porch, which has a ☞ fun swing built for two; then gently sway under the brightly lit stars as you watch the dim lights of Galena far below. It's really quite romantic.

Eating breakfast in Linda's elegant dining room is itself a treat. Standard fare includes rolls, juice, and coffee. Linda's suggestions also will ensure you a fine evening meal; the Kingston Inn is a good bet.

Make sure that you reach the house via its rear walkway on High Street, behind the building. I came off Prospect and had to climb more than sixty steep steps to get to the top of the bluff, and the inn. Either way, you might be greeted by the wagging tail of Murphy or Bogart.

How to get there: Enter Galena via U.S. 20 and turn north on South High Street until you reach the inn. There's a sign on the wall of a garage building showing you've arrived.

The Henry Fricke
Guest House
Galena, Illinois
61036

Innkeeper: Bill Hunt
Address/Telephone: 119 South Bench Street; (815) 777–1193 or
  9430
Rooms: 2, with shared bath.
Rates: $45. Includes full breakfast. Children OK. Well-behaved pets
  only.
Open: All year.
Facilities & Activities: Near most of the historic sites and specialty
  shops in Galena, an 1850s town with fascinating architecture.

Sometimes you can have the most fun exploring a new
inn all by yourself. That's how I got to know The Henry
Fricke Guest House.

Bill told me he'd be out of town during my daytime visit,
but he left my key with neighbors next door. I drove up to
this handsome home one-half block from the heart of Galena's historic district and was immediately excited by what I

saw. A ☞ magnificent decorative iron-rail fence surrounding the property signaled something special.

Inside, I found a quiet elegance that soothed my nerves from the three-hour drive from Chicago. It was obvious that Bill had carefully selected his antiques and materials to render this restoration faithful to the period. In fact, Bill said he'd spent more than five years completing this landmark residence.

In the parlor, ☞ tall windows are crowned with golden velvet draperies. A rich Oriental rug covers a hardwood floor. A victorian sofa sits snugly by a cozy fireplace. The Victorian finery almost approaches museum quality. I just sat there drinking in all the wonderful antique pieces.

I found quiet here, a peacefulness that allows everyday tension to just fall away. The loudest sound was the ticking from a ☞ magnificent antique pull-chain clock resting in the dining room.

Breakfast is taken in the dining room, filled with Empire-style furniture, oak woodwork, and the original plank floor. Bill serves up a hearty feast, with bacon, eggs, pancakes, waffles, fruit, muffins, and beverages. Afterward, a walk in the home's rock garden is a good way to burn off the calories.

Upstairs, the guest rooms are decorated in steep Victorian tradition, with period antiques conjuring up an atmosphere of a wealthy gentleman's residence. The ☞ rooms seem to exude privacy, and the tranquility is striking. Bill is happy to recommend Galena restaurants that cater to your particular tastes.

How to get there: Take U.S. 20 into Galena. Whether coming from the east or west, turn north on South Main Street and continue to Hill Street. Turn west, going one block to Bench Street. Turn south. The inn is on the right side of the street.

Log Cabin Guest House
Galena, Illinois
61036

Innkeepers: Linda and Scott Ettelman
Address/Telephone: 11661 West Chetlain Lane; (815) 777–2845
Rooms: Authentic, 2-room 1800s log cabin; 2-room historic Servant's House.
Rates: Cabin: $45 per night double occupancy; $10 extra for each additional adult; $50 for families. Servant's House: $40 per night double occupancy. Two-night minimum (Friday and Saturday) during summer season. Wheelchair access to cabin.
Facilities & Activities: Very private location; near old barn, fields, woods. A short drive to historic attractions, specialty shops, museums, and restaurants of Galena.

It's not often Midwesterners get to step inside an authentic log cabin. Most have been destroyed by man's "progress" as he battled to conquer this stubborn land. The few that remain usually belong to local historical societies, and most of these can be viewed only from the outside.

That's why this cabin, built in 1865 by a Civil War veteran who later came to the booming lead-mine town of Galena to try his luck, is so special.

I pulled open its old latch door to find a room dominated by a ☛ huge stone hearth and with a massive stone floor covered by a braided rug. A large antique spinning wheel sat in one corner, and black kettles hanging from iron rails hovered over the remains of a toasty fire in the hearth.

The ☛ logs are whitewashed inside to give the quarters a bright, airy look, with cheery tieback curtains on the small windows. An antique spindle bed is tucked into the far corner of the room.

Upstairs is a sleeping loft, spartanly furnished with two three-quarter-sized rope beds—real pioneer spirit, here. I tried one out, and it actually felt quite comfortable. (Scott explained that it's all in how the ropes are strung.) A small corner crib adds more sleeping space for babies.

The Servant's House was built on the property between 1832 and 1834 by the father of Civil War General Augustus Chetlain, one of nine Galena native sons who reached that rank in the Union Army's war against the South. Scott said that in all Galena only his home (next to this building) is older than the servants' quarters. In fact, Scott said that it's the oldest farmstead in northern Illinois, constructed in 1832.

Inside the Servant's House a charming potbellied stove caught my fancy. I also liked the original plank floors, spindle beds adorned with quilts, lace curtains on the windows, and floral-print wallpaper. A kitchenette and indoor plumbing are the only bows to the twentieth century.

There's no breakfast or dinner served here, but Scott recommends the Farmers' Home Hotel for hearty, reasonably priced morning meals and the Kingston Inn for evening feasts. Both are located downtown, a short drive away, and Scott will give you directions.

How to get there: Take U.S. 20 west through Galena to Chetlain Lane and turn left. Go ¼ mile and you'll find the farmstead on the left.

☙

B: *A peaceful, history-laden hideaway.*

Mother's Country Inn
Galena, Illinois
61036

Innkeeper: Pat Laury
Address/Telephone: 349 Spring Street; (815) 777-3153
Rooms: 7; 1 with private bath.
Rates: Inn: $35 single, $45 double; children, $10. Includes continental breakfast. Two-night minimum on weekends, Memorial Day through Christmas Day. Guest House: 3-night stay. $120 for six people.
Open: All year.
Facilities & Activities: Antique shop on first floor. Short walk to all historic Galena attractions, restaurants, and shops. Ten-minute drive to alpine and nordic ski facilities.

When I walked into Mother's Country Inn, Shotzie started barking at me. "She's my doorbell," said Pat, patting her pretty puppy on the noggin. "And I've got her well trained. Once you pay for your room, she won't bark at you."

All kidding aside, Pat has done a fine job restoring this 1838 Federalist townhouse. Its quiet country antique charm has already attracted much attention, from eager inn hoppers to fellow Galena innkeepers.

After a long fireside chat that warmed me on a cold spring day, Pat gave me a grand tour of the inn. Plank floors harken back to its pre–Civil War construction. I could even see the round pegs in the floorboards.

Windows set in walls nearly a foot thick add to the pioneer feel of the home. I could imagine early settlers huddling next to the fire during harsh Midwestern winters. That's probably why three fireplaces are scattered throughout the house. They still add toasty warmth in the winter months when modern-day guests return from nearby skiing adventures.

I have carried on a long love affair with quilts, and Pat had some beauties adorning her guest beds. Other period antiques completed the guest-room décor.

One of the inn's most attractive spots is The Hospitality Room, which doubles as an antique shop. It's perhaps the most historic room at the inn, with more original pine plank floors and a wide stone hearth. It's fun to breakfast here with your coffee, juice, and rolls while scanning the inn's antique collection for that perfect discovery.

Next to the inn is The Guest Cottage, Galena's oldest frame home. Built in 1830, it's done in Louisiana-French style, has a wood-burning stove and modern kitchen, and sleeps six.

It's just a short walk to nearby restaurants that offer varied dining—from elaborate romantic dinners to pub house sandwiches. Pat will recommend one that'll do your tummy proud.

How to get there: From Dubuque, take U.S. 20 east; go over the bridge at the Mississippi River and continue into Galena. The inn is located at High Street and Highway 20.

⌛

B: This is one of Galena's oldest buildings, in one of the first areas settled by Northwest Territory pioneers.

The Ryan Mansion
Galena, Illinois
61036

Innkeeper: Linda K. Pluym
Address/Telephone: Route 20 West; (815) 777–2043
Rooms: 10; all with private bath.
Rates: $48 to $61. Includes continental breakfast. Children welcome. No credit cards.
Open: All year.
Facilities & Activities: Near to historic homes, architecture, and sites, including home of U.S. Grant. Also near antique, art, and specialty stores. Historic countryside tours, monthly festivals.

The Ryan Mansion has one of the most distinctive and curious profiles of any Illinois country inn: A tall ☞ "onion skin" square cupola stands four stories high like an eerie sentinel guarding the grounds.

Linda has worked hard to restore the 1876 Italianate mansion while retaining its Victorian charm, offering guests a chance to peek back into Galena's rich heritage. Little touches like the ☞ "RM" etched into the glass of the heavy oak hallway entry doors grace this twenty-four-room mansion.

Inside, the chandeliered hallway features sweeping staircases leading to the second- and third-floor guest rooms. Linda has furnished them with rich brass beds, brass lamps, cheery floral wallpaper prints, and antique reproductions.

I soon discovered my favorite, a room with a fine Italian-marble fireplace and a marble-topped dresser with hurricane-style lamps. There were also several ceiling-to-floor windows that flooded the room with sunlight.

Another feature I liked was the sense of space the house offers. For me, this is characterized by a long window-filled hallway at the rear of the home lined with greenery and flowering plants.

These hallway windows also overlook a small horse corral, which was enough to hook me on the Ryan. I'm a city boy who loves horses.

Linda is especially proud of her impressive ☞ Bohemian glass archway window that graces the second-floor stairway landing.

She serves a continental breakfast of rolls, juice, and coffee and will recommend dinner spots for your enjoyment. The Kingston Inn is my favorite Galena restaurant.

The mansion is set far back from the road, with nothing but acres of gently rolling Illinois farmland behind it. It's a welcome respite from Galena's hustle and bustle.

How to get there: From Freeport, take U.S. 20 west until you reach the mansion at the edge of town.

The Victorian Mansion
Galena, Illinois
61036

Innkeeper: Robert George McClellan
Address/Telephone: 301 High Street; (815) 777–0675
Rooms: 6; 1 with private bath.
Rates: $35 to $60. Children over 12 only. Includes coffee served in
  morning.
Open: All year.
Facilities & Activities: All historic attractions of Galena, U.S. Grant
  home, tours of historic houses; art, antique, and specialty
  stores.

Robert led me into his twenty-three-room, 1861 Italianate mansion, long a prestigious address for entertaining important guests in this former boom town along the Fever (Galena) River.

We sat down in the library to chat about this incredible inn, furnished and preserved with museum-quality antiques so authentically displayed that it's as if a photograph of the home in the 1860s had come to life.

I noticed soldiers' boots standing next to a tall coatrack and ☛ Civil war–era Union Army greatcoats slung over the high backs of elegant chairs in the dining room. That's not surprising because General Grant was a confidant of the home's original owner, wealthy smelter Augustus Estey; and a group of the General's cronies often gathered to discuss political issues of the day with the cigar-chomping soldier in the very library where Robert and I were sitting.

"See that black grate above you?" Robert asked, pointing to the ceiling. "Estey had that built into his library ceiling to suck cigar smoke out of the air."

The house is immaculate. Walking through the front door, I passed a beautiful highboy secretary only to be confronted by a 10-foot-tall antique grandfather's clock. What especially intrigued me was the hallway's unusual chandelier, which has four graceful swan figurines supporting a large glass shade. But even these wonderful items are overshadowed by the grand oval staircase that spirals all the way up to the third floor.

Second-floor guest rooms exhibit exquisite antique furnishings. My favorite is the Grant Room, with its invitingly huge walnut bedframe, marble-topped bureau, and deeply colored floral-print carpeting. Robert's collection of antique *Harper's Bazaar* political caricatures sniping at the General hang on the walls.

I found elegance everywhere in this magnificent showplace. Plank floors are covered by Oriental-style carpets, some original to the home. Pocket doors (which slide unobtrusively into walls) separate many of the rooms. Historically correct wallpaper, four marble fireplaces, and opulent chandeliers are just some more of the extras.

The Kingston Inn is probably Galena's finest spot for dining. You'll enjoy everything from its special *cioppino*, seafood bathed in spicy tomato-based sauce, to redfish and fine steaks. The homemade cheesecake is a scrumptious dessert.

How to get there: Take U.S. 20 west to High Street and turn left. Go all the way to the top of a steep hill to the mansion, which stands on the left side of the street.

B: *This is simply the most magnificent inn Galena offers and one of the finest in the Midwest.*

The Mansion of Golconda
Golconda, Illinois
62938

Innkeepers: Don and Marilyn Kunz
Address/Telephone: P.O. Box 339, Columbus Avenue; (618) 683–4400
Rooms: 4 with shared bath; 1 fishermen's cottage with private bath.
Rates: $45 to $60. Includes full breakfast. Children OK. Pets not encouraged.
Open: All year.
Facilities & Activities: Full-service dining room, lounge. Short walk to Ohio River, levee drive; short drive to spectacular Shawnee National Forest. Fishing, boating on river; horseback riding, hiking; cross-country skiing in area during winter.

I wandered down to southern Illinois' Ohio River country, some of the most beautiful scenery in the Midwest. This historic corner of the state is also rich in legend, from the trail-blazing George Rogers Clark expedition to the Ohio river pirates of the 1790s who preyed on flatboats from infamous Cave-In-Rock.

Right in the heart of a small river town is The Mansion of Golconda. I was surprised to find that the innkeeper of this

1895 mansion was from my old neighborhood back in Chicago.

Don and Marilyn recently purchased The Mansion and have continued its tradition of fine dining and hospitality. The rose, gold, and blue dining rooms, furnished largely with period antiques, set the mood for what Marilyn proudly calls "The Mansion's dining experience."

Dinner means candlelight and elaborate meals. While selections include sautéed chicken livers, honey-baked chicken, steaks, and frog legs, I recommend the ☛ catfish Almaden for a down-home treat. Marilyn serves dinners in huge old skillets, and loaves of steaming-hot bread served on rough-hewn breadboards add to the home-style "flavor" of the meal.

But hold on! You can't walk away without one of The Mansion's ☛ homemade desserts, which are prepared daily. A real treat is the egg-custard pie.

I also like the inn's enclosed back porch for cheery, informal dining. In fact, homemade pizza is served here every night—and Don says you can often hear the bellowing horns of passing river boats.

Marilyn knows that sometimes travel-weary inn hoppers "want the breakfast to be good" at a country inn. So she caters to both light and hearty eaters. Juice, fruit, toast, and croissants satisfy some guests; ☛ eggs over easy, spicy southern Illinois pork sausage, and biscuits and gravy satiate hungrier guests.

Did I forget to mention lunch on the back porch? How about red snapper with cream sauce or chicken with tomato-wine sauce?

Original stained-glass windows, six fireplaces, fine woodwork, and pocket doors are all architectural features of the inn. The guest bedrooms on the second floor have an eclectic mix of Victorian, antique, and other furnishings.

Don and I later talked in the small bar just off the entrance. "You know, I still get back to the old neighborhood now and then," he said, as we reminisced about our Chicago connection, "but I wouldn't trade this for anything."

How to get there: From north, east, and west, follow Illinois 146 into Golconda and turn right on Columbus Avenue.

Colonial Inn
Grand Detour, Illinois
61021

Innkeeper: James Pufall
Address/Telephone: Rock and Green streets (mailing address: Route 3, Dixon, Illinois 61021); (815) 652–4422
Rooms: 12; 4 with private bath, others share 3 baths.
Rates: $25 to $35. Includes continental breakfast. Children OK. No credit cards.
Open: All year.
Facilities & Activities: Sitting rooms, expansive lawns. In quaint New England–style village. The John Deere historic site is just a short walk down country village roads. Three state parks within a short drive; hiking, boating, fishing, swimming, golfing, biking, cross-country skiing.

Driving into this historic town is like wandering through New England back roads. Quaint houses are strewn about tiny streets, shaded by tall trees; a little stone church built in the 1840s stands amid the homes, still welcoming visitors; friendly people tend to their gardens; families prepare country barbecues in their back yards.

Then there's the charming Colonial Inn, an 1850 red-brick Italianate house sitting on an expansive lawn with huge shade trees, low hedges, colorful flowers, and chirping birds. Owner James Pufall was waiting for his weekend guests when I arrived.

The guest rooms are on the second floor, reached via a labyrinth of angling corridors. "Just when you think they're going to end, they start all over again," he said with a chuckle. They have high ceilings and are furnished with many antiques from James's personal collection, along with an eclectic mix of other styles You'll find quaint country-floral wallpapers, some Victorian headboards, iron-rail and brass beds, Empire dressers, oak crosscut 1920s furniture, and bright curtains on tall windows.

One of my favorite inn treasures is the solid brass chandelier hanging over the stairway in the second-floor hallway; it was handcrafted in England, James told me.

All that wonderful flooring is the original pine plank used in 1850. Most of the other wood in the home is walnut; even the beams that support the house are made of that valuable wood.

In the morning, James serves a continental breakfast featuring homemade croissants, sweet rolls, English muffins, and beverages. For dinner, James can direct you to nearby small towns that have charming restaurants in quaint riverside settings.

How to get there: From Chicago, take the Eisenhower Expressway (I–90) west to Illinois 5. Continue west to Illinois 26 at Dixon and head north. At Illinois 2, turn right to Grand Detour. Illinois 2 becomes River Street in town. Then turn left on Rock Street for a few short blocks to the inn.

B: *I found a walk around the village very soul-satisfying.*

The Bennett-Curtis House
Grant Park, Illinois
60940

Innkeepers: Sam and Charlotte Van Hook
Address/Telephone: 302 West Taylor Street; (815) 465–6025
Rooms: 1; with private bath and kitchen.
Rates: $50 for single or per couple. Includes continental breakfast
  with homemade breads and pastries.
Open: All year. Dinner: Friday and Saturday, 7:30 P.M.; Sunday,
  6:30 P.M. Lunch Wednesday through Saturday, noon; brunch
  Sunday, 11 A.M. to 2 P.M. Spectacular holiday dinner celebra-
  tions and decorations, especially Christmas and Easter.
Facilities & Activities: Good antique hunting in nearby villages.

This sleepy little town is an unlikely place for an inn so
acclaimed for its prodigious eight-course dinners and five-
course brunches. And these meals are served with imagination and flair inside a many-gabled fourteen-room Victorian
mansion filled with antique furnishings.

Sam and Charlotte have lovingly restored this 1900
landmark with the "old stuff" they've collected over the
years. I love the 🖝 long veranda with comfy wicker furniture
padded with iris-patterned cushions. And the large wicker
willow swing was purchased from Marshall Field's in 1918.

I like the inn's tall 🖝 double front "casket" doors (used for home funerals in Victorian times). Inside, antiques literally overwhelmed me; included are some big-city nostalgia pieces like cane chairs from Chicago's old Trianon Ballroom. The living room, music room, and dining room host inn diners. All are decorated with rich, green velvet draperies, antiques, and table settings of rich silver, shining crystal, and fine china. Sam said that the main dining room's 🖝 Victorian walnut side chairs are part of a set of six numbered and stamped "1887."

The intimate breakfast room features particularly attractive wallpaper with an unusual bird design that was copied from a pattern in the Smithsonian.

If you like to eat, this is the place for you. Charlotte prepares a fantastic multi-course dinner that left me bursting at the belt. I loved the cold peach soup, and I tasted raspberried pear for the first time. Then there's crab Newburg, artichoke and mushroom salad, chicken pâté, apple sorbet, cherry-glazed pork roast, and an unusual (but delicious) eggnog pie. And I couldn't pass up more than a few of the inn's famous lemon muffins.

After dinner, I toured the second-floor family museum—five rooms crammed with treasures, including a Civil War document issued to Sam's grandmother and his father's political cartoons that appeared in Illinois newspapers. The third floor holds Charlotte's collection of more than one hundred teddy bears, both antique and contemporary ones.

Sam and Charlotte offer one splendid getaway room (no telephone) in a nineteenth-century country house across the street. It has 🖝 Chippendale reproductions, a canopy bed, romantically draped walls, and antique furnishings that are constantly changing—because they're for sale!

How to get there: The inn is about 45 miles south of Chicago. From various points, go south on Illinois 394 to Route 1, then south to Grant Park. Cross the railroad tracks and proceed west for two blocks. The inn is at the southwest corner, at the stop sign.

B: It's worth a visit to The Bennett-Curtis House just for the lemon muffins!

Old Illiopolis Hotel
Illiopolis, Illinois
62539

Innkeepers: James Browne and Kathleen Jensen-Browne
Address/Telephone: Box 66, 608 Mary Street; (217) 486–6451
Rooms: 5; share 2 hallway baths.
Rates: $18 single, $20 double. Includes continental breakfast. Children welcome. Pets OK. No credit cards.
Open: All year.
Facilities & Activities: Just 19 miles from all the historic sites and museums of Abraham Lincoln's Springfield, the capital of Illinois.

This Midwestern landmark hotel was built in 1854 as a stopover for the passengers and crew of the Great Western Railroad, which passed through Illiopolis. The rail line is famous for Lincoln's Depot in Springfield, from which he often traveled, and made way to Washington, D.C. It's also the line that brought his body back home after his assassination in 1865.

Structurally, the building hasn't changed, noted Kathleen, who with her husband, James, bought the old hotel in

1981. They've reopened the hotel doors to travelers and re-created the friendly feeling of bygone days.

The parlor room has an old player piano with rolls of music that the innkeepers like to play for guests. "We like them to feel a bit like family," Kathleen said, "share a glass of wine with them, play some music, give them an oral history of the house, and a tour, if they like. Of course, some travelers are so tired from their trips that they head straight to their rooms. We want them to feel comfortable no matter what they choose to do."

The upstairs guest rooms harken back to those railroad days and are furnished in country antiques that the innkeepers collected from local shops and flea markets.

Weekday breakfasts generally include English muffins, fruit, toast, hard-boiled eggs, and sweet rolls. Kathleen often delivers it on a tray to guests up in their rooms.

Weekend breakfasts might feature all the above, plus pancakes, eggs, and sausage. The innkeepers will recommend Springfield and other area restaurants to suit your dinner tastes.

How to get there: Get off I–72 at exit 19 and follow into Illiopolis. Turn right on Matilda Street, then left on Fifth Street. At Mary Street, turn right and proceed to the hotel.

B: *Why not stay at an historic hotel when visiting the historic Lincoln sites at nearby Springfield?*

Hotel Nauvoo
Nauvoo, Illinois
62354

Innkeeper: Elmer Kraus
Address/Telephone: Route 96, P.O. Box 398; (217) 453–2211
Rooms: 12, with 1 suite; all with private bath.
Rates: $24.95 single, $31 to $41 double. Children OK.
Open: March 16 to November 16.
Facilities & Activities: Located in historic Mormon town. Tours of many historic homes and architectural attractions including site of old temple. Specialty store, antique shops. Just off the Great River Road, a scenic drive along the Mississippi River. About a 1½-hour drive to Hannibal, Missouri, home of Mark Twain.

Elmer and his family bought this 1840 landmark example of early Mormon architecture in the mid-1940s and have been extending their family-style hospitality ever since.

Nauvoo continues to be a family-conscious community, largely in keeping with its historical roots. This town on the Mississippi River was the center of the family-oriented Mormon culture in the mid-1800s. Founder Joseph Smith had a general store not far from here. In fact, bricks from that historic structure are said to have been used in the construction of the Hotel Nauvoo.

So the fact that the inn, along with many other historic Mormon buildings in town, is still sturdy and strong is no surprise. Just what you'd expect from these industrious people.

I walked through solid walnut entry doors and was immediately confronted by a long staircase. I followed it, and it led to a wonderful find: a third-story cupola crowning the building, a great place from which to survey this interesting old river town.

Elmer's guest rooms are simple and functional, with original period décor sprinkled with near-antiques.

But the special treat is the Nauvoo dining room, where the Krauses serve up family-style dinners. There's also a wall here built of historic bricks kilned nearby that still bear the mason's fingerprints.

I marveled at the heaping bowls of delicious blueberry muffins that rested on my table. How did Elmer know that these goodies were my favorites?

I also loved the channel catfish, which is a local specialty, although I was tempted by the home-baked turkey served with the inn's fabulous wild rice—and I shouldn't forget the Nauvoo grape jelly served with home-baked rolls.

Later I toured some of the historic Mormon sites. A town orientation is held at the Nauvoo Restoration Visitor Center, and twelve miles south on Illinois 96 is the old jail where Smith and his brother died at the hands of an angry mob before his followers headed for Utah.

How to get there: From Chicago, take I–55 to Illinois 136. Go west to the Mississippi River; then north on Illinois 96 to Nauvoo. The inn is on this road, in the center of town.

※

B: *Don't forget to try some of the area's famous blue cheese.*

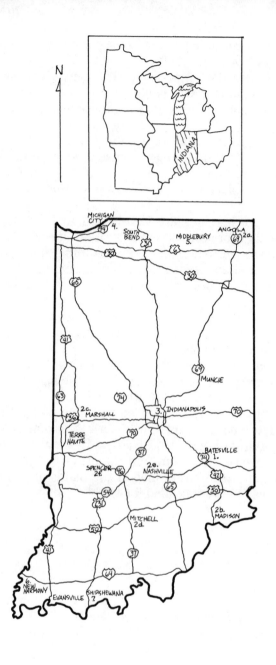

N

Indiana

Numbers on map refer to towns numbered below.

The Sherman House
Batesville, Indiana
47006

Innkeepers: Bertha Vogt and Jim Dittger
Address/Telephone: 35 South Main Street; (812) 934-2407
Rooms: 25, with 4 suites; all with private bath.
Rates: $32 to $40 single, $37 to $50 double, $80 to $90 suites. Children welcome. Pets not encouraged.
Open: All year.
Facilities & Activities: Large public dining room, private dining rooms, cocktail lounge. Nearby fishing. One hour's drive to Indianapolis or Cincinnati.

I didn't expect to find, in the middle of small-town Indiana, an 1852 landmark building dedicated to the Civil War's tough Union Army general William Tecumseh Sherman that resembles a European old-world chalet. But this was just another surprise on the country-inn trail.

Renovations made in 1953 covered The Sherman House's original pioneer timber frame, whose thick yellow poplar girders had remained sturdy through the years. And that's when the hotel adopted its old-world décor, complete with 🔊 peaked eaves, leaded-glass street-side windows, and half-timbered façade. In fact, the Old Vienna Café (the hotel's restaurant) was designed by studying sketches of European cafés.

But the hotel has kept its ☛ collection of antique Sherman prints, which continue to grace its walls today. And its reputation for good wholesome food is still strong.

During my visit, the dining room was jammed with Sunday diners all gussied up for a special treat. The Sherman House specializes in German ethnic foods, particularly all kinds of *wurst* (sausage).

There's also sauerbraten with potato pancakes and heaping bowls of red cabbage. Of course, standard fare includes a choice of steaks and seafood. But I challenge you to leave the dinner table without trying one of the inn's fabulous golden-nugget ice-cream sundaes.

The guest rooms are furnished in a conservative, contemporary style, and I found them comfortable and quiet.

How to get there: From Indianapolis or Cincinnati, take I–74 to the Batesville exit, which turns into Walnut Street. Continue straight to East Pearl Street and turn left. Then turn right on Main Street and proceed to the hotel.

Indiana State Park Inns

I've discovered that Indiana state park inns are some of the most enjoyable places one could experience in the entire state. You get panoramic vistas, deep forests, rolling hills, outstanding outdoor recreation opportunities, naturalist-led hikes and lectures, and a varied cultural arts program of music, dance, and theater.

All the inns are open year round, offering winter-season fun, too. Guest room accommodations are more than acceptable, especially if you have a large family. Most inns offer full-service restaurants, some with mighty tasty fare.

Reservations are always recommended, as the parks fill up very quickly.

a. Potawatomi Inn

☛ English-style lodge with especially good wintertime activities; long toboggan slide and cross-country ski trails. Indoor pool, sauna, home-cooked meals. (Pokagon State Park, Route 2, Box 180, Angola, Indiana 46703; [219] 833–1077.)

b. Cliffy Inn

☛ Private balconies in the Riverview section overlook the grand Ohio River and the historic town of Madison. Cherry-paneled dining room specializing in broasted chicken and homemade desserts. (Cliffy Falls State Park, Box 387, Madison, Indiana 47250; [812] 265–4135.)

c. Turkey Run Inn

In the heart of 👉 covered bridge country; a massive annual festival (October) in nearby Rockville celebrates these remnants of a bygone era. Inn rooms and cabins. Private pool and Olympic-sized pool, tennis courts, hiking trails. (Turkey Run State Park, R.R. 1, Marshall, Indiana 47859; [317] 597–2211.)

d. Spring Mill Inn

A 👉 reconstructed pioneer village, hiking trails, caves, the Virgil "Gus" Grissom Memorial. Heated indoor–outdoor swimming pool. (Spring Mill State Park, Box 68, Mitchell, Indiana 47446; [812] 849–4081.)

e. Abe Martin Lodge

Brown County State Park is one of my Midwest favorites, with incredible scenic vistas, rolling hills, and a charming rustic lodge and cabins. There's even a luxurious retreat up on Skunk Ridge. The dining room features homemade cobblers and pies. Just a short ride from the 👉 quaint town of Nashville, filled with specialty shops and summer playhouse theater. (Brown County State Park, Box 25, Nashville, Indiana 47448; [812] 988–4418 or 988–7316.)

f. Canyon Inn

Indiana's first state park. Recreation center and swimming pool. Dining room. Special weekend-getaway packages during winter season. (McCormick's Creek State Park, P.O. Box 71, Spencer, Indiana 47460; [812] 829–4881.)

Room rates typically range from $27 to $50 at the inns. For more specific information, contact the inns directly or call, within Indiana, (800) 622–4931. Outside Indiana, call (800) 2–WANDER.

Hollingsworth House Inn
Indianapolis, Indiana
46254

Innkeepers: Susan Muller and Ann Irvine
Address/Telephone: 6054 Hollingsworth Road; (317) 299–6700
Rooms: 5, with 1 suite; all with private bath.
Rates: Rooms, $65 to $85; suite, $110. Includes continental breakfast. No children.
Open: All year.
Facilities & Activities: Near Indianapolis Union Station, renovated train station filled with specialty shops; football stadium for Colts' NFL games; Conner Prairie historic settlement; golf courses.

Susan and Ann have made a business of buying historic properties, restoring them, and then putting them back on the market hoping for a tidy profit. But when they bought the Hollingsworth house, "something clicked inside our heads," Susan said. "We decided to live here and open an elegant country inn."

The two women pioneered the concept of a country inn (or B&B) in the Indianapolis area, Susan explained, as she recalled the wrangling with town fathers over building codes before transforming the historic property into the charming way station that now greets travelers.

"We went to all kinds of antique stores, flea markets, and estate auctions," Susan said, "sometimes waiting more than twelve hours to bid on just the right piece of furniture. At the same time, we worked on painting, stenciling, wallpapering, and plumbing."

It was worth their time and effort because the inn is a delight. Susan led my wife, Baby Kate (our two-month-old daughter), and me into an elegant ☛ front parlor with an inviting manteled fireplace, poplar hardwood floors, Chippendale sofa, and assorted antiques.

It's the breakfast room that will capture your imagination, as it did mine. Pure country delight, it's done in Williamsburg-blue trim, with a manteled fireplace, table, and barn-red chairs.

I found the guest rooms equally charming. The largest has a four-poster bed and period floral wallpaper. A salmon-colored room has light rose down-filled satin comforters, which match the room's décor. And there are claw-footed tubs in some of the bathrooms.

Susan and Ann are quite talented decorators, and they use lots of antique lace (discovered at estate sales) for quilt trim, curtains, wall hangings, coverlets, and more. Ann did all the handsome wall stenciling that graces some of the rooms.

Imagine ☛ breakfast served off a sparkling antique German silver service. That's the treat in store for you, along with fresh fruit, scrambled eggs, ham, cheese, beverages, and Susan's freshly baked pecan rolls. There are many fine restaurants in Indianapolis serving lunch and dinner; Susan and Ann will be happy to recommend one to you.

How to get there: From east or west, exit at the I–65/I–465 junction (Lafayette Road) and go northwest to 71st Street. Turn east to Georgetown Road and head south. Turn west on 62nd Street to Hollingsworth; then turn south to the inn.

☗

B: *The 1854 farmhouse sits on acreage listed in a land grant of 1826 signed by John Quincy Adams.*

Creekwood Inn
Michigan City, Indiana
46360

Innkeeper: Mary Lou Linnen
Address/Telephone: Route 20–35 at Interstate 94; (219) 872–8357
Rooms: 12 rooms, 1 suite; all with private bath.
Rates: $75 to $85 single, $80 to $90 double, $125 to $135 suite. Includes continental breakfast. Children OK. Wheelchair access.
Open: All year except March 4 to 13. Closed Christmas Day and New Year's Day.
Facilities & Activities: Dinner served in parlor on weekends to guests only. Short drive to southeastern shore of Lake Michigan, Indiana Dunes State Park, Warren Dunes State Park in Michigan. Charter fishing, swimming, boating. Antiquing in nearby lakeside communities. Area winery tours. Old Lighthouse Museum. A short drive to heart of southwestern Michigan's "Fruit Belt" for U-pick fruit and vegetable farms.

The Creekwood Inn is nestled amid thirty-three acres of walnut, oak, and pine trees near a fork in tiny Walnut Creek. The winding wooded roadway leading to the inn is breathtaking, especially in the fall when nature paints the trees in rainbow colors.

Done in English Cotswold design, the inn is warm, cozy,

ing beams on the main floor were taken from an old area toll
bridge by the original owner, who built the home in the
1930s. The parlor has a large fireplace, surrounded by comfortable sofas and chairs—a perfect setting for afternoon teas
or intimate midnight conversation. Wood planking covers the
floors. And you can gaze out a bay window that overlooks the
estate's lovely grounds.

Innkeeper Mary Lou Linnen said she wanted to com-
bine the ambience of a country inn with the modern amenities that people have come to expect. She has done better
than that; she has established a first-class retreat. Twelve
large guest rooms are tastefully decorated in a mixture of
styles; some have fireplaces and terraces. All have huge beds,
overstuffed chairs, and mini-refrigerators.

Mary Lou serves a tasty continental breakfast. I especially like her homemade oatmeal cookies, along with freshly
baked breads, pastries, fruit, and coffee.

Late-afternoon tea in the parlor offers more cookies and
some delicious pastries. You may even have a cup of hot
chocolate at bedtime on a blustery winter night, stretching
before the fire and toasting your toes.

Mary Lou can arrange for special weekend dinners at
the inn. She'll also recommend area dining spots. I suggest
that you take a short drive along the lake to New Buffalo and
try a famous gourmet hamburger at the renowned "Redamak's."

How to get there: Heading northeast to Michigan City on I–94, take
exit 40B. The inn is at Route 20–35, just off the interstate.

47

The Patchwork Quilt
Country Inn
Middlebury, Indiana
46540

Innkeeper: Arletta Lovejoy
Address/Telephone: 11748 County Road 2; (219) 825–2417
Rooms: 3; none with private bath.
Rates: $35 single, $45 double. Includes continental breakfast. No
 children. No credit cards. No smoking.
Open: All year, Tuesday through Friday only. Closed all holidays
 and three weeks in January/February (depends on the
 weather).
Facilities & Activities: Renowned restaurant. Located in Amish
 countryside; farm and craft tours. Crystal Valley is the heart of
 Indiana Amish crafts and quilt and specialty shops. Near Shipshewana, where numerous festivals are celebrated throughout
 the year.

 The Patchwork Quilt Country Inn serves quintessential
home cooking that most people only dream of finding at
country inns.
 It's tucked away on the back roads of northern Indiana's
Amish country, where black horse-drawn carriages clip-

clopped past me as I strolled down country roads. Surrounded by the Lovejoy family's 260-acre working farm (it's been in the family more than one hundred years), I knew that the food had to be farm-cooking-good at this charming inn.

Arletta's specialties include ☛ family-style buttermilk-pecan chicken, Burgundy steak with all the trimmings, and baked ham with escalloped pineapple.

And then there are the "trimmings": ☛ home-grown fruits and vegetables from the Lovejoys' garden out back; steaming homemade bread and rolls fresh out of the oven; dessert creations like Rhubarb Mousse and Sweet Cherry Bavarian; home-blended jams, jellies, and marmalades; and Arletta's cinnamon-pecan rolls that ooze sweet spices, nuts and raisins, and gooey icing.

If that's not enough, The Patchwork's guest rooms add more country charm to your visit. The Meadow is a handsome room with wattled walnut paneling. There's an ☛ early American cannonball bed topped by a canopy made from a hand-stitched apricot quilt that I thought would look great in my bedroom back home. And a leather-topped desk is decorated with Pigeon Forge pottery.

Another room boasts double four-poster beds. But it's the Treetop Room that draws "oohs and ahs" from many of the guests. Women especially enjoy the canopied bed, with its fabrics a splash of pastel colors and lacy trim, with a bright quilt to warm up toes on frigid winter nights. A pastel velvet chair sits next to a Franklin fireplace.

Some of the inn's freshly baked breads, rolls, homemade jellies and jams, morning cakes, fruit, and juice make up the breakfast served every morning to room guests. Then it's time to explore the Amish countryside. You can either drive up and down the back roads as I did, watching farmers break the soil with three-horse teams pulling a hand plow in age-old fashion, or sign up for one of the inn's guided tours. The tours enable you to observe Amish farm life up close, as well as watch skilled craftspeople at work making quilts and furniture and repairing the ever-present buggies.

How to get there: Take I–80/90 to Middlebury at exit 13–131. Take Indiana 13 north to County Road 2; turn west and go 1 mile to the inn.

The New Harmony Inn
New Harmony, Indiana
47631

Innkeeper: Nancy McIntire
Address/Telephone: North Street; (812) 682–4491
Rooms: 90; all with private bath.
Rates: $34 to $67. Includes continental breakfast. Special winter
    packages. Children welcome. Wheelchair access.
Open: All year.
Facilities & Activities: Indoor swimming pool. Located in historic
    small town renowned for its early nineteenth-century Utopian
    society community. A magnificent modernistic visitors' center
    distributes information on historic buildings that dot the settle-
    ment and conducts audio-visual presentations and walking
    tours. Also nearby are specialty shops and fine restaurants.

    As I drove across a bridge leading from southern Illinois
into Indiana, a scripted sign arched high above the steel girders proclaimed "New Harmony, Ind." Now I know why the
town elders make that announcement. Driving into quiet
New Harmony can lead to culture shock.
    Amid the historic structures that are a reminder of a
long-ago Utopian religious community stands The New Har-

mony Inn, blending harmoniously with its cultural surroundings. It's all dark brick, and its simple lines immediately call to mind Shaker styling. Surrounded by tall trees, it looks unbelievably peaceful.

I talked with Nancy in her office across the street before I entered the inn. She said The New Harmony's goal is to provide "simple rest and relaxation" for its guests. That's exactly what I experienced.

Like all guests, I walked into the Entry House, a welcoming area that features a large open sitting area, high balcony, and a ☛ chapel intended for meditation. Rooms are located in buildings across expansive lawns.

My favorites are rooms with ☛ wood-burning fireplace and a sleeping loft that's reached by a spiral staircase. Others have kitchenettes and exterior balconies overlooking the grounds.

The spartan furniture reflects the strong influence of Shaker design. Rocking chairs, simple oak tables, some sofa beds, and area rugs on hardwood floors complete the décor.

I immediately headed for the "greenhouse" swimming pool that's open all year. It's just a short walk from the rooms and a great way to relax after a long drive.

The inn serves a simple continental breakfast of fruit juice, coffee, and rolls to overnight guests. Nancy recommends the Red Geranium for wholesome dinner delicacies. You can choose down-home dishes like baked chicken, grilled ham steak, and braised brisket of beef with vegetable.

How to get there: New Harmony is located at the point where Indiana 66 meets the Wabash River, 7 miles from I–64. In Indiana, take the Poseyville exit; in Illinois, take the Grayville exit.

The Rockport Inn
Rockport, Indiana
47635

Innkeepers: Emil and Carolyn Ahnell
Address/Telephone: Third Street at Walnut; (812) 649–2664
Rooms: 6, with 1 suite; all with private bath.
Rates: $26 to $39. Includes continental breakfast. Children welcome. No credit cards.
Open: All year.
Facilities & Activities: Full-service restaurant. Rockport is a small Ohio River town rich in Abe Lincoln lore. The Lincoln Pioneer Village, a re-created mid-1800s homestead, is nearby. The Old Rockport Little Theater presents a variety of productions throughout the year. Fishing, boating on the Ohio River; and cross-country skiing in the bluff-filled surrounding area during winter.

When I arrived at the charming Rockport Inn, a wedding-shower party had just gathered in the lobby, waiting to be seated in a private dining room. The room vibrated with loud, friendly chatter, which seemed to perfectly characterize the quaint small-town atmosphere that the inn calls to mind.

I met Emil back in the kitchen, where he was helping the cook ready luncheon plates and mimosa for the shower. In between his slapping tomatoes and lettuce on sandwiches, he told me that the 1855 inn is ☞ one of the oldest remaining buildings in this history-filled Ohio River town.

He excused himself and took a platter of sandwiches out to the dining room. When he returned, Emil told me that the building still rests on the original hand-hewn logs and beams used to build the house. I saw the old square-shaped iron nails that hold it together.

Later, as we walked up the stairs and down a long hallway to reach the guest rooms, we discovered that we're "Big Ten" brothers, both having completed studies at Northwestern University's graduate school. So we had lots of catching up to do before we proceeded any further.

Inside the rooms, I first noticed the ☞ original poplar hardwood floors that have survived all kinds of renovations. Emil and Carolyn have decorated with antique beds, oak dressers, sitting chairs, and Oriental-style rugs. Even with the party going on downstairs and a dining room full of customers, it was quiet and peaceful here.

The inn prides itself on excellent food. Prime rib, tournedos, beef *bordelaise,* and stuffed pork chops are just some of the entrées offered here. A daily special is announced by waiters at the dining tables.

Homemade pies and cookies are another treat at the Rockport. A good way to work off dessert is to walk to the foot of the two-hundred-foot bluff at the end of Main Street. An historical marker notes that it was from here that young Abe Lincoln left on his famous flatboat trip to New Orleans.

How to get there: From Evansville, take Indiana 66 into Rockport; then turn right on Linda. At Main Street, turn left and continue to Third Street. Turn right to the inn.

♟

B: *The Rockport Inn was one of the first area buildings to have glass windows. If you look closely, you'll see wavy lines in the old lead glass.*

Old Davis Hotel
Shipshewana, Indiana
46565

Innkeeper: Alvin Miller
Address/Telephone: 228 West Main Street, P.O. Box 545; (219) 768–7300
Rooms: 6; 1 with private bath.
Rates: $25 single, $50 double. Includes continental breakfast. Children and well-behaved pets OK.
Open: All year.
Facilities & Activities: Nearby renowned Shipshewana Auction & Flea Markets, with more than 900 outdoor vendors, every Tuesday and Wednesday, May to November. Massive antique and livestock auctions year round. Area festivals in warm months only. See May corn planting, June–August haymaking, mid-June–mid-July wheat harvest, October–November corn harvest in surrounding Amish fields.

As I walked into the shop area of the Old Davis Hotel, Alvin was showing a piece of antique fabric to a customer looking to make a quilt. The woman smiled broadly to herself at her good fortune.

I also smiled because I'd stopped in to visit the historic

hotel that Alvin purchased a few years ago and was delighted at *my* good fortune.

The 1891 building is right on Main Street in Shipshewana, the heart of Indiana's Amish country. From the hotel's front porch, I watched horse-drawn buggies pull off the street to a metal hitching rail. Here horses snort, chew on their bits, and paw the ground as they wait for their simply clad Amish owners to hop aboard for the ride home.

Even from some of the rooms, you can hear the clip-clopping of horses' hooves on the pavement.

Six guest rooms are spartan and simple: double beds covered with hand-stitched quilts (naturally), and Victorian-style dressers. The ☞ historic character of the hotel remains intact, with creaky staircase, long second-floor hallways, and high-ceilinged rooms. There are historic photos of the town and hotel on one wall.

Breakfast is continental style, according to Alvin's daughter Kristine, who manages the hotel. She bakes home-made breads and muffins to go along with cheeses, meats, fruits, and "whatever else we decide for the day." She'll recommend an area restaurant for home-cooked dinners; the Patchwork Quilt Country Inn near Middlebury (just twelve miles away) serves incredible down-home food.

The hotel also ☞ offers buggy rides "right off the front porch" into the Amish countryside during the good-weather season.

How to get there: Off I–80/90, exit at Indiana 15 and go south to U.S. 20. Go east to Indiana 5 and drive 2 miles north to Shipshewana. At Main Street, go right to the hotel.

B: Downtown Shipshewana looks like a one-hundred-year-old photograph of the town come to life.

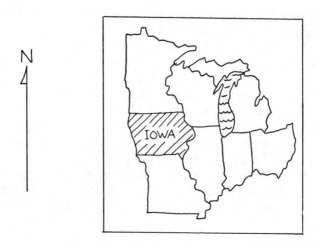

N

IOWA

SIOUX CITY

WATERLOO

DUBUQUE 4.

MISSOURI RIVER

MISSISSIPPI RIVER

STONE CITY 10. CEDAR RAPIDS

1. ADEL

ELK HORN 5.

DES MOINES

HOMESTEAD 6.

TIPTON 11.

2. AVOCA

PELLA 9.

MOUNT PLEASANT 8.

KEOSAUQUA 7.
BENTONSPORT 3.

Iowa

Numbers on map refer to towns numbered below.

Walden Acres
Adel, Iowa
50003

Innkeepers: Phyllis and Dale Briley
Address/Telephone: R.R. 1, Box 30; (515) 987–1338 or 987–1567
Rooms: 3; all with shared bath.
Rates: $30 single, $40 double. Includes hearty farm-style breakfast.
   Children $10. Pets boarded, $5. Horses boarded.
Open: All year.
Facilities & Activities: Recreation room–solarium. Outdoor trampoline. Forty acres of rolling hills with 6-acre horse-shaped lake for fishing. Four-room antique shop. Stable for 18 horses; kennel runs.

   I'm a baseball fanatic. That's why I believe Walden Acres is a special kind of baseball shrine.
   The shrine is an old barn standing on the historic Bob Feller homestead. Inside the weathered structure, the Hall of Fame pitcher for the Cleveland Indians threw that incredible fastball to his dad when he was just an Iowa farmboy with a live arm.
   The farmstead is home to Phyllis and her country-vet husband, Dale (who has a small cottage clinic for his animals

far away from the main house), and to their guests who stay overnight at this idyllic forty-acre spread.

On my visit, Dale was tending to his patients; an Irish setter was an especially happy fellow, licking his owner's face in thanks that she'd come to retrieve him. ☞ What with a kindly, soft-spoken country vet, horses in a corral behind the main house, and bales of hay strewn in the fields, I couldn't help but feel that I'd stepped into a scene right out of James Herriot's animal tales.

Phyllis and Dale share a stately English-style home with guests. Phyllis showed me the charming guest rooms: One was soft and delicate, with Oriental rugs, ceiling fans, a lacy bedspread and curtains, and a fireplace; another was more rough-hewn, laden with ☞ attractive antiques and folk art.

I was particularly taken with a large antique basket hanging on the wall. Phyllis told me that it had been used by field hands harvesting tobacco.

If you like farm breakfasts, you're in for a treat. Phyllis serves "stick to your ribs" Iowa breakfasts to guests in her English country kitchen. That means eggs, sausage, flapjacks, bread, rolls, and hot coffee. (It's just a short ride to Des Moines for lunch and dinner spots.)

Of course, I toured the historic barn that is crucial to the Bob Feller legend. The one-hundred-year-old building now boards horses, as Walden Acres is a B&B for four-legged travelers, too! I especially liked watching the animals being turned out to pasture daily.

Phyllis said that people often stop along the road just to take a glimpse inside the Feller barn and soak up some baseball history.

Funny—that's exactly how I discovered Walden Acres.

How to get there: Take I–80 to the Waukee/Booneville exit (#117) and go south on Rural Route 22 for 1 mile. At the top of the hill turn right down a gravel road and proceed for 1 mile until you come to the barn and home on the left side of the road.

ꗦ

B: *Bob Feller often stops by the home during summers to visit. Wouldn't it be great to run into a Hall-of-Famer on "Backroad, U.S.A."?*

TAYLOR

Victorian
Bed and Breakfast Inn
Avoca, Iowa
51521

Innkeepers: Andrea and Rodney Murray, owners; Nancy McCarthy,
   manager
Address/Telephone: 425 Walnut Street; (712) 343–6336
Rooms: 5; with two shared baths.
Rates: $38 to $44. Includes full breakfast. Children over 12 OK.
Open: All year.
Facilities & Activities: Area tours of grain and livestock farms ar-
   ranged by request. Just east of Avoca is the "biggest little an-
   tique center in southwest Iowa," with 12 shops. An hour's
   drive away is Carstens Memorial Farm, a 100-year-old farm-
   stead; DeSoto National Wildlife Refuge; Elk Horn Danish
   Windmill; and Botna Bend Park.

   I immediately liked this gracious turn-of-the-century
Queen Anne Victorian. Nancy pointed out the ☛ magnificent Southern yellow pine woodwork and floors that literally
sparkle. They're easily the most outstanding features of the
home.

Finely carved pine columns in both the parlor and elegant dining room are highlighted by large windows that let the sunlight in, adding luster to the pine adornments. Nancy adds her personal touch with beautiful flower arrangements in both rooms.

All the guest rooms have names of flowers, like Jasmine and Apple Blossom, and they're reached by climbing a hand-turned pine staircase. One room has fine antique ☞ walnut Eastlake treasures, while others boast brass beds, floral-print wallpapers, and other decorating goodies. They're happy and friendly spaces.

Nancy also pointed out the ☞ handmade quilts, fashioned by her mother-in-law. The innkeeper herself chose wallpapers to match those wonderful treasures.

My favorite is the Wild Rose Room, resplendent in pink pastels and washed in white furniture that includes an iron-rail bed; what makes it so is the ☞ little alcove with tall windows that look out onto the quiet street.

☞ Hearty farm-fare breakfasts are Nancy's specialty. You'll be treated to eggs, meats, homemade rolls and breads, fruit, and juices. She'll arrange special dinners for $35 per couple. A typical feast includes slaw *béarnaise,* breast of chicken stuffed with country ham, Amaretto sautéed apples, Swiss potatoes, apple-rye bread, and tart green-apple-and-grape pie. If she hadn't had a full house, I would have invited myself to dinner.

How to get there: Take I–80 to U.S. 59. Go south to Avoca. U.S. 59 turns into Walnut Street in town. The inn is just past the downtown section, on the right side of the street.

☒

B: Look for the Murphy bed hidden in an oak cabinet and the imposing Northwind walnut sideboard, both dating from the 1800s.

Mason House Inn
Bentonsport, Iowa
52565

Innkeeper: Kathy Fisher, manager
Address/Telephone: Rural Route 2, Bentonsport, Keosauqua, Iowa
   52565; (319) 592-3133
Rooms: 8; with 2 shared baths.
Rates: $35 single, $45 to $55 double. Includes full breakfast. Children OK. Well-behaved pets only. No credit cards.
Open: All year.
Facilities & Activities: Entire village declared National Historic
   District by Department of Interior in 1972. Walk to 1852 Post
   Office; 1853 Greef Store; 1867 Greef House, at that time the
   town's showplace.

   If you look upstream from the bridge in this historic river-front village, you'll see ripples on the water marking the site of the old dam. It's a reminder of the days when the Des Moines River teemed with riverboat traffic, mills lined the winding banks, and nearly fifteen hundred people lived in the town.

   Now only twenty-six people live here. "Twenty-five, since a woman just threw her husband out of the house," said a chuckling Kathy. "In a town this small, you can't help but know these things."

The Mason House Inn was originally built to serve steamboats navigating the winding channels of the river. Its cozy Georgian stylings provide a warm welcome for big-city visitors.

The parlor appears much as it did in its heyday, with many original furnishings. Kathy is especially proud of the inn's beautiful 🖝 silk-upholstered sofa and chairs, and the hanging oil lamp. She said there was no electricity here until the 1950s!

We spent lots of time chatting in the antique-filled dining room, a tiny room where a long wooden table almost guarantees conversation among guests.

The guest rooms boast many antiques, including a 🖝 massive walnut headboard that stretches almost to the ceiling—10 feet high. Kathy explained that you won't find any closets here because they were taxed as regular rooms in pioneer days, so you use clothes hooks on the walls.

I especially like room number five; it looks out over the river and was a favorite of namesake Lewis Mason's son, a state senator who liked to gaze out at the old wharf while watching steamboat traffic pass by. Number seven is another beauty, with a 🖝 tall walnut headboard on a large bed, Victorian dressing mirror, fainting couch, and wood-burning stove—all original to the inn.

Kathy's breakfasts are a treat. How does broiled French toast, grilled grapefruit, eggs, sausage, homemade biscuits, and muffins sound? Specially arranged dinners at the inn are romantic affairs, with dishes like Greek baked chicken a guest favorite.

How to get there: Take Iowa 1 south through Keosauqua, cross the river, and go uphill to J40. Then go east to Bentonsport. Turn right on any village road that heads toward the river. The inn is along the bank.

B: *Don't miss the copper-lined pull-down bathtub that unfolds from a kitchen wall cabinet opposite the stove. Its position kept bathers nice and toasty on frigid Midwestern nights.*

63

The Redstone Inn
Dubuque, Iowa
52001

Innkeeper: Gail Naughton
Address/Telephone: 504 Bluff Street; (319) 582–1894
Rooms: 15, with 5 suites; all with private bath.
Rates: $45 to $105 single, $55 to $120 double. Includes continental breakfast. Children OK.
Open: All year.
Facilities & Activities: Afternoon teas and luncheons for guests and other visitors. Dubuque attractions include downhill skiing, Mississippi riverboat cruises, riverboat museum, Cable Car Square (specialty shops in an historic location, scenic railcar climbing 189-foot bluff with view of three states).

If you ever had dreams of piloting a paddle-wheeler down the mighty Mississippi, you can get the next best thing in Dubuque. In this historic river town, you can ply the waters on the stern-wheeler *Spirit of Dubuque,* tramp the decks of the side-wheeler *William M. Black,* and immerse yourself in the exhibits of the F. W. Woodward Riverboat Museum.

And there's no better way of continuing a "living history" visit than by staying at The Redstone Inn, an 1894 Victorian mansion restored to all its splendor.

I registered in a rich oak-paneled hallway on a first floor that retains much of the home's original ambience. The mauve, deep blue, green, and burgundy colors are used to complement The Redstone's many ☞ original stained-glass windows, Gail told me.

Since no two guest rooms are alike, Gail will help you select your favorite from a color-photo portfolio kept at the reception area.

I'm in good shape, so the almost forty steps it takes to get to the third-floor rooms were no problem. (In fact, I enjoyed the exercise.) My room was like many offered at the inn—antique furnishings with ☞ walnut beds, balloon curtains, period lighting fixtures, muted floral wallpapers, and bed quilts. Mine had a whirlpool, which I headed for immediately; some also have fireplaces, with free logs.

Gail serves breakfast downstairs in a small dining room opposite the parlor. Starched white table linens and fresh flowers adorn the tables. I munched on chewy homemade caramel rolls, croissants, and bagels.

Afternoon teas feature a variety of English teas, dainty finger sandwiches, tarts, biscuits, and a dessert of the day— maybe gingerbread-cherry pie, an inn specialty. One of the dinner restaurants Gail recommends is the elegant Ryan Mansion, just a short drive away.

Be sure to peek at the inn's parlor, an exquisite example of Victorian elegance. It took me a few minutes to get comfortable in this very formal room, with its ☞ ornate furniture, Oriental-style rugs, and tile fireplace with an elaborate mantel. The gas chandelier is original to the home, as are the cherub figurines that gaze down from the plaster-cast ceiling. Gail said they're finished in gold leaf.

How to get there: Whether entering Dubuque from the west via U.S. 151 or from the east on U.S. 20, pick up Locust Street at the bridge and proceed to University. Turn left and drive to Bluff; then turn left again. The inn's on the street's left side.

B: *Victorian elegance at its finest.*

The Stout House
Dubuque, Iowa
52001

Innkeepers: Jim Borden and Barbara Kopperud
Address/Telephone: 1105 Locust Street; (319) 582–1890. (Register at The Redstone Inn, 504 Bluff Street; [319] 582–1894.)
Rooms: 5; 1 with private bath.
Rates: $45 to $55 double occupancy. Includes continental breakfast. Children OK.
Open: All year.
Facilities & Activities: Main-floor library. Near Mississippi River; riverboat excursions, water activities. City has many architecturally interesting and restored buildings. Riverboat museum. Scenic railway to top of high bluffs and panorama of 3 states and river; Cable Car Square specialty shops. Near ski areas.

This is one of the most fabulous mansions I have ever seen—where architecture is *the* attraction.

An 1891 masterpiece built by a local lumber baron at the then-fantastic cost of $300,000, The Stout House boasts massive red sandstone blocks, a squared turret, and huge rounded arches among its notable architectural details.

Inside are treasures far beyond words: heavy leaded-glass doors; rosewood, maple, oak, and sycamore woodwork; ornate stained-glass windows; ☛ fireplace hearths of beautiful mosaic tiles; beamed ceilings; Italian marble bathrooms; and lots more.

Purchased in 1909 by the Archdiocese of Dubuque for its archbishop's residence, the house has remained in its almost original condition. Recently bought by a restoration company, it's now open for the public's enjoyment.

The reception hall has a baronial feel, with ornate stained-glass windows, a huge marble fireplace, and ☛ intricately carved, magnificent rosewood woodwork. The tall grandfather's clock encased in carved rosewood was especially hand-carved to set into the woodwork.

I counted five fireplaces on the main floor; all hearths are made of imported mosaic tile. The original dining room has a huge oak quarter-sawn table—that seats eighteen!

The most impressive room is the main-floor library. There's wonderful oak paneling, and a ☛ heavy beamed ceiling is supported by four magnificent green onyx columns, which themselves are trimmed in decorative mosaics.

I particularly like the second-floor guest rooms. Colorful stained-glass windows threw rainbow light onto my bed. Imported Italian-marble bathrooms (the marble sinks have German-silver legs) made me feel like a visiting dignitary. The inn's largest bath has a beautiful mosaic tile floor with a center medallion. Some rooms have fireplaces.

There's also a "mystery" room, which is done in light colors, French Provincial style—very feminine. It is totally out of character with the rest of the mansion.

Guests must go to the nearby Redstone Inn for a breakfast of morning sweet cakes, croissants, and tea. For one of Dubuque's finest dining experiences, try the Ryan Mansion.

How to get there: Enter Dubuque from the west via U.S. 151 or from the east on U.S. 20. Pick up Locust Street at the bridge and proceed to the Stout House.

B: *Staying at The Stout House is like living out a fairy tale in a home that's an overwhelming testament to nineteenth-century extravagance.*

The Travelling Companion
Elk Horn, Iowa
51531

Innkeepers: Karolyn and Duane Ortgies
Address/Telephone: 4314 Main Street; (712) 764–8932
Rooms: 3, with 1 suite; shared baths.
Rates: $40. Includes full breakfast. Children OK. No credit cards.
Open: All year.
Facilities & Activities: Authentic 1848 working Danish windmill
   downtown, General Store Museum, historic Bestemor's House,
   Hans Christian Andersen statue, and Danish ethnic foods in
   area restaurants.

I never expected to see an authentic Danish windmill in
the middle of an Iowa cornfield. But there it was.

When I found out that the town was basically a Danish
ethnic community, some of the shock wore off. In fact, at The
Travelling Companion, the innkeepers have named each
room for a fable of the town's celebrated champion, Hans
Christian Andersen.

The Ugly Duckling Room has antique walnut furniture,
with a high Victorian bedstead and handmade quilts. The
fainting couch in the corner of the room's small sitting area

belonged to Duane's grandfather. Karolyn showed me his name stamped on the bottom.

The Thumbelina Room is cozy, with pressed-back oak furniture. The bed is so high that you might have to step onto a stool to reach it. Karolyn said a guest once told her the higher the bed off a floor, the more prominent the family. At least, that was the rule of thumb in older days.

Another room is dusted in warm rose colors, with two full-sized white iron-rail beds.

I asked about the teddy bears sitting on the stairs leading to the guest rooms. These charming fellas were made by Karolyn's sister, who fashioned most of the inn's many country crafts.

There is a lot to enjoy here, including a small antique shop. Karolyn set off the inn's player piano for me, to get me into the antique-browsing mood.

Karolyn prepares a hearty Danish breakfast for her guests. A special treat is her *strata* (egg-soaked bread stuffed with cheese, baked to a puffy delight). She also offers Danish pastries (of course) and fruit cups.

The Danish Inn restaurant just down the street is Karolyn's favorite going-out-to-dinner spot. Some of her menu suggestions are *aebelskiver* (crispy browned pancake served in spheres), *rullepolse* (onions and spiced beef), and *medisterpolse* (browned pork shoulder sausage).

How to get there: Take I–80 to the Elk Horn exit (#54), and go north 7 miles on Iowa 173 into town. Iowa 173 turns into Main Street, and the home is just a short drive past the windmill, on the left side of the street.

※

B: Take a peek behind the home's front door to see a beautiful antique Danish corner wardrobe made of pine. It's one of the finest of its kind I've ever seen.

Die Heimat Country Inn
Homestead, Iowa
52236

Innkeepers: Don and Sheila Janda
Address/Telephone: Main Street; (319) 622–3937
Rooms: 19, including 5 deluxe; all with private bath.
Rates: $24.75 to $37.75; deluxe, $35.75 to $42.75. Includes breakfast from April 15 to November 15. Children OK. Only well-behaved pets.
Open: All year.
Facilities & Activities: Nearby are the 7 historic villages of the Amana Colonies, with antique and specialty stores, an open-hearth bakery, museums, furniture shops, and woolen mills.

Homestead is a peaceful little village off a busy interstate in the historic Amana Colonies, settled in the 1840s by German immigrants seeking religious freedom and a communal lifestyle. And as soon as I turned off the highway to reach Die Heimat Country Inn, I became absorbed in the quiet of this century-old agricultural community.

Whatever pressures might have been building inside me during the long drive to Iowa disappeared once I stepped inside. Sheila greeted me at the desk, full of good cheer and

chatter. She's generously decorated her charming lobby with
☞ nationally famous Amana furniture (the sofas are original
to the 1854 inn) and a large walnut Amana grandfather's
clock ticking softly in the corner of the room.

☞ Soothing German zither music wafted through the
inn, and I immediately began to feel at home. (*Die Heimat* is
German for "the homestead" or "the home place.") On the
way to my room, Sheila pointed out the cross-stitchings
hanging on many of the walls; they're ☞ German house
blessings, many brought from the old country.

My room was small and cozy, with sturdy Amana furniture, an electric kerosene lamp, writing desk, rocking chair,
and brass-lantern ceiling lamp. It's so quiet that you'll probably wake up in the morning to the sound of chirping birds, as
I did.

I also woke up to a breakfast of ☞ Oma and Opa (German for grandmother and grandfather) rolls with frosting
and fruit toppings, fresh fruit, juice, and coffee. Then I
started the day by swaying on the unique Amana platform
swings out in the yard.

Later I explored the thrumming communities of the
seven Amana Colonies' villages, with all kinds of historical
and commercial attractions, including fabulous bakery goods
and meat shops. Sheila can point out the "can't miss" stops.

Bill Zuber's restaurant, just down the street from the
inn, was one of her recommendations. Zuber was a pitcher
for the New York Yankees, a hometown boy discovered by
scouts when he was seen tossing cabbages during a local
harvest. I liked the menus in the shapes of baseballs, and the
home-style cooking was scrumptious. My baked chicken with
fried potatoes, veggies, and green peas in thick gravy would
be hard to beat. Also served are Amana ham, pork, and baked
steaks.

How to get there: Take I–80 to exit 225 (151 north), and go about 5
miles. At the intersection of Highways 6 and 49, turn left past Bill
Zuber's restaurant to the inn just down the block.

Hotel Manning
Keosauqua, Iowa
52565

Innkeepers: Edgar, Janet, and Peggy Weber
Address/Telephone: 100 Van Buren Street; (319) 293–3232
Rooms: 22 historic rooms, 2 river-view suites; 8 with private bath.
Rates: $20 single, $25 to $50 double. Children welcome. Limited
　　wheelchair access.
Open: All year.
Facilities & Activities: Short walk to oldest Iowa courthouse
　　(1840). Near golf, tennis, canoeing, swimming, hiking. Na-
　　tional Historic District of Bentonsport 6 miles away. Across the
　　river is Lacey-Keosauqua State Park.

　　I stepped out onto the ☛ wraparound second-floor veranda of this historic hotel to gaze at the fast-moving Des
Moines River. I imagined a paddle-wheeler churning down
the horseshoe-bend channel, its whistle shrilly piercing the
air to signal its arrival in town.

　　Well, steamboats are a thing of the past, but the Hotel
Manning still stands on the river bank, not much changed
from that riverboat era of long ago.

　　It's a magnificent example of 1854 ☛ riverboat-style architecture. I found high 14-foot ceilings in a rich oak-filled lobby that had a genuine pioneer feel. Those high ceilings also meant that it took a lot of step climbing to reach the second-floor guest rooms.

But my reward was ☞ antique-filled rooms, with floral wallpapers, plank floors covered by braided rugs, walnut highboys, and iron-rail and sleigh beds covered in hand-stitched postage stamp–style quilts. Next time I'm here, I want to stay in one of the hotel's suites that overlook the river.

Another treat is good Midwestern home-style cooking served in the huge, antique-filled dining room. An inn specialty is Edwin's Choice, a bacon-wrapped filet mignon; another favorite is the Mercantile Special, a 16-ounce, char-broiled T-bone steak. The hotel's homemade rolls are a local favorite.

How to get there: Reach Keosauqua from the north or south on Iowa 1, and the hotel is one block from that highway. From the north, turn left on Van Buren just before the bridge in the heart of town; from the south, turn right onto Van Buren to the inn.

♉

B: *The lobby piano was shipped from New Orleans by steamboat in the 1850s.*

Harlan House Hotel
Mt. Pleasant, Iowa
52641

Innkeepers: Mike and Lynette Richards
Address/Telephone: 122 North Jefferson Street; (319) 385–3126
Rooms: 38, with 3 suites; 14 with private bath.
Rates: $35 single, $55 double, $75 suite. Children welcome. Well-
   behaved pets only.
Open: All year.
Facilities & Activities: Harlan Club, a beautifully restored food-
   and-drink room done in rich oaks and historic-print wallpaper.
   Dinner and lawn concerts.

   One of the unique features of this 1857 inn is its tradition of an 🖝 "open cash register" in the dining room. Often
guests simply pay the price of their meals and make their
own change in the register. "And it's never short," says Lynette. "In fact, when I checked it today, it was 35 cents over."
   That's the kind of atmosphere you'll find here in Main
Street, USA. It's got a town square, a train station—and the
historic Harlan House Hotel.
   Lynette showed off her recently restored lobby, decorated in soothing shades of pink and white, with an 🖝

74

arched 12-foot ceiling and crown moldings. We sat on high-back sofas in front of a wide fireplace while a pianist played soft classical music on the lobby's baby grand.

She told me about the hotel's Abe Lincoln connection. Seems that the daughter of the hotel's namesake married the eldest son of the late president in 1868. James Harlan had always been a close confidant and adviser to Lincoln.

That's why the hotel has its own Lincoln Room, with a portrait of Lincoln over the working fireplace and other historic documents and photographs decorating the walls. The room is most often used for private parties.

Mike is impassioned about showing how the Harlan House restoration actually mirrors the hotel's golden era. He led me to comfortable guest rooms furnished with antiques and reproductions and decorated with historic wallpaper designs searched out by Lynette.

Food in the dining room is down-home good, with dishes like stews, meatloaf, and country pork chops; and there are great homemade pies.

How to get there: Mt. Pleasant can be reached from the north or south on U.S. Highway 218. Then go west on U.S. 34 to Washington Street; make a right on Washington and another right on Jefferson to the hotel.

❧

B: *For decades, people have come from miles around on Saturday evenings just for a slice of the inn's scrumptious lemon meringue pie. It was my misfortune to arrive on a Tuesday.*

Strawtown Inn
Pella, Iowa
50219

Innkeepers: Roger Olson and Ken Howard
Address/Telephone: 1111 Washington Street; (515) 628–2681
Rooms: 7, with 1 suite; all with private bath.
Rates: $45 to $65. Includes full breakfast. Children welcome.
   Wheelchair access.
Open: All year.
Facilities & Activities: Five dining rooms, including a third-story
   barroom. Gift, antique, and country-store shops next door.
   Surrounding town has many old-world Dutch-front buildings.
   Thousands of tulips planted in beds throughout town. Massive
   klokkenspel (several Dutch figures performing to the accom-
   paniment of a carillon) at Franklin Place. Annual Tulip Time
   festival in May. A 45-minute drive to Des Moines.

   I visited the Strawtown Inn during the spring, when
thousands of ☛ blooming tulips planted along walkways and
in gardens create swirls of rainbow colors and fragrant scents
for lucky guests. (They're replaced by bright red geraniums
in summer.)
   This is just one way the inn honors its ethnic heritage.

Another is the inn's name: Mid-1800s Dutch settlers built huts on this corner of the then-tiny village from long slough grass and covered them with straw woven into a stick frame.

The guest rooms are delightful. Each *kamer* (room) is artfully decorated and has its own personality. The *Bedstee kamer*, with its ☞ Dutch prints, pastel floral wallpaper, and Dutch beds built into the wall, is one of my favorites. Stenciling fans will love the *Pannigen kamer*, with its Dutch border stencils on walls and ceilings.

And the *Juliana kamer* is a long room with a slanted ceiling, skylight windows, walnut antique reproductions, and a photograph of former Netherlands Queen Juliana hanging on the wall. It was named for the queen to commemorate her May 1942 visit to Pella.

I cannot think of a better place to enjoy a Dutch breakfast than in the inn's bright morning room. Ladder-back chairs, rich oak woodwork, cheery pastel colors, and scatter rugs covering plank floors add to the old-world ambience. A cold-meat tray is a real treat, along with Dutch cheeses, breads, rolls, beverages—and, of course, a hard-boiled egg.

Five antique-laden rooms host inn lunches and dinners; one even has double Dutch ovens. The ☞ food is celebrated, having received recommendations from diverse publications like the *Des Moines Register, The New Yorker, Holiday Travel,* and *The Saturday Evening Post.* I was especially intrigued by stuffed pork chops with apple-walnut dressing and mushroom sauce, Dutch spiced beef, and pheasant under glass carved tableside.

The inn also holds special international gourmet-dinner weekends in April and November.

How to get there: Pella is reached off Iowa 163. Follow that to Washington Street. The inn is on the west side of town.

B: *Many of Pella's stores have Dutch fronts; you can see wooden shoes being carved at the Historical Village; and authentic Dutch street organs pipe happy tunes for visitors.*

The Inn at Stone City
Stone City, Iowa
52205

Innkeepers: Cheryl and Randy Leclere
Address/Telephone: Route 1, Anamosa; (319) 462–4733 or 462–2119
Rooms: 9; 6 in the main house, 3 in the general store; 1 with private bath.
Rates: $35 single, $55 double. Children and pets OK.
Open: All year.
Facilities & Activities: Breakfast, lunch, and dinner available in the dining room. Nearby canoeing. Buggy and sleigh rides. Winter: rent skis for nearby 12 miles of groomed cross-country trails. Countryside peace and quiet.

Cheryl was cradling a little baby rabbit as I rode up the winding driveway of The Inn at Stone City. "We've got so many animals in these woods," she said as I approached the house after parking my car. "You can't help but cuddle all God's creatures."

The Inn is nestled in the ☞ rolling hills and quiet river valley of the Wapsipinicon River that inspired many of Grant Wood's paintings. Stone City has hosted internationally known writers and artists who want a secluded retreat that offers a complete getaway from workday pressures.

I asked Cheryl about The Inn's striking architecture. It's not often that I find a massive stone building with a distinct urban feel way out in the woods in a region of small family farmsteads. She told me the 1903 home was built by an Irish immigrant stone baron who owned local quarries and wanted the finest home in the country.

Randy added that The Inn's extreme privacy led to its use as an art colony by Grant Wood in 1931 and 1932; women lived in the house, and men stayed in wagons.

Both Cheryl and Randy led me through The Inn's six main-house guest rooms. They're furnished with an eclectic group of antique items; there's even a shared whirlpool spa to soak away the day's cares.

The expansive first floor, with all its open space, wonderfully conveys The Inn's sense of friendliness and down-home warmth. You'll often find Trivial Pursuit and all kinds of cards being played in the game room. It sports antique tavern tables (with small compartments below the table top for your spirits) and chairs, plank floors, and ceiling fans.

And I asked Randy about the three unusual dark-stone fireplaces here. He explained that they're made of soapstone, darkened by soot and ashes that seep into the porous surface.

Meals are served on request. Cheryl likes to whip up scrambled eggs, gingerbread-apple pancakes, and homemade muffins for breakfasts. Dinners are served family-style and can feature anything from roast beef to crab legs.

Other guest rooms are located at the nearby, newly restored General Store, whose lower-level pub is said to be a frequent gathering place for Iowa's top folk musicians.

How to get there: Take I–151 to Iowa 1 and turn right toward Stone City or Anamosa. Then follow the signs (if they're still there) or ask someone.

B: *Best of times here: reading out on the lawn under the huge evergreens; wandering in the woods shared by wild turkeys; watching the stars peek out from under an azure sky.*

Victorian House of Tipton
Tipton, Iowa
52772

Innkeepers: Robert and Christine Gelms
Address/Telephone: 508 East 4th Street; (319) 886–2633
Rooms: 5; with 3½ shared baths.
Rates: $35 single, $55 double. Includes full breakfast. Children
  welcome.
Open: All year.
Facilities & Activities: Two dining rooms: Luncheons, gourmet
  meals served with advance notice for both house guests and
  other visitors. Inn provides bikes to guests; near Cedar River
  canoeing and fishing; riding stables nearby. Short ride to Her-
  bert Hoover Presidential Birthplace, Amana Colonies; Mississippi River just 35 minutes away.

This massive Eastlake-style Victorian mansion domi-
nates a block peppered with fine turn-of-the-century homes.
It has splendid examples of Victorian architectural touches,
from the 10-foot-tall etched-glass double front doors that
open into the gingerbread-filled foyer, furnished in rich mahogany and with the original kerosene chandelier, to ☞ the

chalk-paint frescoes that grace many of the home's walls and ceilings.

The 1883 home, built at an original cost of $9,000, has lost little of its architectural integrity over the years. ☞ I love the solid brass butterfly and arrowhead door hinges found throughout the house and the vinegar-painted doors. Stained- and tinted-glass windows cast muted colors into the high-ceilinged rooms.

Guest rooms on the second and third floors are antique-laden, large, and airy. A bathroom on the second floor features an inviting clawfooted tub facing a window that overlooks the oldest oak tree in Cedar County, estimated to be at least 250 years old.

Christine and Robert are refugees from Chicago's corporate rat race. They showed me ☞ Robert's collection of gold records and photos with rock stars that he gathered as program director for a major Chicago radio station. Get them to talk about their legendary St. Patrick's Day parties, where scores of people often lined up outside their Chicago home to catch a glimpse of rockers like Bob Seeger or Frank Zappa.

Christine grew up next door to the mansion and has lots of wonderfully funny stories about Victorian-era occupants. ☞ Especially entertaining are the tales she weaves about a notorious Tipton figure who used to steal water from the outdoor faucet of her next-door neighbors under the cover of night to avoid paying money to the city for water.

Inn breakfasts include omelets, German apple pancakes, homemade rolls, fruits, and coffee. Christine's scrumptious dinners feature the likes of broiled swordfish or filet mignon, with Vichy carrots, cheddar potatoes, rice pilaf, homemade rolls with hand-churned butter, and chocolate mousse for dessert.

How to get there: Exit I–80 at Iowa 38, going north to Tipton. In the city, take a right on 4th Street; drive until you reach the house.

B: *If you can't have fun with Robert and Christine while enjoying their wonderful Victorian home, you're just not trying.*

Michigan

Numbers on map refer to towns numbered below.

Watervale Inn
Arcadia, Michigan
49613

Innkeeper: Dori Noble Turner
Address/Telephone: Watervale Road; (616) 352–9083; winter mailing address: 20265 Cottagewood Road, Excelsior, Minnesota 55331; (612) 474–8558
Rooms: 20, all with shared bath; 12 cottages, all with private bath.
Rates: Rooms, $35 to $40 per person, with 2-day minimum. Includes breakfast and dinner. Weekly rates available for rooms and cottages. Children OK. No credit cards.
Open: May through October.
Facilities & Activities: Tennis courts. Located on lake; rowboats, canoes, sailboats, and sailboards available. Nearby woods and high sand dunes.

It seems as though we have the same people return year after year," Dori said. "It's almost like our own little family."

The Watervale Inn is ☞ one of Michigan's best-kept secrets. The main lodge (an historic boarding house for lumberjacks) and its outlying cottages (homes for loggers with families) make up the entire historic 1880s logging town of Watervale, hugging lakes Lower Herring and Michigan among spectacular shorelines of high bluffs and shifting sand dunes.

Dori said that schooners once loaded cut timbers off a long wharf built into the lake. She pointed out into the water; I could still see some pier posts peeking out from under the waves.

When the lumber company went bankrupt in 1893, the town was abandoned. In the early 1900s, Dori's Uncle Oscar bought the town, and restoration began on some of the buildings. He eventually used it as a discreet vacation hideaway.

Today, the handsome pale-green clapboard boarding house with dark-green shutters neatly trimmed in white continues to be a special retreat. A long veranda faces the lake; it's a perfect spot to enjoy cool evening breezes.

Dori has decorated the upstairs guest rooms in a cozy, plain, and quaint style. ☛ Iron beds with chenille spreads give them a homey look. Comfy rocking chairs are a great way to enjoy a breathtaking view.

Historic family homes can be rented by families and couples; they're also "cozy cute," and some have fireplaces. All have names like "Margaret" and "Barbara." Said Dori: "For Uncle Oscar's old girlfriends, probably."

Hearty breakfasts and dinners, included in the price of the rooms, are served in the old boarding-house dining room. The inn's private chef prepares dinner treats like duck à l'orange with wild rice, and chateaubriand with a special sauce. Dori will even serve up a vegetarian feast for guests on special diets.

No one can go hungry after an inn breakfast of hot or cold cereal, eggs, pancakes, bacon and sausage, toast, juice, and other beverages.

Later, I climbed Mt. Baldy, down at the end of the road; my reward was a breathtaking view of the rugged Lake Michigan shoreline not often seen.

How to get there: From Detroit, take I–75 north to U.S. 10 and go west. At Scottville, take U.S. 31 north to Michigan 22 and continue north to the Total gas station/general store. You've gone too far! Turn around and count six telephone poles to Watervale Road. Turn road and then turn right again at the tennis courts to the inn.

The Terrace Inn
Bay View, Michigan
49770

Innkeepers: Suzanne and Roger McCloud, owners; Roman and
  Becki Barnwell, managers
Address/Telephone: 216 Fairview; (616) 347-2410
Rooms: 30, with 6 suites; 26 with private bath.
Rates: $38 to $78 double occupancy. Includes continental breakfast. Rates vary with season and choice of full bath, half-bath,
  or hall bath. Children welcome.
Open: May 15 to October 15.
Facilities & Activities: Within walking distance of weekly chamber
  music concerts, Sunday-evening vespers program, drama and
  musical theater productions. Nearby hiking trails on 165 acres
  of virgin forest; tennis; swimming at private beach; Saturday
  evening movies at the Auditorium. Gaslight Shopping District
  five minutes away. Near town of Harbor Springs with fancy
  boutiques, golf, horseback riding, sailing, fishing. Mackinac
  Island about 45-minute drive north of Bay View.

    Entering The Terrace Inn is like walking into the past.
That's because the 1911 inn, located on a quiet street among
tall beech, oak, and maple trees, is part of the historic Bay
View community.

What makes Bay View and The Terrace Inn so special? The entire town is listed on the National Register of Historic Places. "There are more than four hundred Victorian summer homes here built between 1875 and the turn of the century," Becki said. "If you're a fan of Victorian homes and like lots of gingerbread, you'll almost go crazy."

I spent lots of time walking along gently curving streets lined with buildings graced with intricate gingerbread finery. It's as if the ☞ entire town is a frozen snapshot, stopped still at the turn of the century.

The inn sits high on a terrace off Little Traverse Bay. It's one of the last buildings constructed by the Methodist Church, which established the Bay View Association in 1875 as part of its traveling Chautauqua arts series. That dedication to the arts continues here today.

Massive trees flank a high front stairway and hide the inn's four stories. Becki showed me ☞ antique oak furniture purchased from Albert Pick and Company of Chicago; the pieces are still in use today.

There's a ☞ great fireplace in the parlor that warms guests on chilly summer nights. And rocking chairs are everywhere.

Guest rooms have iron-rail beds, cheery bright quilts, oak dressers, and high ceilings. I especially like the ☞ transom windows; I could relax on my bed while gazing out at the sky.

Becki's breakfast includes juice, coffee, special teas, fresh fruit, and home-baked muffins. I recommend Stafford's Bay View Inn for terrific home-cooked dinners; the honey-mustard shrimp is fabulous, as is the Lake Superior whitefish broiled in lemon butter.

How to get there: From the south, take U.S. 31 east through Petoskey. Upon leaving the city limits and entering Bay View, the road jogs to the right and crosses a railroad track. Turn right at the first road after the track (the main entrance to Bay View). Turn right again at the first street (Lakeview) and turn left at the Glendale Street stop sign. The rear entrance to the inn is ¼ mile down Glendale on the left. From the north, take U.S. 31 south. The main entrance to Bay View is the second street past the pedestrian overpass. Then follow the above directions.

The Bridge Street Inn
Charlevoix, Michigan
49720

Innkeepers: Doug and Penny Shaw
Address/Telephone: 113 Michigan Avenue; (616) 547–6606
Rooms: 9; 3 with private bath.
Rates: $50 to $70. Includes continental breakfast. Two-night minimum stay during special holiday weekends. Off-season rates available. No children. No smoking.
Open: All year.
Facilities & Activities: Charlevoix is a colorful harbor town on Lake Michigan. Huge marina, fleet, pleasure boating, and charter fishing. Specialty and antique shops. Swimming and picnicking on Lake Michigan and Lake Charlevoix beaches. Ferry boats to Beaver Island. July Venetian Festival; August Art Fair; Fall Color Cruises.

Penny has created a whimsical world of antique attractions inside this magnificent building that boasts spiky gables, leaded- and stained-glass windows, and a long wraparound porch. "We shipped 20,000 pounds of antiques here from [her previous home in] California," she said.

These include a colorful 1950s Wurlitzer jukebox sitting

next to the fireplace, a huge, round time clock almost covering an entire wall, and an antique baby carriage with oversized wheels that would be just about perfect for my daughter, Kate.

I immediately noticed a vintage Underwood typewriter sitting invitingly on a table. "It's just waiting for guests to peck out a message to friends," Penny said. She also encourages guests to "just pour yourself a glass of sherry from the crystal decanters on the fireplace mantel, and get about your task."

The nine guest rooms are warm and friendly, with hardwood plank floors dashed with antique floral rugs. Penny adds a special touch with fresh flowers in each room, individually decorated with more antiques.

In the Autumn Leaves Room, I found a quarter-sized cigar-store Indian and a genuine humpback steamer trunk. The Harbor Rose Room has oak and cherry furnishings and a view of the lake. But I'll take the Evening Glow Room, where I had a spectacular view of Charlevoix's great sunsets.

Breakfast is served in the dining room, or you might open the French doors and take your meal to a cozy sitting area. Penny's spread includes smoked whitefish, bagels, cream cheese, tomatoes, onions, fresh fruit, croissants, cheese plates, and beverages. I like the nearby Grey Gables Inn for dinners, especially their Lake Superior whitefish.

The home (once called the Baker Cottage and intended as the personal residence of the namesake family who built the grand Beach Hotel—long since demolished) has a terrific view of Lake Michigan, Lake Charlevoix, and the downtown drawbridge.

How to get there: From Chicago, take I–94 north to I–196 and continue north. At U.S. 131, go north; then at Michigan 66, turn northwest. At U.S. 31, go north into downtown Charlevoix. Here the road also is called Michigan Avenue. Take 31 one block north of the drawbridge to Dixon and the inn.

☀

B: Maybe you're in the mood for a dinner cruise on the Star of Charlevoix?

Charlevoix Country Inn
Charlevoix, Michigan
49720

Innkeepers: David C. Campbell, Doug Goulait, and Kathy Ingle
Address/Telephone: 106 West Dixon Avenue; (616) 547-5134
Rooms: 8, with 2 apartment suites; all rooms share bath.
Rates: $56 to $95. Includes continental breakfast. Children OK.
Open: All year.
Facilities & Activities: The northwestern Michigan coastline is
    known as the "Land of the Million-Dollar Sunsets." Lake
    Michigan water sports and activities abound, including charter
    fishing. Specialty shops, antique stores, fine restaurants. A
    huge protected harbor makes this one of the most favored ports
    on the lake. Ferry boat to Beaver Island.

The inn is located just off the lake at the end of a quiet
dead-end street. I could feel the mist off Lake Michigan, hear
the soundings of lighthouse foghorns, and see a magnificent
sunset.

The boxlike gray-and-white inn, its stories stacked like
the decks of a ship, reminds me of a captain's pilothouse.
Built in 1896, it once was the private summer cottage used
by special guests of the esteemed Beach Hotel, which no
longer exists.

90

It's warm and cozy—all slate blues, squeaky clean whites, and informal country atmosphere. The innkeepers have individually decorated each guest room with a number of special touches. For example, the ☛ Bike Room has pink-and-white wallpaper with designs of bicycles on the wall borders.

One suite has a manteled brick fireplace, country-styled furniture, cute wall borders resembling stenciling, and ☛ great windows for watching fabulous sunsets.

It's also not surprising that quaint country crafts dot the rooms throughout the inn. That's because "The Parlor," a ☛ country-craft gift shop, is located just off the inn entrance.

A light continental breakfast comes with a room. The Grey Gables Inn serves great prime-rib dinners; Tom's Café, home of Tom's Mom's cookies, features quiches and *nouvelle cuisine*. Both are in town, just a short drive away.

How to get there: From Chicago, take I–94 north to I–196 north. Continue north on U.S. 131 and turn west on Michigan 32. At Michigan 66, go north into Charlevoix; then turn north on U.S. 31 and continue to Ainsile. Turn east and follow Ainsile, which turns into Dixon, to the inn.

Dearborn Inn
Dearborn, Michigan
48124

Innkeeper: Gerald Snider
Address/Telephone: 20301 Oakwood Boulevard; (313) 271–2700,
toll free in Michigan (800) 221–7237, outside Michigan (800)
221–7236
Rooms: 179, with 4 suites; all with private bath. Includes rooms in
main building, historic homes, and motor houses.
Rates: $76 single, $90 double, $190 suites. Kids under 13 free when
using same room facilities with parents. Cribs free. Pets allowed in historic homes and motor houses.
Open: All year.
Facilities & Activities: Full-service dining rooms and restaurants.
Inn situated on 23 quiet acres. Large outdoor pool, tennis
courts, playgrounds, shuffleboards. Golf and other athletic facilities nearby. Two-minute ride to Henry Ford Museum and
Greenfield Village. Short ride to Fairlane Town Center, one of
the world's largest indoor shopping malls.

My wife and I drove up the sweeping circular driveway
that leads to the graceful porticoed entrance of the Dearborn
Inn. It reminded me of a grand mansion of a wealthy colonial
gentleman.

Henry Ford built this inn and its surrounding guest houses in 1931. It was the nation's first "airport hotel" (a small airport was across the street), serving visitors to the Henry Ford Museum and Greenfield Village just down the street.

I easily recognized Ford's love for early America. Our suite in the main building was decorated in colonial fashion with four-poster beds, wing and Windsor chairs, wooden chests, and brass lamps. Particularly fun are five historic colonial-home replicas out back—honoring Edgar Allan Poe, Patrick Henry, Barbara Fritchie, Walt Whitman, and Revolutionary War hero Oliver Wolcott.

My favorite is the Poe Cottage, a modest white clapboard that often serves as a honeymoon suite. A delightfully eerie touch is the ☛ black iron raven "hovering" above the doorway.

Dining here is a real treat. The Early American Room is romantic, with tall Georgian windows, glittery chandeliers, and crisp white linen tablecloths. Fresh flowers on each table add a pampering touch. We dined on Rock Cornish Game Hen Madeira and Country Pork Loin Applejack, while a three-piece, tuxedo-clad combo provided music for evening dancing—as they do every Saturday night.

Less formal is the Ten Eyck Tavern, styled to resemble a colonial public house. Traditional American fare rules here. The next evening we tried the old-fashioned chicken shortbread with garden vegetables, then headed to the "Snug," a lounge where liquor bottles are still kept below the copper-topped bar—in deference to Ford's lifelong opposition to alcohol.

How to get there: When approaching Dearborn, follow the green-and-white directional signs of Greenfield Village, neighbor of the inn on Oakwood Boulevard. From points west via I–94, head east on I–94 to the Oakwood Boulevard exit. Then turn left on Oakwood and proceed 2 miles to the inn. From points west and south via the Indiana and Ohio toll roads, go east to Ohio exit 5 (I–280) and north on I–280 to I–75; continue north on I–75 about 50 miles to Southfield Freeway (Michigan 39). Then turn left on Southfield and go about 5 miles to the Oakwood Boulevard exit; turn left on Oakwood and continue about 2 miles to the inn.

The Kirby House
Douglas, Michigan
49453

Innkeepers; Loren and Marsha Konto

Address/Telephone: Center Street and Blue Star Highway (mailing address: P.O. Box 1174, Saugatuck, Michigan 49453); (616) 857–2904

Rooms: 10, with 1 suite; share 4 baths.

Rates: $55 weekdays, $65 weekends. Includes breakfast. Children and pets OK.

Open: All year.

Facilities & Activities: Common room, swimming pool, hot tub. Near attractions of art colony in Saugatuck; Allegan Forest; Grand Rapids antique markets; Holland's ethnic Dutch villages, museums, specialty shops. Cross-country skiing close by.

The grand Kirby House is an irresistible Victorian pleasure. It just "jumped out" at me with its 🖝 turrets, gables, leaded- and stained-glass windows, and a quaint white picket fence surrounding the grounds.

Marsha has preserved the elegant Victorian interiors, which really impressed me. Especially fetching are 🖝 leaded-prism windows that fling shards of sunlight on origi-

94

nal hardwood floors. I was particularly taken with the ☞ parlor fireplace (one of four in the house). Marsha told me that it was of an unusual cast-iron design.

The home was built in 1890 by Sarah Kirby, who made her considerable fortune from farming ginseng. She wanted to be rid of troublesome pitchers and wash basins, so she replaced them with corner sinks in the bedrooms; some remain to this day.

In 1932 the home became a community hospital and operated in that capacity for thirty years. In fact, the old hospital operating room is now named for Jackie Onassis. Ask Marsha to explain that one.

I almost lost my head over the Anne Boleyn Room. Marsha surmised that it was the maid's room in older times because a dumbwaiter was located in the corner. Now it's bright and airy, with a fabulous oak sleigh bed and pleasant period pieces.

Breakfast means croissants, cheese Danish, old-fashioned sticky buns, fresh fruit, and juices—all served buffet style. (Marsha will be glad to recommend one of many fine restaurants in nearby Saugatuck.) By early morning, many of Marsha's guests were already enjoying the ☞ inn's backyard deck, where lounge chairs, hot tub, and swimming pool await.

How to get there: From Chicago, take I–94 north to I–196 north and go to exit 36. Go north on Blue Star Highway into Douglas. Turn left at the only traffic light and you're there.

ᄇ

B: *Kirby-Bird is the inn parrot; Hundl (Old English for "dog") is the home's English sheepdog. One of them can say his name.*

The Rosemont Inn
Douglas, Michigan
49406

Innkeepers: Ric and Cathy Gillette
Address / Telephone: 83 Lakeshore Drive (mailing address: P.O. Box
   541); (616) 857-2637
Rooms: 14; all with private bath.
Rates: $55 to $70. Includes continental breakfast. Children OK.
Open: All year.
Facilities & Activities: Garden room, swimming pool. Nearby: char-
   ter fishing, boating, scenic supper cruises; golf; hiking the
   Lake Michigan dunes; summer theater; cross-country skiing in
   winter. Close to fine restaurants.

On a cool late-spring day, I drove to The Rosemont Inn.
Foghorns sounded off Lake Michigan, which is just across
the tiny road and down a steep bluff. Lake winds rustled tall
trees that shade the inn's landscaped acre. A touch of sun
peeked through the clouds.

☛ If there's a more perfect location for an inn, I'd like
to know about it.

The inn stands like an inviting friend, a turn-of-the-
century Queen Anne–Victorian that got its start as an 1886

tourist hotel. French doors open onto a small formal sitting room, with an elegant hardwood column fireplace the focal point.

I walked out back to the ☞ Garden Room, perhaps my favorite spot. It's bright and sunny, with cathedral ceilings, and a ceiling-to-floor glass wall that looks out onto the swimming pool. This is where Ric and Cathy serve a buffet-style continental breakfast of juice, rolls, and Danish pastry. They can also suggest some fine dinner spots in nearby Saugatuck.

Country antiques fill the comfortable guest rooms; ☞ nine have gas fireplaces that add a cozy touch. Brass beds adorned with charming bed quilts of rich country prints supply a pinch of colorful pizzazz. Some rooms boast a view of the lake through the tall maples that ring the grounds.

How to get there: From Chicago, take I–94 north to I–196 north. At exit 36, near Douglas, take Ferry Street north to Center Street. Turn east on Center Street and go to Lakeshore Drive; then turn north to the inn.

☒

B: *One of my favorite pastimes is reading a good book on the long veranda.*

The House on the Hill
Ellsworth, Michigan
49729

Innkeepers: Buster and Julie Arnim
Address/Telephone: Box 206, Lake Street; (616) 588–6304
Rooms: 3, all with shared bath.
Rates: $60. Includes full breakfast. No children. No credit cards.
Open: Memorial Day to Mid-December.
Facilities & Activities: Huge turreted veranda overlooking St. Clair Lake. Boating, fishing, swimming. Two gourmet restaurants nearby. Lake Michigan is 5 miles away.

Magnolia Blossom greeted me first. That's the inn's low-to-the-ground basset hound, who's equipped with a foghorn instead of a bark.

Buster and Julie are from Texas. Didn't take a genius to figure that one out, what with their delightful Texas twang and the Lone Star State flag flying high from a pole in the back yard.

Buster grabbed my hand and gave me a welcoming whomp on the back. "We specialize in ☛ old-time Southern hospitality," he told me. I soon discovered there couldn't be two more gracious hosts around.

Their one-hundred-year-old renovated farmhouse is 🖝 perched atop a high hill overlooking St. Clair Lake like an imposing sentinel. "It's part of a chain of lakes," Buster said. "You can hop from one to another all day."

The Arnims decided to become innkeepers after touring a number of inns during a swing through New England. A relative in Michigan told them about this home. After doing research on the area (while still in Texas), the Houston natives put a down payment on the house without ever setting foot in Michigan!

The guest rooms are full of country charm, with antique furnishings and country crafts set about in lively combinations. The Blue Room has a thick blue patchwork quilt, fanciful draped curtains, a rocking chair, and charming wall borders.

My favorite is the Anniversary Room, bright and cheery, with a view of the lake. And the Mustard Room exhibits some of the innkeepers' 🖝 collection of art of the Southwest.

"We serve a good 🖝 Texas breakfast," Buster said. "I don't let anyone go away hungry." Get ready for fresh fruit, ham, sausage, eggs, homemade breads, and Julie's delicious strudels.

"One of the reasons we decided on this location is because we're right between two gourmet restaurants that may be the finest the state has to offer," Buster said. The Rowe Inn and Tapawingo are landmarks that draw crowds from miles away. Gourmet delights include rhubarb-strawberry soup, spinach-and-Montrachet tart, breast of pheasant *chasseur,* and white-chocolate mousse with raspberry sauce.

How to get there: From Grand Rapids, take U.S. 131 north to Michigan 32. Turn west, and near East Jordan, go west on County 48 to the inn.

B: *The long gingerbread-laced wraparound porch, from which you can view the lake far down the hill, has comfy wicker rockers.*

Botsford Inn
Farmington Hills, Michigan
48024

Innkeeper: John W. Anhut
Address/Telephone: 28000 Grand River Avenue; (313) 474–4800
Rooms: 75 rooms, 3 suites; all with private bath.
Rates: $50 and $60 single, $60 and $65 double, $100 to $125 suites.
　　Special "Historic Weekend" packages, October through April,
　　$110 per couple. Children OK. Wheelchair access.
Open: All year except Christmas Day and New Year's Day.
Facilities & Activities: Coach House restaurant with 5 private din-
　　ing rooms; serves breakfast, lunch, and dinner daily, except
　　Christmas Day and New Year's Day; also has a ballroom. Henry
　　Ford Museum and Greenfield Village nearby. Also nearby
　　Henry Ford Fairlane Estate, Franklin Village, Northville, his-
　　toric specialty shopping areas. Shopping at Hunter's Square
　　and Twelve Oaks Mall 10-minute-drive away. "Blitz Strip," ele-
　　gant and sophisticated shops along Northwestern Highway,
　　short drive away.

　　　I swung open the heavy oak door in ☛ one of Michigan's oldest inns. My heels clicked on plank flooring that
stretches to a huge hearth crackling with a warming fire,
with two Windsor chairs huddled around the blaze. A mas-

sive oak desk runs almost the length of the room, and in an office behind it is a 🖛 table once used by Abe Lincoln. History is everywhere.

The 1836 white clapboard house, converted into a tavern five years later, quickly became a popular stagecoach stop on the Grand River plank road, about sixteen miles from the then-young city of Detroit.

Known as the Sixteen Mile House, it was a resting spot for farmers and drovers heading toward the city. But only traveling "gentlemen and ladies" could sleep in rooms; rougher elements had to stretch out on the taproom floor.

The inn became a favorite courting spot in the 1920s for Henry Ford and his future wife, Clara, who attended country dances in the inn's ballroom.

The inn owes many of its antiques to Ford's restoration efforts: Original Hitchcock chairs grace the parlor; a rare turn-of-the-century 🖛 Chickering square piano is said to have belonged to *the* General Custer's sister; and there's a buffet from General Robert E. Lee's home.

John purchased the inn in 1951, adding rooms to the original structure while preserving its pioneer roots in a number of historic suites. I was especially fascinated by the suite created for and used by Thomas Edison, filled with oversized carved-oak furnishings.

Make sure to get a room in the restored historic wing. The hallway is long and narrow, dotted with sitting benches, velvet couches, and antique prints. My room had stenciled Victorian wallpaper, a huge walnut bed, a "pie safe" used as a chest of drawers, and more. John's pampering touches include fresh flowers and bright calico bed quilts.

The Coach House taproom and restaurant serves good Midwestern staples prepared by longtime chef Mattie Miller. These include pan-fried chicken, veal supreme, honey-baked ham and roast duck with wild rice. I was delighted with a house specialty, Botsford chicken pie. Hot cherry cobbler with vanilla ice cream topped off my tasty dinner.

How to get there: Follow I–96 from Detroit and get off at the Farmington Hills exit. From Chicago, follow I–94 to Michigan 39 and continue north to I–96; then go west. The inn is located at the intersection of Eight Mile Road and Grand River Avenue.

Winter Inn
Greenville, Michigan
48838

Innkeeper: Robert King
Address/Telephone: 100 North Lafayette Street; (616) 754–3132
  or 754–7108
Rooms: 15, with 1 suite; all with private bath.
Rates: $38 to $48 single, $45 to $76 double. Includes continental
  breakfast. Children OK.
Open: All year.
Facilities & Activities: Near several ski areas and Grand Rapids'
  Gerald R. Ford Presidential Museum.

The lobby is filled with elegant Victorian antiques. Handsome nineteenth-century Victorian couches and chairs, cut and stained glass, magnificent tapestries, and ceiling-high hallway mirrors celebrate the inn's heritage.

The Winter Inn is an unusual find, tucked on a busy commercial street of this small town. It seems that lumbermen who worked the Big Woods would come to the "city" for some rest and relaxation. They'd take stagecoaches from the city train station to the hotel on "Main Street."

The 1902 inn was one of Greenville's two first-class

hotels. I could see lots of evidence toward that claim. For example, the lounge contains one of my favorite inn antiques: an immense Brunswick oak-and-mahogany bar made in the 1880s, complete with a long brass foot rail. With the lounge's pressed-tin ceiling, solid oak floor, and a collection of antique prints, oil lamps, and memorabilia, it made me feel as though I had just stepped into an authentic Victorian pub.

The dining room boasts more handsome surroundings. Tables are cast with the warm glow of light filtered through stained-glass windows, and there's lots of greenery. A light breakfast of fresh fruit, doughnuts, and coffee comes with your stay. And dinner fare is all-American, small-town good, featuring seafood like walleye pike, home-baked chicken, and tasty steaks.

Guest rooms are furnished in contemporary style and remain comfortable and cozy. All have extra-long beds, especially attractive to someone like me who stands 6'2".

How to get there: From Chicago, take I–94 north to I–196 and continue north to U.S. 131. Go north to Michigan 57 and turn east, continuing to Greenville. The road turns into Lafayette Street in the city.

B: *It's fun to browse among the inn's historic photos on the second floor that depict a long-ago era.*

Harbor Inn on the Bay
Harbor Springs, Michigan
49740

Innkeeper: Thomas Mooradian
Address/Telephone: 200 Beach Road; (616) 526–2107
Rooms: 62; all with private bath.
Rates: $53 to $55 single, $68 to $70 double. Includes breakfast.
  Special packages available. Children welcome. Wheelchair access.
Open: All year.
Facilities & Activities: Full-service dining rooms, live entertainment, private sand beach, tennis, swimming pool. Nearby golf, horseback riding, boating. Short drive to chic boutiques of Harbor Springs downtown area, Petoskey's famous Gaslight Shopping District, *Star of Charlevoix* dinner-cruise ship, and more.

It seemed like a long drive from the main road to the inn. The winding back road was lined with tall scrub pines, and it was a while before I spotted the hotel sign. I wasn't prepared for what I saw.

Harbor Inn on the Bay is stacked like a giant wedding cake on the shore of Lake Michigan's Little Traverse Bay. The huge white turn-of-the-century hotel recalls a time when fancy Victorian vacation retreats of the Great Lakes resort era catered to the Midwest's wealthiest families.

The imposing structure—complete with ☞ Victorian tower—originally attracted visitors to the area because of its fine harbors, pollen-free air, and scenic woods.

Today, it not only is a state historic site, but it still offers the warm hospitality and gracious living of bygone days. Its ☞ lakeside setting is spectacular. Mist coming off the lake enveloped my face, and I took in deep breaths, smelling the sweet scent of a landscape studded with tall pine trees. The air was cold and fresh. And it was absolutely quiet.

The inn's well-secluded location allows for a peaceful respite. I found the sitting area's massive stone hearth a cozy spot to warm up on this chilly day. Maybe cards or a table game would suit you more in the comfortable sitting room. At night, the pulsating rhythms of a live band's dance beat will help you heat up the dance floor. Or just take a romantic hand-in-hand walk along the shoreline, under a canopy of twinkling stars. There's always something to do.

The guest rooms are comfortable, with mostly contemporary furnishings. Many of the ☞ window views over the blue bay waters are inspiring.

A full breakfast buffet is another treat. The all-you-can-eat feast includes the likes of eggs, bacon and sausage, pancakes and French toast, fresh fruit, juice, and other beverages.

For dinner, Lake Superior whitefish is an inn specialty.

How to get there: From Detroit, take I–75 north to Michigan 32. Then go west to U.S. 131. Continue north to Michigan 119 and then onto Beach Road, following signs directing you to the inn.

Old Wing Inn
Holland, Michigan
49423

Innkeepers: Chuck and Chris Lorenz
Address/Telephone: 5298 East 147th Avenue; (616) 392–7362, toll
    free (800) 547–1463
Rooms: 5; all with shared baths.
Rates: $40 to $46 single, $46 to $55 double. Includes continental
    breakfast. Children OK. Off-season rates available November 1
    to April 30.
Open: All year.
Facilities & Activities: Dutch town celebrates Tulip Time each May
    with massive tulip displays, wooden-shoed *klompen* dancers,
    ethnic foods, parades, and more. Also year-round attractions
    like Windmill Island, wooden-shoe factories, Dutch Village,
    museums, and specialty shops.

    Chuck said that this is an old Indian mission, built in
1844 by a minister to an Ottawa Indian colony that moved
here from Allegan, Michigan, which makes this modest
white clapboard home the ☞ oldest historic landmark in the
area.
    Named after one of the Reverend's Indian converts, it
also was a base for Dutch settlers who stayed here before

building their own homesteads. Of course, Dutch customs prevail in this predominately ethnic town, where an ☞ annual May Tulip Festival draws a half million people to see millions of colorful tulips, authentic windmills, wooden-shoed *klompen* dancers and traditional street scrubbers.

All that hubbub won't affect you here. I took a long drive off the main road, out to fields of swaying corn populated only with chirping birds, to find the Old Wing Inn.

Chuck and Chris have fashioned five cozy guest rooms in the historic home. I found country antiques and period décor; I especially liked the ☞ lacy curtains and lace-hoop decorations catching sunlight from the windows. I felt a sense of history throughout this landmark building.

The upstairs bedrooms are named for the five Smith children who grew up here. Mary Jane's Room is the coziest. Doorways are rather low, so watch your head.

In season, the innkeepers pamper guests with fresh flowers in the rooms. There's also a small library filled with history tomes penned by local authors.

Breakfast is taken in the pioneer kitchen, with coffee, tea, juice, and a sweet roll standard fare. You can use the kitchen for snacks, as well. I'm sure first-timers will want to try one of the Dutch restaurants in Holland; Chuck and Chris will recommend one to suit your tastes. For something different, drive to nearby Point West, whose dining room features a spectacular view of Lake Macatawa. I found the chicken Kiev (an inn specialty) delightful.

How to get there: From Chicago, take I–94 north to I–196 north and take exit 49. When Michigan 40 jogs left, turn right onto 48th Street and go east to Waverly. Then continue north ½ mile to 40th Street. Turn east to 147th Street, and about ½ mile over the hill, you'll see the house.

Grist Mill Guest House
Homer, Michigan
49245

Innkeepers: Judy Krupka and Allene Downing
Address/Telephone: 310 East Main Street; (517) 568–4063
Rooms: 6, all with shared baths.
Rates: $40 weekdays, $50 weekends. Includes breakfast. Children 13 and older only. No credit cards.
Open: All year.
Facilities & Activities: The True Grist Dinner Theater, located just in back of the guest house, features a professional acting troupe starting its second decade of entertainment. All the Victorian homes, historic sites, and antique stores of Marshall, Michigan, are a short drive away. Nearby area golf course and great back roads for country biking.

Judy showed me a ☛ steam tunnel that formerly connected the house to the mill across the road. "That was so the mill owner could check on the factory's power output right from his house," she said. "And if they were using too much, he could shut it right down." I saw the curious steam gauges in the hallway.

I love the elaborate Victorian oak woodwork and leaded-glass windows in the parlor of this turn-of-the-century house.

The guest rooms also are charming, featuring antiques that Judy and Allene found throughout the area.

Judy especially likes to hunt for the beautiful antique quilts that grace the beds, antique lace curtains, and hand-crocheted lace linens that are used in creative ways. There's an 1810 four-poster bed, a canopied bed—even a curious hand-carved walnut Victorian bed-and-dresser set that came from Jackson State Prison, according to Judy.

Breakfast is a fun affair, and the house is filled with the scrumptious aroma of Judy's home baking. She features hearty dishes like eggs Benedict, and ham and sausage with cheese potatoes. Her sweet treats may send you to heaven.

The innkeepers offer a country-inn-canoeing weekend package that's pure fun. You begin with a Friday-evening "gourmet style" meal, enjoy two champagne breakfasts, and feast on a gourmet picnic along the St. Joseph River with your personal/guide instructor. Complete canoe outfitting is included.

For nightly inn guests, I suggest a walk across the street to the True Grist Dinner Theater. Here you can take in a performance by the professional acting troupe that puts on musicals like *A Chorus Line* and *Gigi*. The theater is housed in the old 1887 Homer Mill. I toured the building during theater rehearsals and saw much of the early construction, with exposed hand-hewn walnut and oak beams everywhere. Victor flour bags hanging on the theater walls are reminders of the Homer Mill's own brand of flour.

The theater offers a hearty dinner menu, featuring steaks, Grist fried chicken, pork chops, and cured ham steaks.

How to get there: From Chicago, take I–94 east to Marshall; then head south on old U.S. 27 (South Kalamazoo Street) for 11 miles to the four-way stop at Tekonsha. Turn left on M–60E, go approximately 10 miles, and turn in at the theater entrance. The inn is in front of the old mill. From Detroit, take I–94 west to Jackson. Take exit 136 (M–60W, Spring Arbor exit) to Homer, approximately 20 miles.

B: Local legend says that the federal government wanted to condemn the mill during World War I and fashion the still-sturdy wood beams into airplane propellers.

Stuart Avenue Inn
Kalamazoo, Michigan
49007

Innkeepers: Bill and Andrea Casteel
Address/Telephone: 405 Stuart Avenue; (616) 342–0230
Rooms: 6; all with private bath.
Rates: $42 to $47. Includes continental breakfast. Children 12 and
  over only. No smoking.
Open: All year.
Facilities & Activities: Kalamazoo often is a festival-crazed city;
  there's seemingly a celebration each week. It's about an hour's
  drive to Lake Michigan beaches and resort towns.

I wasn't in the best frame of mind as I drove up to the
Stuart Avenue Inn. I'd come a long way in a powerful thun-
derstorm. I was tired and cranky. Then I had to make a long
run to the entrance at the side of the building, and I got
soaked. But once inside, I forgot about all that. This charming retreat was just the cure for a trying day.

The 1889 Queen Anne–style building is part of the
Stuart Avenue Historic District of prosperous Kalamazoo
homes. Bill and Andy have said many times that their goal is
to provide travelers with a unique and pleasant experience in

an elegant, friendly home. They've succeeded, lovingly restoring their Victorian inn with comfortable, well-appointed antique furnishings.

All guest rooms have fun names. The Mayor's Room (named for a former owner who happened to be a three-term mayor of the city) is the largest. I especially liked the antique ☛ Eastlake bedroom suite, complete with high headboard and marble-topped dresser.

The Deer and Rabbit Room, less formal, features ☛ hand-printed wall coverings and an iron-and-brass bed. Another favorite of mine is the Arboretum, a romantic spot with many windows and a cozy fireplace.

A special gathering spot for guests is the lovely Eastlake Sitting Room, with its handsome beaded-glass window. The breakfast room also is terrific, with ten windows that let you start a clear day with lots of bright sunshine. Here Bill and Andy deliver a special breakfast treat: ☛ freshly baked goods from the famous Sarkozy Bakery. The innkeepers can recommend good area restaurants for dinners.

How to get there: From Detroit, take I–94 west to exit 81, which turns into Kalamazoo Avenue. Continue west to the inn at the corner of Stuart and Kalamazoo. From Chicago, take I–94 east to U.S. 131. Go west to West Main Street and continue for 2 miles. Just past the Kalamazoo College Tennis Courts, turn left onto Stuart Avenue and continue one block to the inn.

The Pebble House
Lakeside, Michigan
49116

Innkeepers: Jean and Ed Lawrence
Address/Telephone: 15197 Lakeshore Road, P.O. Box 62; (616)
469–1416
Rooms: 9, 4 with private bath; 2 cottage suites, each with private
bath.
Rates: $45 to $65, main building; $65 to $85, cottage suites. Includes Scandinavian breakfast. Wheelchair access. Children
over 12 allowed in main building; younger children in suites
only. No credit cards.
Open: January through March, closed two weeks in April; then
open May through December.
Facilities & Activities: Private tennis court on grounds. Access to
beach across road. Hiking, boating, fishing, charter fishing for
chinook and coho, sailing, golf, biking, horseback riding. In
winter, downhill and cross-country skiing, snowmobiling, tobogganing. Warren Dunes State Park nearby. Antique shops in
lakeside towns. Winery tours. Pick-your-own-fruit farms. Hang
gliding in Warren Dunes.

I like this inn for its peaceful, laid-back ambience. It's as
comfortable as your favorite easy chair, a good place to just

wind down and relax. And it's located in the heart of ☛ Michigan's dune-swept Harbor Country, with Lake Michigan just across the road.

"We call it a European-style inn," Jean said, "because of our Scandinavian breakfasts." That's a special treat, with European breads, imported cheeses, smoked sausages, herring—and Jean's fresh muffins and home-baked pastries.

The main building dates back to the turn of the century, located in a tranquil village with rolling countryside noted for its farms, orchards, and vineyards. I could ☛ see the lake from the porch and from some of the guest-room windows.

One of my favorite spots is an ☛ enclosed porch with a large fireplace, perfect for nighttime reading by a crackling fire.

The guest rooms have self-descriptive names. The Rose Room has lace curtains, rose borders, and a wicker rocker in front of a ☛ floor-to-ceiling etched-glass window that overlooks Lake Michigan.

Perhaps the most fun room is the loft apartment of the Coach House, where there's a wood-burning stove to keep cuddly warm. Downstairs is the Art Studio, which looks out through leaded-glass windows onto the garden. Here you'll probably find Jean's paintings in progress; guests also are invited to work on their own masterpieces.

For meals, try Redamak's, featuring "the hamburger that made New Buffalo famous," nearby. I also suggest a visit to the Harbert Swedish Bakery, in Harbert on Red Arrow Highway. The freshly baked Danish butter-pecan sweet rolls, pineapple-bran muffins, pecan brownies, and elephant ears are a delight to anyone with a sweet tooth.

How to get there: Take I–94 to the Union Pier (exit 6) and turn left to Lakeside Road. Continue on Lakeside Road, crossing Red Arrow Highway, until you reach the stop sign at Lakeshore Road. Turn left and continue for ¼ mile. The Pebble House is on the left.

⏳

B: *Notice the natural stone fence. The small rocks used for the inn's exterior trim are the same kind used for the porch fireplace. That's how Pebble House got its name.*

The Riverside Inn
Leland, Michigan
49654

Innkeepers: Edward and Barbara Collins
Address/Telephone: 302 River Street; (616) 256–9971
Rooms: 8; 4 with private bath.
Rates: $32 to $70 midweek, $35 to $80 weekends.
Open: Warm-weather season (opens sometime in spring, depending on weather).
Facilities & Activities: Near historic Fishtown, home to charter fishing boats, commercial fishing fleets, specialty stores, antique shops. Summer boat trips to Manitou Islands.

Ed is a sculptor; Barbara is a photographer. Together they've done an artful job of restoring The Riverside Inn.

This country charmer, surrounded by a white picket fence and tall trees, is a little bit of New England in the Midwest. I love the ☛ backyard terrace that stretches down to the bank of the Leland River—it makes for great sunsets.

It's history stretches back to 1901, when another inn occupied this site. The present building was converted from a 1920s dance hall.

Inside is a cozy, comfortable country look, with rustic

antique furnishings, Oriental-style rugs, quaint wallpapers, and intriguing prints. The entryway has a distinctive colonial feel, with its old candle chandelier. Don't overlook the historic photo of the inn hanging here on the wall.

An enclosed side porch (or solarium) offers more country comfort, with white wicker furniture, ceiling fans, and tables for games and cards.

Barbara has fashioned guest rooms in the same kind of cheery country motif; a neat idea are the 🖝 electric blankets for frequent chilly nights.

Wholesome breakfast treats served in the comfortable dining room include pancakes and French toast smothered in local maple syrup, and home-baked breads and rolls. Breakfast is served on Barbara's collection of 🖝 Vermont Bennington pottery.

I would not miss the 🖝 fish boil, a major inn event that takes place twice on Friday evening and twice on Saturday evening. It's a variation on the Door County, Wisconsin, fish boil, part of Ed's boyhood past. For about forty minutes, water is boiled in a huge iron cauldron (usually used for making maple sugar) over a wood fire on the outside lawn. A Master Boiler adds red-skinned potatoes, onions, and— eleven minutes before the cooking stops—whitefish steaks. Eight minutes later, the fire is doused with kerosene, creating a giant plume of fire reaching to the sky. This helps boil any remaining oils over the pot's side. It also provides a spectacular show.

The youngest child present traditionally rings the dinner bell, and it's time to chow down. The meal usually includes coleslaw, homemade rye bread, and fruit-and-nut bread. Dessert is hot cherry pie à la mode.

How to get there: From Detroit, take I–75 north to U.S. 10. Continue north to Michigan 115. Continue northwest to Michigan 22. Go north to Leland's River Street and turn right to the inn.

Grand Hotel
Mackinac Island, Michigan
49757

Innkeeper: John M. Hulett III
Address/Telephone: Mackinac Island; (906) 847–3331
Rooms: 275; all with private bath.
Rates: $100 to $160 per person; children in same room with 2 persons, $12.50 to $55 per child. Includes breakfast and dinner.
Open: Mid-May through October.
Facilities & Activities: Main dining room, Geranium Bar, Grand Stand (food and drink), Audubon Bar, Carleton's Tea Store, pool grill. Magnificent swimming pool, private golf course, bike rentals, saddle horses, tennis courts, exercise trail. Carriage tours, dancing, movies. Expansive grounds, spectacular veranda with wonderful lake vistas. Nearby: museums, historic fort, and other sites, guided tours; specialty shops. There are no motor vehicles allowed on historic Mackinac Island; visitors walk, or rent horses, horse drawn carriages and taxis, and bicycles.

The Grand Hotel, built in 1887, has been called one of the great hotels of the railroad and Great Lakes steamer era. Its ☛ location high on an island bluff provides magnificent vistas over the Straits of Mackinac waters.

Its incredible, many-columned veranda is 880 feet long (it claims to be the longest in the world) and is decorated with huge American flags snapping in the wind, bright yellow awnings that catch the color of the sun, and colorful hanging plants everywhere. Many guests simply sit in generous rockers, sip on a drink, relax, and enjoy cooling lake breezes. I also like to admire the hotel's hundreds of acres of woodland and lawns, finely manicured with exquisite flower gardens and greenery arrangements.

At the Grand Hotel, I feel immersed in a long-ago era of luxury and elegance. Even the attire of hotel attendants is impressive; they're dressed in long red coats and black bow ties. Once I rode the hotel's 🖙 elegant horse-drawn carriage (the driver wore a black top hat and formal "pink" hunting jacket) from the ferry docks, up the long hill, to the grand portico.

Inside, the hotel is all greens, yellows, and whites, with balloon draperies on the windows, high-back chairs and sofas everywhere in numerous public rooms, and a healthy dash of yesteryear memorabilia hanging on hallway walls. One 🖙 1889 breakfast menu especially caught my eye, listing an extraordinary selection of foods, including lamb chops, lake fish, stewed potatoes in cream, and sweetbreads.

Special services are legion and include and complimentary morning coffee, 🖙 concerts during afternoon tea, horse-drawn-carriage island tours, dinner dances, and much more. It seems the pampering never stops.

Many of the 🖙 guest rooms have spectacular lake views. Rates include breakfast and dinner, with Lake Superior whitefish an evening specialty. A dessert treat—the Grand pecan ball with hot fudge sauce—almost made me melt.

How to get there: From either Mackinaw City from the Lower Peninsula or from St. Ignace on the Upper Peninsula, a 30-minute ferry ride brings you to Mackinac Island. Dock porters will greet your boat. There's an island airstrip for chartered flights and private planes.

B: Simply one of the "Grand"-est inns imaginable.

117

Haan Cottage
Mackinac Island, Michigan
49757

Innkeeper: Mary Ellen Jerstrom, manager
Address/Telephone: Box 1268, Front Street (winter address: P.O. Box 1014, Marco Island, Florida 33937); Michigan telephone (906) 847–3403
Rooms: 7, with 2 suites; 5 with private bath.
Rates: $48 to $80; suites, $160 to $240. Single occupancy, 10 percent discount. Off-season discounts of 10 to 20 percent. Includes continental breakfast. Children OK. No credit cards.
Open: May 15 to October 15.
Facilities & Activities: Located off Front Street, the main street of Mackinac Island, one of the Midwest's most famous summer resort communities. Short walk to historic sites, specialty shops, restaurants, ferry boats, other attractions.

The Haan Cottage is easily my favorite Mackinac Island inn. A stately Greek Revival design with tall white columns, it dates all the way back to the 1830s. That's when the island was a point of contention between England and French colonial troops.

In fact, the home was once owned by Colonel William

Preston, the last physician at the historic English settlement of Fort Mackinac. (I never pass up a chance to tour this historic fort, which stands sentinel atop the island overlooking the straits.)

The exterior is a gem. Once a frontier log cabin, the Greek Revival influences and the wing were added in 1847. Mary Ellen pointed out the ☞ original tongue-and-groove walls and the wavy lead windows made in the early 1800s.

Her guest rooms are furnished in striking authentic period antiques, beautiful pieces that call to mind the island's rich legacy. Such historic items as ☞ Colonel Preston's original desk and bed grace the premises.

The rooms are named after significant island figures. The Lafayette Davis Room has ☞ twin four-poster cannonball beds made in the 1700s. And can you guess which bed is filled with horsehair? It also has fine English prints. "We found old newspapers, dating to the 1840s, inside the walls during restoration," Mary Ellen said. "They were used as a crude insulation against the frigid winter cold."

Anne's Garden View has a handcrafted antique double bed with English bedspreads, and a rare butternut chest; a screened-in porch offers ☞ a view of the garden of neighboring St. Anne's Church. (The church, dating from 1695, was the first one dedicated in this part of the country.)

Breakfast is taken in the parlor or out on the porch. It includes home-baked breads and muffins, coffeecakes, juice, and other beverages. Mary Ellen will recommend one of the island's many restaurants for dinner fare.

Did I mention that no cars are allowed on the island? You must walk, rent a horse or horse-drawn carriage, hansom (horse-drawn taxi), or bicycle. There are miles of rugged lakeshore to explore.

How to get there: Catch a ferryboat from the Upper or Lower Peninsula, off I–75, at St. Ignace or Mackinaw City. Once on the island, walk east down Front Street (the island's main road) to the inn.

B: *This is an historically significant inn, elegantly furnished with some of the finest antiques, and situated on a magical island that has frozen the hands of time.*

Hotel Iroquois
Mackinac Island, Michigan
49757

Innkeepers: Sam and Margaret McIntire
Address/Telephone: Front Street; (906) 847–3321
Rooms: 47; all with private bath.
Rates: Full season: standard, $88 to $135; deluxe, $155; deluxe suites, $185 to $210. Early and late season: $52 to $170. Special packages available. Children welcome.
Open: May 16 to October 20.
Facilities & Activities: Full-service restaurant, bar, and lounge. Swimming at private beach or public pool. Nearby: golf course, tennis, biking, hiking, island tours, museums, specialty shops, historical sites, horseback riding, boating, and charter fishing. Mackinac Island is an historic site—home of a British Revolutionary War fort and former fur-trading center.

Every time I ride the ferry across the Straits of Mackinac to Mackinac Island, the sight of this white, gabled Victorian building shimmering in the mist ahead always sends shivers down my spine. The hotel literally sits on the beach, the lake waters lapping its grounds out on the point.

This marvelous vision of the Hotel Iroquois always stays with me, so I never miss the chance to visit this turn-of-the-century house that offers 🖙 spectacular guest-room views at the water's edge.

The hotel always seems to be expanding, but it never fails to maintain the charming appeal of an earlier era. And while it's an expensive inn, the location and resulting ambience are unsurpassed. You can hear seagulls crying during sun-drenched summer days, and foghorns faintly sounding romantic calls at night. There is a large lakeside sundeck and 🖙 rooms that seem to stretch right out over the water; in fact, some suites with daring alcoves do just that.

The guest rooms are cheerful, decorated in bright floral wallpaper, with wall-to-wall carpeting, and mostly contemporary furnishings.

The hotel's dining room is quite spectacular; you can look out over the water, alive with the flickering lights of pleasure boats and the shadows of massive freighters passing far in the distance. A candlelight dinner in this setting is especially romantic.

Lake Superior whitefish, an island specialty, is really a tasty dinner treat; so is the country-style chicken. Then there are all the home-baked breads and rolls. The dessert tray can drive you mad.

How to get there: Off I-75, there's ferryboat service from St. Ignace on the Upper Peninsula and from Mackinaw City on the Lower Peninsula. The hotel's dock porter meets all boats and transfers luggage to the hotel. It's only a short walk to the hotel, or you can take a horse-drawn taxi.

Metivier Inn
Mackinac Island, Michigan
49757

Innkeepers: Kirk and Cynthia Henshaw, owners; Irma Kujat, manager
Address/Telephone: Market Street, Box 285; (906) 847–6234
Rooms: 11, with 2 efficiencies; all with private bath.
Rates: Rooms, $65 to $85; efficiencies, $120. Includes continental breakfast. Children welcome.
Open: May to early November.
Facilities & Activities: Located a short walk from the main street on Mackinac Island, a unique summer resort community. No motor vehicles are allowed—only horses, carriages, bicycles. Many specialty shops, historic island sites. Horseback riding, swimming, golf, tennis nearby.

This handsome 1877 building, situated on one of the most history-laden streets on historic Mackinac Island, borrows heavily from the colonial English and French influences that saturated the region in the 1700s and 1800s.

Irma pointed out that most of the furniture is from the Ethan Allen ☞ English pine collection. It's perfectly suited to the inn's styling. There also are a number of original antiques gracing both common and guest rooms.

The guest rooms are enchanting, especially if you want to enjoy ☞ country-inn ambience without sacrificing modern conveniences. Each room is named for an historic island figure. The John Jacob Astor Room (a building used as one of his historic fur-trading offices is located just down Market Street; it's now a preserved historic home) has a four-poster bed, wicker chairs, and soothing rose-colored wallpaper. A special touch: I could see the bay waters from a ☞ romantic turret alcove.

Other rooms have antique headboards and iron-rail beds, marble-topped dressers, tulip lamps, padded rockers, and more.

I enjoyed relaxing in a wicker rocker on the expansive front porch and watching the parade of island visitors pass by. You might want to explore the island's six square miles of unique beauty. Just walk, ☞ rent a horse or horse-drawn carriage, or rent a bicycle. There are no motorized vehicles allowed on the island.

Breakfast fare is light: fruit, croissants, coffeecake, juice, and other beverages. For dinner, I put on my best dinner jacket and headed for the famous Grand Hotel. Its luxurious formal dining room offers a wonderful Mackinac whitefish.

How to get there: Take a ferryboat to Mackinac Island. Ferries run from both the Upper and Lower Peninsulas, off I–75. From the Sheppler ferry dock, follow the road leading up the hill; turn right on Market Street to the inn.

B: *Staying overnight on Mackinac Island is like stepping into a long-ago world, filled with history and surprises.*

Leelanau Country Inn
Maple City, Michigan
49664

Innkeepers: John and Linda Sisson
Address/Telephone: 149 East Harbor Highway; (616) 228–5060
Rooms: 10, with 2 shared baths.
Rates: $35 to $45. Includes continental breakfast. Children OK.
Open: All year.
Facilities & Activities: Full-service dining room. Area winery tours.
 Near Sleeping Bear Dunes National Lakeshore, Glen Lake,
 Lake Michigan.

If Bob Newhart's television inn ever moved to the Midwest, it might look just like this.

The gabled clapboard house has all the comforts needed for a restful stay in the country, including front and side porches that boast comfy chairs. Tall trees shade the grounds, and seasonal flowers burst in rainbow colors everywhere. I found Linda in the garden doing yet more planting.

This house is an old farmstead that was built in 1891. Pictures of the then–newly built structure hang on inn walls. Linda pointed out ☛ photos (hanging on walls throughout the house) of all the families that have lived here. And she said that the granddaughter of the original owners now lives right across the street.

The inn began serving traveling families from Chicago. Linda has an ☞ early-1900s guest register. "Some deal," she laughed. "Guests paid $1 per day for a room and three meals."

While the prices may have changed, I found the same kind of warm hospitality that must have welcomed turn-of-the-century guests to this charming country retreat.

Although there are three dining rooms, my favorite is the long enclosed porch that's done in lively colors, offering a view of the flowers and grounds out front. The inn specializes in ☞ seafood, which John has flown in fresh from Boston. Another inn specialty is homemade pasta. Favorites like roast duckling with walnut-mint sauce and blackfish Provençal are served regularly.

Linda has fashioned guest rooms that are simple, quaint, and charming. The plank floors made me feel as though I were back at my aunt's Wisconsin farm. Fancy bedspreads and wall wreaths add splashes of color, and the old-fashioned rocking chairs are fun.

Breakfast includes fresh fruit, freshly made croissants, rolls, coffee, and tea.

How to get there: From Chicago, take I–94 north to I–196 north. Continue to U.S. 31 north. Turn north on Michigan 22 and continue north just past County Road 667. Turn right into inn driveway.

The National House Inn
Marshall, Michigan
49068

Innkeepers: Sharlene and Jack Anderson; Barbara Bradley, man-
ager
Address/Telephone: 102 South Parkview; (616) 781–7374
Rooms: 16, with 2 suites.
Rates: $52 to $73 single, $58 to $79 double; all but 2 rooms with
private bath. Includes continental breakfast. Children OK.
Wheelchair access.
Open: All year except Christmas Eve and Christmas Day.
Facilities & Activities: The Tin Whistle Gift Shoppe. Many fine examples of historic Victorian homes throughout town, with 12
national historic sites and 35 state historic sites. Museums, including the Honolulu House. Antique stores. Stage productions at local theaters. Boating, fishing, swimming at nearby
lakes. Winter cross-country skiing. Monthly town events and
annual celebrations.

Stepping into The National House Inn is like entering a
way station on nineteenth-century frontier back roads:
Rough plank wood floors, hand-hewn timbers, and a ☛ massive brick open-hearth fireplace with a 13-foot single timber
mantelpiece bring back visions of the Old West.

126

And why not? The house was built in 1835 as a stage-coach stop. As it stands, it's the oldest operating inn in Michigan.

More history? Barbara told me that the inn is reputed to have been part of the "Underground Railroad" and once also functioned as a wagon factory. Now it provides a glimpse into the past for travelers and is furnished with antiques and Victorian finery.

The rooms are named after local historical figures. "Color schemes are authentic to the early 1800s," Barbara said. So you'll see muted salmons and blues—all taken "from original milk-paint colors that were made from wild berries to achieve their hue."

The elegant Ketchum Suite is formal Victorian, with a high bedstead and a tall, marble-topped dresser. Other rooms reveal iron- and brass-rail beds, elaborate rockers, and balloon period curtains.

I was overwhelmed by the huge armoire in the Charles Gorham room; it must stand 9 feet high. Still more rooms evoke pure country charm, with bright quilts that complement pine, maple, and oak furniture, and folk art portraits that grace the walls.

Continental breakfast in the nineteenth-century-styled dining room features five different pastries (including bran muffins, bundt cake, and nut breads), apple sauce, juice, and other beverages. Ask the innkeepers to suggest an area restaurant; there are several good ones nearby.

How to get there: From Detroit, take I–94 west to the Marshall exit. At the Fountain Circle, jog right and follow the road around to the inn.

☀

B: *I love touring the town, which is teeming with all sorts of Victorian-era homes, histories, and legends.*

127

TAYLOR

The Helmer House Inn
McMillan, Michigan
49853

Innkeeper: Robert Goldthorpe; Marion Schroeder, manager
Address/Telephone: County Road 417, "on the creek"; (906)
  586-3204
Rooms: 5; sharing 2 baths.
Rates: $20 to $32. Includes full country breakfast. Children OK.
Open: April to November.
Facilities & Activities: Full-service dining room. Near Upper Peninsula attractions: Tahquamenon Falls, Devil's Slide, agate
  beaches of Grand Marais, sand beaches of Lake Michigan, Pic-
  tured Rocks, mouth of Two Hearted River. Also swimming,
  fishing, sailing, biking.

Deep in the Upper Peninsula's spectacular Hiawatha
National Forest on Manistique Lake, The Helmer House
harkens back to a time of simple country comforts.

It's a rather ordinary-looking white clapboard house
built in the late 1800s by a Presbyterian minister. (It has
been a mission house for early Michigan settlers, a general
store, a U.S. Post Office, and a resort hotel.)

128

But there's nothing ordinary about the inn's hospitality, friendliness, and terrific home-style meals.

Marion showed me a unique inn feature. "It's called the ☛ Salesman's Room," she said. There was a tiny space for a white iron-rail bed and oak dresser. "We still have people— salesmen traveling on business—ask especially for the room." Why not—it's one of the Midwest's best country-inn bargains at $14 per night. And that includes a full breakfast of bacon, eggs, toast, fruit, and coffee!

Other upstairs guest rooms feature more antique furnishings. There are big black iron beds and brass beds, oval reading tables, cane chairs, and writing desks.

"I've got the perfect thing for you," Marion said, leading me to a room with a lovely antique brass shaving stand. "It's one of my favorite pieces and would be a good thing to help you shave without ruining your bushy mustache."

An enclosed porch serves as the inn's dining room, crowded with antique oak tables and chairs and cheered by lacy curtains. Dinner choices include hearty country fare like Helmer's old-fashioned fried chicken and "Grandma's best spaghetti" at hard-to-beat prices.

A common room with ☛ original inn furniture (red velvet covered couches and deeply cushioned chairs) is a nice place for an evening chat with other guests.

How to get there: From Chicago, take I–94 north to I–196 and continue north to U.S. 131. Go north to U.S. 31 and continue north to I–75. Go north to Michigan 28 and turn west, heading toward McMillan. Turn south on County H–33; then turn right on County 417 to the inn.

ᗺ

B: Michigan's Upper Peninsula is pure, magnificent wilderness—some of the Midwest's most unspoiled acres. Be ready for a startling starlight sky show and unbelievable quiet.

The 1873
Mendon Country Inn
Mendon, Michigan
49072

Innkeepers: Jane and Lewis Kaiser
Address/Telephone: 440 West Main Street; (616) 496–8132
Rooms: 9; 7 with private bath.
Rates: $22 to $52. Includes continental breakfast. Children 12 and
  over.
Open: May through October, weekends and holidays only.
Facilities & Activities: Rooftop garden with view of creek; antique
  shop. Near antique market and Shipshewana, Indiana, Auc-
  tion and Flea Market; local Amish settlement. Golf, tennis,
  fishing, boating, museums, winery tours also nearby.

The 1873 Mendon Country Inn is everything I imagine
a county inn should be. Others must feel the same way: It
was featured in the January 1986 issue of *Country Living*
magazine.

Lewis welcomed me, like all newcomers, to the Indian
Room, a gathering place on the first floor with Indian artifacts strewn about. "People come here to turn off the speed

in their lives," he said, "for a quaint at-home feel—like they're part of a family." He gave me area maps that identify local points of interest—restaurants, specialty stores, historical attractions—just about everything I needed to enjoy my stay in this quaint town.

He told me that the inn was built as a frontier hotel in the 1840s, then rebuilt with locally kilned St. Joseph River clay bricks in 1873. It was ☞ called The Wakeman House, a name the locals still use for the inn today.

Guest rooms are decorated thematically. The Amish Room has a beautiful antique Amish quilt. The Nautical Room features country-pine furnishings, with a swag of fishermen's netting used for the bed canopy; it also has a creekside porch. But my favorite is The Wakeman Room, of ☞ elegant post–Civil War design—including 8-foot-tall windows, a 12½-foot-high ceiling, and fine oversized Empire furnishings.

The ☞ best bargain is the Hired Man Room, a small space in country-style décor with a three-quarter bed and a half-bath—for only $22. That includes a breakfast of juice, rolls, and coffee.

The inn's Roof Top Garden affords another view of the creek and is great for sunbathing or private late-night moon gazing.

There's lots more. But I think you've already got the idea.

How to get there: From Chicago, take I–94 north, then west outside of Benton Harbor, to U.S. 131. Go south to Michigan 60/66. Head east into Mendon. M–60/66 is called Main Street once in town; follow it to the inn.

☒

B: *Each room comes with a livery canoe in case you want to float down the creek on a hot summer day.*

Stafford's Bay View Inn
Petoskey, Michigan
49770

Innkeepers: Stafford and Janice Smith; Judy Honor, manager
Address/Telephone: P.O. Box 3, U.S. 31; (616) 347–2771
Rooms: 21, with four suites; all with private bath.
Rates: $51 to $70 single, $71 to $86 double. There are weekday, weekend, and seasonal rates. Includes full breakfast from regular dining-room menu. Special packages available. Children OK. Wheelchair access.
Open: Daily, mid-May through October. Also open during winter sports season.
Facilities & Activities: Located just outside Bay View, a city whose Victorian architecture qualifies it as a National Historic Site. Near Petoskey's famous Gaslight Shopping District and ritzy Harbor Springs boutiques. Bay View chautauqua programs feature concerts and lectures throughout summer. Biking in summer; cross-country skiing, ice boating, snowmobiling in winter. Sailboat charters on lake; golfing nearby.

Stafford's Bay View Inn, overlooking Little Traverse Bay, calls itself a "Grand Ol' Dame of the Victorian resort era." It's certainly steeped in rich Victorian traditions; in fact, it ☛ sits next to a village that may have a treasure of Victorian gingerbread architecture unmatched anywhere.

Built in 1886, this elegant white clapboard inn has served North Country hospitality to four generations of discerning travelers. It's a ☛ classic summer house, in the sense that it offers cool breezes due to its bayside location, all kinds of outdoor activities, and an ambitious community program of music, drama, and art. Did I forget great shopping, too?

Some highlights include the following:

A long sun porch overlooking the bay, furnished with oversized wicker pieces.

Several dining rooms serving food with a fine reputation, including fresh Great Lakes whitefish and local specialties, such as honey-mustard shrimp and Veal Louisiana in creole-mustard sauce, which have been featured in *Gourmet* magazine.

Guest rooms filled with antiques and reproductions that reflect the styles of the Victorian era. Room 3 has a ☛ four-poster bed so high that even I had to use a stepstool to climb atop it—and I'm 6′2″. You'll also find brass beds and sleigh beds, and inviting flower wreaths on room doors.

A full breakfast ordered from the regular menu is included in the price of the rooms. That means choices like malted waffles or whole-wheat pancakes with Michigan maple syrup, and biscuits with sausage gravy.

Stafford's also offers food at two other nearby locations: The new One Water Street, on Lake Charlevoix in Boyne City, offers specialties like Trout Hemingway and cold black-cherry soup, as well as various game selections; Stafford's Pier Restaurant is in Harbor Springs, near one of Michigan's most scenic drives along Michigan 119, north from the village.

How to get there: From any direction, the inn is right on U.S. 31, just outside Bay View.

B: The fancy boutiques in nearby Harbor Springs are a hot spot for the "oh, so chic."

St. Clair Inn
St. Clair, Michigan
48079

Innkeeper: Mike LaPorte
Address/Telephone: 500 North Riverside; (313) 329–2222 or (313) 963–5735
Rooms: 97 rooms, with 20 suites; also riverside Captain's House and Annex, all with private bath.
Rates: $50 single (available weekdays only), $55 to $90 double, $65 to $150 suite, $275 suite in Captain's House. Children OK. Wheelchair access.
Open: All year, except Christmas Day.
Facilities & Activities: Six dining rooms; breakfast, lunch, and dinner available; special holiday brunches. Winter: cross-country skiing. Summer: water sports, charter fishing, hiking, golf, tennis. Antique and specialty stores across the street.

The St. Clair Inn hugs fast to the shore of the St. Clair River overlooking the woods of Canada, just across the channel. Built on the site of an old sawmill in 1926, the inn luxuriates in its English Tudor architecture, while providing a comfortable vantage point for viewing a constant parade of merchant ships that ply these waters leading to Great Lakes ports.

Opening the inn's heavy oak doors, I stepped onto a cobblestone floor. ☞ Four massive oak pillars support a rough-hewn beamed ceiling, calling to mind the spine of a sailing ship. Two huge stone fireplaces flank large windows that look out over the river. Each has the required high-back chairs nearby for cozy conversation or serious reading.

Later that evening, fog horns sounded upriver, and I ran out from my room to the ☞ inn's dock (touted as the "world's longest freshwater boardwalk").

A massive freighter, seemingly an arm's length away, almost scraped both shorelines as it moved through the mist-shrouded channel. I waved to a sailor standing on the high aft deck. He tipped his cap and waved back.

I ate breakfast on the South Porch, whose ☞ riverside picture windows stretch almost the full length of the inn. The "Inn on the River," as it's also called, has become one of southeastern Michigan's favorite places for dining, so don't be surprised to see lots of visitors during the dinner hour.

The menu owes a great deal to the inn's proximity to Lake Huron and includes northern Canadian walleye, lake perch, and red snapper. Other dishes prepared by chef Warren Zimmer, who's been at the inn for thirty years, include pork chops, an inn specialty. Fresh strawberry pie topped with a sea of whipped cream and whole strawberries defies willpower.

The guest rooms in the main building are mostly carried out in a contemporary style with a nautical theme. There are also several pine-paneled cottages facing the river, a three-bedroom ☞ Captain's House with sunken lounge, fireplace, sun porch, Jacuzzi, and wet bar, and Annex rooms with outside river-front decks.

How to get there: Follow I–94 to exit 257. Turn right on Fred Moore Highway and follow to Clinton Avenue; then go right on North Riverside. Turn left on North Riverside and follow to the Inn. It's a drive of about one hour from Detroit and one hour from Detroit Metropolitan Airport.

Fly in by commercial or private plane (St. Clair County Airport is 6 miles away).

Boat in and dock at the inn's spacious waterfront boardwalk. However, the channel's closed to water traffic from December through February.

Kemah Guest House
Saugatuck, Michigan
49453

Innkeepers: Terry and Cindi Tatsch
Address/Telephone: 633 Pleasant Street; (616) 857–2919
Rooms: 4, with 1 suite; all share baths.
Rates: $65 to $85. Includes continental breakfast. No children.
Open: All year.
Facilities & Activities: Rathskeller (for guests only). Located on a quiet hill, high above the hustle of this lakeside Midwest art-colony village. Short drive to antique and specialty shops, art galleries, beaches, swimming, boating, dune exploring, and more.

The Kemah Guest House is 🖝 one of the most intriguing residences in the lakeside village of Saugatuck. It reminds me of traditional European homes and combines an 🖝 old-world German flair with touches of Art Deco—and Frank Lloyd Wright!

Built by a German sea captain, the home is named for its site on a breezy hill. (*Kemah* is a Potawatomi Indian word meaning "teeth of the wind.") Cindi said that the captain, ever a superstitious seaman, wanted to ensure that his sails would always billow with the winds, so he graced his home with a good-luck moniker.

It was remodeled in 1926 by William Springer, a Chicago Board of Trade member. You can see his initials carved everywhere—from wood panels in the rathskeller to the massive wrought-iron arched doorway.

There are so many highlights:

Many stained- and leaded-glass windows depict sailing scenes.

Hand-carved wooden landscapes on the solarium paneling depict the house's various appearances through the decades.

A bricked, semicircular solarium with a running fountain was designed by T. E. Tallmadge, a disciple of Frank Lloyd Wright, and captures the master's Prairie School architectural style.

Beamed ceilings, cornice boards, and a fireplace (of Pewabic tile) recall the Art Deco era.

Have a drink in a genuine rathskeller, with the home's original wine casks, wall stencils, and leather-strap and wood-frame chairs hand carved in Colorado in the 1930s.

Can you find the secret panel that hid whiskey and spirits during Prohibition days? A hint: Look at the windows near the arched door and kitchen.

There's a cave on the grounds and an Indian grave on the side of the hill.

Cindi has fashioned charming guest rooms in rich individual styles. One is done in fine lace; another recalls a gentleman's room, filled with oak furniture and a 6-foot-tall Victorian headboard on the bed.

My favorite room features a four-poster bed and an ☞ eleven-piece bedroom set made in 1918, one of only two like it ever made. It's all walnut, of gorgeous craftsmanship. Can you find the secret jewelry drawer in the dresser?

There are rolls and coffee for breakfast. If you wish, the innkeepers will recommend one of many good area restaurants, too.

How to get there: From Chicago, take I–94 north to I–196. Exit at Saugatuck on Blue Star Highway and go south to Pleasant. Turn right and continue to the inn.

Maplewood Hotel
Saugatuck, Michigan
49453

Innkeepers: Vivian and Scott Holford; Grant Smith, manager
Address/Telephone: 428 Butler Street (mailing address: P.O. Box
1059); (616) 857-2788
Rooms: 12, with 4 suites; all with private bath.
Rates: $45 to $124 May through September, $35 to $124 other
months. Includes continental breakfast. Children OK.
Open: All year.
Facilities & Activities: Saugatuck is one of the major art colonies in
the Midwest. It has many art galleries, specialty shops, and antique stores; also many fine restaurants, sand dunes, and
breathtaking lake views. Swimming, yachting, sightseeing
cruise aboard an old stern-wheeler down the Kalamazoo River.
Tours of area vineyards and cellars. Historic-home tour in fall.

I have some great news for fans of this landmark Greek
Revival building ☛ prominently located on the village green
of this lively art-colony lakeshore village. Some major restoration and refurbishing is taking place, with completely new
public-room décor and totally redecorated guest rooms. Also
on tap is a ☛ swimming pool, sun room, and gazebo.

Grant showed me one of the almost-completed "new" suites. It's an attractive three-room suite with floral wallpaper, a comfy bed placed near a tall window, and a cozy fireplace that transforms cold weather into cuddly nights. My favorite new addition is a ☛ double Jacuzzi, which is planned for most rooms.

I was especially fond of all the Baker furniture used throughout; it's locally made and nationally renowned.

But then the Maplewood Hotel always has gotten a lot of attention. Built in 1860, its ☛ downtown location makes it an ideal spot for shop hopping; and it's close to restaurants, art galleries, and the chain ferry on the Kalamazoo River that goes to famed Oval Beach.

Breakfast usually includes rolls, croissants, and coffee. Grant is planning to add a kitchen; then you'll be treated to homemade muffins and breads as well.

How to get there: From Chicago, take I–94 north to I–196 north and exit at Blue Star Highway. Go south to Allegan Road; then west to Butler and the hotel.

The Newnham Inn
Saugatuck, Michigan
49453

Innkeepers: George Iski and Ron Benkert
Address/Telephone: 131 Griffith Street, P.O. Box 1106; (616) 857–4249
Rooms: 6; 2 with private bath; also a 2-bedroom cottage.
Rates: Seasonal room rates, $45 to $65. Two-night minimum required on weekends. Includes continental breakfast. No children.
Open: All year.
Facilities & Activities: Hot tub, swimming pool. Located in the heart of Saugatuck's business district, within walking distance of art galleries, specialty shops, restaurants, and just minutes from Lake Michigan beaches.

The inn has a ☛ much-coveted location in the heart of gala shops and specialty stores of this lakeside art colony, and it's just a short walk to Lake Michigan swimming holes; in other words, a perfect home away from home.

George has rescued the original wooden sign that has greeted visitors to this historic 1920 former boarding house for more than six decades. It now hangs out front.

The whole inn feels like home. There are comfy chairs, vintage magazines strewn about, and a quaint dining room that has a welcome lived-in look.

One first-floor guest room contains reproduction period pieces, with a ☞ handsome four-poster bed as the room's centerpiece. A nice touch is the ☞ small porchlike sitting room. Another room contains the ☞ Newnham's original bedroom set.

To reach other rooms, George and I walked through the country kitchen and up the back stairs that led to the maid's quarters in days gone by. Iron-rail and brass beds are among the fun antiques.

A light breakfast of fresh fruit, muffins, and coffee means not much waiting before diving into the ☞ in-ground swimming pool out back. The new deck also has a hot tub. The innkeepers will recommend one of the many fine area restaurants for dinner.

How to get there: From Chicago, take I–94 north to I–196 north and exit at Blue Star Highway. Go south to Lake Street; then right on Griffith.

The Park House
Saugatuck, Michigan
49453

Innkeepers: Lynda and Joe Petty
Address/Telephone: 888 Holland; (616) 857–4535
Rooms: 7; all with private bath.
Rates: May through October: $50 to $55 weekdays, $60 to $65 weekends (2-night minimum on weekends). November through April (off-season): rates available on request. Includes hearty continental breakfast. No children. Wheelchair access.
Open: All year.
Facilities & Activities: Short drive to beaches, swimming, boating, specialty stores, art galleries, and other attractions in this major Midwest art-colony village hugging Lake Michigan.

When I arrived at The Park House, Lynda and Joe were muscling up railroad ties and timbers, landscaping their garden and grounds. Nobody else was working that hard on a hot Sunday afternoon in this fun-filled Lake Michigan resort town.

So it's not suprising that The Park House is a treasure. Built in 1857 by a local lumberman, the two-story clapboard home is 🖝 Saugatuck's oldest historic residence.

Lynda told me a great story of how the inn got its name. Seems a former owner fenced the home's almost eight acres and stocked the pasture with deer. Their grazing cropped the grass, giving the grounds a manicured look. People started calling it the "park" house.

Want more history? Susan B. Anthony stayed here for two weeks in the 1870s and helped form the county's first temperance society. In fact, Joe laughingly said that Anthony was responsible for closing down half the bars in Allegan County!

The house is built from original timbers that once stood on the property. Some special touches include the original wide-plank pine-wood floors, pretty wall stencils done by Lynda, a wide fireplace, and antique furnishings throughout the home. French doors in the parlor open onto an herb garden. All in all, it's a real country charmer.

Each cozy guest room is distinctly decorated, and all have queen-sized iron-rail beds and warm oak furniture.

Lynda serves breakfast at an antique oak table in a gathering room dotted with country crafts and antiques. Get ready for freshly baked muffins, granola, fruit, and the Pettys' own blend of coffee. They'll also suggest a few "can't miss" dinner spots.

How to get there: From Chicago, take I–94 north to I–196 and continue north to exit 41 (Blue Star Highway). Turn west and continue on Holland (where Blue Star turns left) to the inn.

B: During the *Christmas season, all the guest rooms are decked out in holiday finery.*

Singapore Country Inn
Saugatuck, Michigan
49453

Innkeepers: Mike and Denise Simcik
Address/Telephone: 900 Lake Street; (616) 857–4346
Rooms: 10, with 1 suite; all with private bath.
Rates: May 1 to Labor Day: $45 to $50 weekdays, $60 to $70 weekends. Off-season rates available. Includes continental breakfast. Two-night minimum on weekends during summer season. No children under 5 during summer season or on weekends.
Open: All year.
Facilities & Activities: Short walk or drive to art galleries, specialty shops, antique stores, beaches, swimming, boating, and more.

Denise explained that her inn originally stood on a hill across the Kalamazoo River. One winter it was moved across the frozen waters by mule team and log sled to Saugatuck.

She laughed. "After all that trouble, the owners thought they'd put it too close to a road. So they moved it again to its present location."

The inn is named for a genuine Midwest ghost town. The old logging town of Singapore hugged a spot on the dune-filled eastern shores of Lake Michigan that is now oc-

144

cupied by Saugatuck. But when the trees had been cut down, lumber interests left, and the town was abandoned. Eventually the crumbling buildings were buried under tons of ever-shifting sand dunes. Now the old town is just an historical footnote.

The 1870 inn is built from timbers cut in the old Singapore sawmill. And it was ☞ designed by the same architect who built the magnificent Grand Hotel on Mackinac Island.

The local arts-and-crafts association headquarters in the dining room. So it's not surprising that cute antiques and crafts are everywhere.

I love the old ☞ pressed-tin ceilings, walls, and wainscoting, which is quite an unusual find. Add to that a common-room fireplace surrounded by comfy chairs, sofas and rockers, and the atmosphere is just right for lazing away a weekend.

The guest rooms are lovingly furnished, each distinctive and warm. The Wicker Room, of course, has wicker chairs, and is brightly decorated in shades of yellow—quite a sight on a sun-drenched morning—while the Cape Cod Room features beautifully crafted pine furniture made by Mike. But my favorite is the Dutch Room, ☞ all tulips and Dutch blue colors, with 1914 furniture made in Gettysburg, Pennsylvania.

A light continental breakfast is served buffet style in the dining room. Or you can eat out on the long porch and watch boats sail out of the village harbor. Good hearty dinners are served up in area restaurants; Denise can recommend the spot for you.

How to get there: From Chicago, take I–94 north to I–196. Continue north to exit 36 and go north on Blue Star Highway. Turn left on Lake Street and continue to the inn.

Wickwood Inn
Saugatuck, Michigan
49453

Innkeepers: Sue and Stub Louis
Address/Telephone: 510 Butler Street; (616) 857–1097
Rooms: 11, with 2 suites; all with private bath.
Rates: $75 to $110 May 1 through October 31, $60 to $95 November 1 through April 30. Includes continental breakfast, afternoon tea, complimentary bottle of wine. No children. Wheelchair access.
Open: All year.
Facilities & Activities: Sunken garden room, library/bar. Located in the resort town of Saugatuck, with the wide, sandy beaches of Lake Michigan nearby, as well as specialty stores, antique shops, restaurants, golfing, boating, fishing, cross-country skiing in winter.

Staying at the Wickwood Inn is almost like taking a mini–European vacation. That's because it was 🖙 inspired by a visit to the grand Duke's Hotel in London. Sue and Stub vowed to open an equally exquisite inn back home in the United States.

The result is outstanding. All 🖙 linens, wallpapers, and

fabrics are from British designer Laura Ashley's collections. There are elegant pieces from Baker Furniture's "Historic Charleston" collection. Complimentary soaps and shampoos by Crabtree & Evelyn of London are provided in every bathroom.

I discovered more British influences. The library/bar calls to mind an English gentlemen's club. And Stub sometimes whisks away visitors in his 🖝 authentic London taxicab for tours of this lively and colorful coastal village. It's usually parked right in front of the inn.

These are some of the finest guest rooms I have ever seen. Exquisite walnut, pine, and cherry antique furnishings are outstanding. The Carrie Wicks Suite features a 🖝 magnificent four-poster Rice bed. In the Master Suite, I found a cherry-wood canopy bed with an antique white eyelet spread and hand-crocheted canopy. Its sitting room contains an Empire-styled couch, with finely carved swan heads gracing the arms. Beautiful!

Other rooms feature scalloped wallpaper borders, brass and hand-painted headboards, hand-rubbed paneling, primitive sailing-ship prints, braided rugs, and more.

One of my favorite gathering rooms is the 🖝 sunken garden, with its vaulted beamed ceiling and greenery everywhere; and the toy room holds Stub's antique toy-train collection.

Continental breakfast includes homemade coffeecakes, juice, and other beverages. There's also a special Sunday brunch. The innkeepers will find a dinner spot perfect for you.

How to get there: From Chicago, take I-94 north to I-196. Continue north to exit 41; turn southwest on Blue Star Highway, just outside Saugatuck. At the fork in the road, take Holland Street (to the right) into town. Turn right at Lucy; then left at Butler to the inn.

B: *The inn's screened gazebo demands nothing of you, except to relax in oversized California redwood furniture and enjoy the evening's cool breezes.*

The Last Resort
South Haven, Michigan
49090

Innkeepers: Wayne and Mary Babcock
Address/Telephone: 86 North Shore Drive; (616) 637–8943
Rooms: 10, with 4 suites; all with shared baths.
Rates: $38 to $42 single, $42 to $46 double. Includes continental
breakfast. Two-night minimum on weekends. Children 12 and
older OK. No credit cards.
Open: Mid-April to November 1.
Facilities & Activities: Located one block away from North Beach.
South Haven is a Lake Michigan resort village, with terrific
beaches, waterfront sports, charter fishing, tennis, golf, specialty shops, antique stores, fine restaurants, and more. Also
many annual festivals, including the National Blueberry Festival in July.

"During our first summer together, we found this little
arched door washed up on the lakeshore," Mary said. "It
must have been part of a shipwreck. I convinced Wayne to
take it home with us. I just felt that someday we'd be able to
use it someplace really special."

That's the romantic tale of how The Last Resort got its

little arched door, now just past the entryway. And it's an example of the innkeepers' notion of "specialness."

The Babcocks' historic 1883 inn is pretty special itself. (Built by a Civil War captain to entertain his big-city friends, it actually was the *first* resort in South Haven.) It has ☛ views of both the village marina and Lake Michigan on South Haven's North Beach Peninsula. The area has ☛ genuine beach-town flavor, with skateboarders, people dressed in Hawaiian shirts and flowered shorts and sporting deep tans à la Southern California's surfing havens.

Wayne and Mary opened the inn during the 1983 season on its one hundredth anniversary. With tongue firmly in cheek, they had referred to their massive restoration project as the "last resort" in their efforts to fix up the place before calling in the wreckers. The name stuck.

Charming guest rooms are ☛ named after steamers and schooners built in South Haven from 1874 to 1904. All have scenic views of the lake or harbor. They're furnished with antiques, boasting oak valets, lacy curtains, and cheery wallpaper. There's also a downstairs sitting room furnished with an eclectic assortment of furniture—in true beach-house style.

Continental breakfast includes juice, freshly ground coffee, sweet rolls, and croissants—all ☛ served on dishes used in the original inn. There are many good restaurants in town. Clementine's is a favorite for hearty sandwiches and mugs of beer. I think Venezia's has the best thin-crust pizza around, outside of Chicago's famed pizzerias. Or you can dine on fine cuisine on board a stern-wheeler at Idler Riverboat Restaurant.

How to get there: From Chicago, take I–94 north to I–196. Continue north; then get off at exit 22 (North Shore Drive). Follow North Shore Drive to the inn.

B: *Wayne is an artisan specializing in beautiful "Bronze by Babcock" jewelry. "The Inn Gallery" also features fine arts and crafts done by Michigan artists.*

Clifford Lake Hotel
Stanton, Michigan
48888

Innkeepers: Norm and Dyane Eipper
Address/Telephone: 561 West Clifford Lake Drive; (517) 831–5151
Rooms: 4 with shared bath; 1 2-room suite with private bath; 3 cottages.
Rates: $45 single, $55 double. Inquire about higher rates for suite and cottages. Includes continental breakfast. Children OK.
Open: All year.
Facilities & Activities: Full-service dining room, bar, large basement gift shop. Located on the shores of 200-acre Clifford Lake. Boating, fishing, golf, antiquing, cross-country skiing in season.

"We went fishing last night and got about fifty small ones," Dy said. "This is a good lake for bluegills."

And I *love* bluegill filet chips.

It's all part of the lakeside charm at the Clifford Lake Hotel, built in 1881 and now ☞ an official state historic site. This area once held great promise of becoming an important Michigan town. (It was formerly called Richard's Point, and a horse-drawn bus line ferried passengers to the area, while a steamboat plied the lake waters.)

But now the only legacy left from the Richard's Point era is the historic hotel—and for that I'm grateful.

The sunny yellow clapboard building has a 🐾 big white porch facing the lake. Dotted with hanging flower pots and shaded by tall trees, it's a great place to enjoy a cold drink.

The upstairs guest rooms are each decorated with antiques, old-fashioned corner sinks, and country furniture. Norm said that the plank floors are original. One room has a red velvet couch, and there are displays of country stenciling on the walls. Three rooms overlook sparkling Clifford Lake.

Downstairs, I sat sipping a beer in a fun bar built to resemble an old saloon. There are animal trophies and mounted horns that create a strange compulsion to belly up to the bar cowboy-style and raise a glass of suds.

The dining room is a picture of country comfort, with high ceilings, country antiques, and tulip-shaded chandeliers. One 🐾 entire wall of windows fronts the lake. A special Prime Rib Dinner on weekends has earned the kitchen many fans, and the Clifford Charburger is a lunchtime favorite.

How to get there: From Grand Rapids, take U.S. 131 north to Michigan 46; then turn east. At Michigan 66, go south to Stanton. Take Main Street west to Clifford Lake Drive and turn right to the inn.

The Victorian Villa
Guest House
Union City, Michigan
49094

Innkeepers: Ronald and Susan Gibson
Address/Telephone: 601 North Broadway Street; (517) 741–7383
Rooms: 8, with 2 suites; some share baths.
Rates: $55 with shared bath, $65 with private bath. Includes continental breakfast. Children OK. No smoking.
Open: All year.
Facilities & Activities: Forty-five quality antique shops within 25 miles. Six Victorian homes/museums, nineteenth-century historical walking tours, 3 summer stock theaters, country auctions, fishing, summer festivals.

Steady yourself before entering The Victorian Villa for the first time. The grandeur of its elegant Victorian appointments is overwhelming. I could manage only a long stare and a silly "Wow!"

This Italianate mansion, built in 1876 at the then-whopping cost of $12,000, is nestled in the quaint river village of Union City. Its formal Victorian décor makes it an 🖙 absolutely perfect romantic hideaway.

Ronald and Susan have done a masterful restoration job. The formal entrance hallway, with a winding staircase, is all dark woodwork, highlighted with hurricane lamps, red velvet curtains, and gingerbread transoms.

The "informal" parlor is absolutely elegant. Heavy red-velvet high-back chairs are placed around a marble fireplace. Tall hurricane lamps and tulip-shaped chandeliers cast a warm glow over the room. One of my favorite touches is a 🖙 massive gingerbread arch over the doorway.

The guest rooms are equally impressive. The 1890s Edwardian Bedchamber has a 🖙 headboard almost 8 feet high, with antique quilts and pillows, dark rose wallpaper, a marble-topped dresser, and more. The 1860s Rococo Bedchamber has a working fireplace, Tiffany-style lamps, an antique armoire, and a tall Victorian rocker.

Two Tower suites are decorated in country Victorian and separated by a small sitting room. I like the rough-hewn country feel, with iron-rail beds, exposed brick walls, and round tower windows.

Breakfast in a magnificent formal dining room includes Susan's special treats: imported teas, home-baked Amish pastries, fresh fruit in season, and juice. Afternoon English tea also is part of Villa tradition. And you'll find fancy chocolates on your bed pillows at turn-down time.

How to get there: From east or west, take I–94 to I–69 and go south. Turn west on Michigan 60 (exit 25) and continue 7 miles to Union City. There Broadway Street is the town's main street.

B: The inn's 🖙 "Old-Fashioned Christmas" is celebrated the first three weekends of December. That means pine-cone garlands, scented candles, mistletoe, and a gala sprawling feast—and an incredible Christmas tree decorated with handmade Victorian baubles. The holiday-weekend special includes a Victorian Christmas buffet, featuring roasted goose with herb-and-forcemeat stuffing; wassail, caroling, and a chestnut roast; Christmas tea with steamed plum pudding, English trifle, and hot wassail; parlor music and a magic show; a Victorian tree-decoration party, and lots more.

The Gordon Beach Inn
Union Pier, Michigan
49129

Innkeeper: Colleen Recor
Address/Telephone: 16240 Lakeshore Road; (616) 469–3344
Rooms: 13, with 2 suites; 5 rooms with bath down the hallway.
Rates: $35 to $70; suite $85. Includes continental breakfast. Two-night minimum on weekends and holidays. Children OK. No credit cards.
Open: All year.
Facilities & Activities: Short drive to Lake Michigan beaches, Warren Dunes State Park, specialty shops, antique stores, restaurants.

Harbor Country is a stretch of small resort villages with quaint names that hug Lake Michigan's southeastern shoreline. With its miles of sandy beaches, framed by shifting sand dunes, fine marinas, and refuge harbors, it's often been called the "Midwest Riviera."

In this idyllic setting you'll find The Gordon Beach Inn, a vintage 1925 resort hotel. The two-story frame building is all blue stucco and clapboard, with white-rimmed windows. It was bought simply on impulse by Colleen.

"I was driving to Warren Dunes [State Park], and I just came upon it," she said. "There was a 'For Sale' sign on the property. And it was painted orange. It was ugly."

Colleen, a former airline attendant who harbored a secret dream to own an inn since visiting European inn hideaways, immediately got to work restoring the once-grand hotel. She removed paint from hardwood floors, fanciful columns, and woodwork; she trashed dropped ceilings and even uncovered ☞ beautiful copper and pewter lamps affixed to the hardwood columns in the Great Room.

The result is a wonderful inn, with a rich, wood-dominated lobby highlighted by a ☞ massive fieldstone fireplace surrounded by high-back chairs and sofas. Various sitting areas are defined by Oriental rugs strewn about.

"You'll love the dining room. It has this classic 1950s 'marble' tile floor," Colleen said. I found it really homey, with its oak tables and chairs, ceiling fans, and a big chrome potbellied stove among antique bric-a-brac.

My favorite suite has a four-poster bed adorned with a colorful country quilt. Its sitting room also boasts an elegant Victorian bench chair.

Another lovely guest room is done in Williamsburg blue, with bold, oversized Empire-style antique furnishings and a high-back rocker. Still others have iron-rail beds. All are charming.

Colleen serves a continental breakfast of fresh fruit, croissants, rolls, and beverages. She'll recommend a good place for dinner. I suggest Redamak's in nearby New Buffalo; the hamburgers are famous and fantastic.

How to get there: From Chicago, take I–94 north to exit 6, Union Pier. Go west to Lakeshore Road and turn left, continuing to the inn.

The Inn at Union Pier
Union Pier, Michigan
49129

Innkeepers: Madeleine and Bill Reinke
Address/Telephone: 9708 Berrien (mailing address: P.O. Box 222);
    (616) 469–4700
Rooms: 9, with 2 suites; all with private bath.
Rates: $65 to $85. Includes continental breakfast. Children 12 and
    older.
Open: All year.
Facilities & Activities: Outdoor deck and dining area; decktop hot
    tub. Located in southwestern Michigan's Harbor Country,
    where lakeshore communities hug Lake Michigan. Walk to
    breathtaking beaches; drive to antique shops, U-pick fruit
    farms. Inn will arrange windsurfing, bicycling, fishing, canoe-
    ing, horseback riding, winery tours. Cross-country skiing in
    winter.

I cannot put out of my mind those ☛ circular, ceiling-
high, wood-burning Swedish stoves that grace each guest
room. These colorful tile masterpieces are so difficult to as-
semble that the inn "imported" an expert from Sweden to
ensure that they were installed correctly.

But that's only one of the highlights of this elegant inn,

located on the eastern shore of Lake Michigan. Just a walk
from the sand castles and sweeps of the lake's beaches—two
hundred steps from the front door—I enjoyed refined hospitality with all the comforts of a well-appointed country home.

The seventy-year-old beach-resort house has been completely redone in spectacular finery by Madeleine and Bill.
Especially elegant touches are the huge ☞ terra-cotta-and-
iron chandeliers in the gathering room. There are also
leaded-glass windows casting prisms of sunlight on the pretty
pastel colors used to decorate the inn. That ☞ massive
pagoda-style Oriental stove in the gathering room is another
Swedish design.

Madeleine's guest rooms are pictures of country elegance. From the polished hardwood floors and comfy country
furnishings to those wonderful Swedish stoves and lacy window curtains, I felt like a country squire.

A long wood deck connects the main house with another guest-room building. Just between these is an ☞ outdoor hot tub, a favorite gathering spot for guests.

Breakfast can be served out on the deck at tables
adorned with white linen and fresh flowers, some more of
Madeleine's attentive touches. It includes fresh fruit, juice,
rolls, and homemade popovers; in winter you can even have
some old-fashioned oatmeal sprinkled with brown sugar. The
innkeepers can recommend many fine area restaurants for
dinners to suit your taste.

How to get there: From Chicago, take I–94 north to exit 6. Go north
on Townline Road less than a mile to Red Arrow Highway. Turn
right; then go a little more than ½ mile and turn left on Berrien.
The inn is about two blocks ahead on the left side of the road.

ᶁ

B: *Snacks like iced coffee, tea, lemonade, and cookies are treats
for summer guests. Potato soup and chili are offered at 4 P.M.
snacktimes during the cold season.*

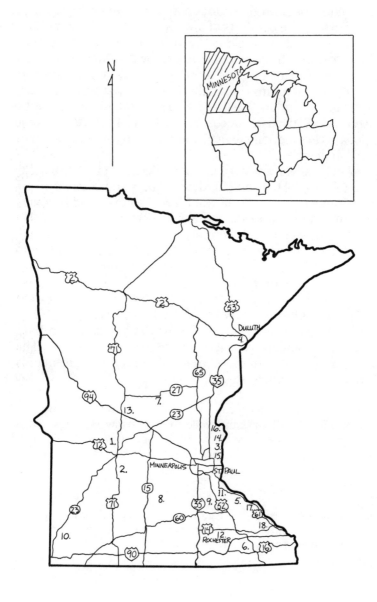

Minnesota

Numbers on map refer to towns numbered below.

Thayer Hotel
Annandale, Minnesota
55302

Innkeepers: Wally and Dotty Houle
Address/Telephone: Downtown on Highway 55; (612) 274–3371
Rooms: 14, with 4 suites; all with private bath.
Rates: $40 winter, $50 summer, double occupancy; $5 less for single occupancy. Includes full country breakfast. Special package rates. Children OK. Wheelchair access.
Open: All year.
Facilities & Activities: Sauna. Full-service restaurant, lounge. Very good antiquing area. Twenty-five lakes within 5 miles. Snowmobiling and skiing nearby.

I walked into the Thayer Hotel and fell in love.

There's something about pioneer hotels and country-Victorian charm that brings to mind tales of the Old West—probably because I always wanted to be a cowboy.

Wally told me that the 1888 building, painted a bright blue and white, was built to accommodate overnight passengers and crew of the Soo Line railroad at this turn-of-the-century resort town. (There are scores of lakes within an hour's drive of the hotel.)

Now I know why all the ☞ handsome glass transoms above the guest-room doors are etched with Soo Line themes—everything from massive locomotives to the line's attractive logo.

Guest rooms ooze country charm. They're spotless and cheery and decorated to convey a turn-of-the-century feel. Some have canopy, four-poster, or iron-rail beds. Others boast ☞ fancy Dutch lace curtains on windows that stretch almost from ceiling to floor. I love the brass clothes hooks and handmade quilts.

One bow to the twentieth century: There's a sauna on the third floor.

Wally suggested I try the hotel's Chicken Oscar as we sat down in a dining room that looks much like a real frontier restaurant. "The woodwork here is rare," he told me. "All made from tamarack—swamp trees. You don't find many swamps around here any more."

My chicken was down-home delicious. Another treat is stuffed pork chops with Burgundy sauce. Then there's a ☞ Shepherd's Dinner featuring spicy meats in a pastry shell.

I'm telling you that the hotel's bakery can do no wrong; in fact, its ☞ delicious pecan pie came close to matching my favorite, which is served in a little café down in Austin, Texas.

How to get there: From Minneapolis, take Minnesota 55 northwest to Annandale. The hotel is located on 55, in the heart of the downtown area.

🍺

B: *I wish I lived closer to the Thayer Hotel. Then I could sample a different home-baked dessert every day.*

Bluff Creek Inn
Chaska, Minnesota
55318

Innkeeper: Marjorie Bush
Address/Telephone: 1161 Bluff Creek Drive; (612) 445–2735
Rooms: 4; all with private bath.
Rates: $55 to $85. Includes elaborate country breakfast. No children.
Open: All year.
Facilities & Activities: Minnesota Renaissance Festival nearby. Ten minutes from Shakopee's Canterbury Downs. Close to Murphy's Landing, historic village.

Marjorie collected the fine antique furnishings of Bluff Creek Inn from shops all over the country, and she's always on the lookout for more treasures to fascinate inn hoppers.

Her charming country-Victorian home is built on land granted in 1860 by Abraham Lincoln; his signature is on the papers. The first white settler in the county was married here.

The yellowish stone used to build the 1886 home is ☛ Chaska brick, Marjorie said. It was ☛ hand-hewn at an historic foundry.

Marjorie is a fun lady. Pointing to a painting of a castle hanging on her wall, she said, "That's where I used to live— my castle on the Rhine." Then she looked at me and winked.

She invited me upstairs to have a chat with ☞ her mascot, a little elf with curly-toed shoes. "It works like this," she said. "When you get here, you turn all your worries over to him. He'll give them back when you leave, but they'll no longer be troublesome."

You are ☞ assured of being pampered during your stay. Marjorie often serves wine and hors d'oeuvres for a special treat. And breakfasts are served in her handsome dining room on Royal Doulton china. One specialty is Yorkshire eggs with artichoke sauce. She'll recommend a special spot for dinner at an area restaurant.

Original pine-plank floors throughout the house lend a rough-hewn country feel. The second-floor guest rooms get special treatment: Marjorie has ☞ bathed all the antique beds in Laura Ashley linens and quilts; one room has a wall of exposed yellow Chaska brick, and I could still see some of the square-headed nails used in the home's original construction.

How to get there: From Minneapolis, take I–494 west to U.S. 169 south. Proceed to the U.S. 212 junction. Go west 1 mile from the junction until you come to a gravel/dirt road. That's Bluff Creek Drive. Turn right and go up the hill to house.

☙

B: *One room boasts an outdoor balcony. What a great place to enjoy breakfast treats.*

Crabtree's Kitchen
Copas, Minnesota
55047

Innkeepers: Terry and Beverly Bennett
Address/Telephone: 19713 Quinnell Avenue, Marine on St. Croix;
(612) 433–2455
Rooms: 4; all with private bath.
Rates: $40. Children 12 and over OK. No smoking. Includes full
breakfast.
Open: All year.
Facilities & Activities: Just a short walk to the restaurant. O'Brien
State Park is connected to Crabtree's by paved hiking and bik-
ing trail; it's one of the state's finest cross-country ski areas.
Canoeing on the St. Croix River; boat tours. Fishing, golf, ten-
nis close by. Near several downhill ski areas. Gift and antique
shops, flea markets in area.

Purely by chance, I wandered into this little red building
with white trim just off Highway 95. It looked like any other
roadside café, except that the parking area was jammed with
cars—a really good sign. It was lunchtime, and I was starv-
ing.
Here I found ☞ some of the best home-cooked food I've
had in a long time. I ordered baked country chicken, and

it came with almost a plate full of homemade mashed potatoes, thick chicken gravy, and green beans. Dee-licious!

Friendly waitresses hovered in old-fashioned uniforms,
bringing mounds of freshly baked bread and sweet butter to
me.

It was a few minutes before I even looked around at the
dining room. Its décor is quite simple, with pine paneling,
padded kitchen chairs, and square tables covered with
freshly starched linens; it made me feel as though I were
back in grandma's kitchen.

All through the main course, I'd been eyeing the incredible desserts that people at surrounding tables had been or-
dering. So I asked for Crabtree's special treat, which turned
out to be hot-fudge cake, just the thing for this rabid
chocoholic. Layers of chocolate-fudge cake are laced with vanilla ice cream, topped with whipped cream, and smothered
in hot-fudge sauce. Wow!

Inn guests choose breakfast off the regular restaurant
menu, which includes goodies like eggs, pancakes, steak,
sweet rolls, and more.

The restaurant building was constructed in 1854. It's
been put to many uses in its lifetime: general store, boat
works—even a brewery during Prohibition.

Behind the restaurant are the guest rooms, comfortably
furnished in down-home fashion with warm turn-of-the-
century antiques. There's a separate entrance, so you don't
have to traipse through the restaurant to reach your room
every night. Come to think of it, I don't know if that's such a
good idea. Something smells awfully good, and I still haven't
tried . . .

How to get there: Take Minnesota 95 whether approaching from
the north or the south. Crabtree's is located on the east side of 95,
between Scandia and Marine on St. Croix, 45 miles northeast of
Minneapolis.

B: *Crabtree's home-style food has been famous in the St. Croix
Valley for thirty-five years.*

The Mansion
Duluth, Minnesota
55804

Innkeepers: Warren and Susan Monson
Address/Telephone: 3600 London Road; (218) 724–0739
Rooms: 9, with 1 suite; 4 with private bath.
Rates: $64 to $130. Includes full breakfast. Well-behaved children
    OK. Wheelchair access.
Open: May 15 to October 15.
Facilities & Activities: Six acres of grounds with 525 feet of gor-
    geous Lake Superior shoreline; includes lawns, woods, and
    gardens. An hour's drive from Apostle Islands National Lake-
    shore.

"It's kind of like a medieval castle," Susan said.

Sure is. The entryway Gallery is all massive plaster-cast
walls sand finished to resemble blocks in a great baronial
hall, with heavy exposed beams adding to the Middle Ages
styling. With its 🖝 spiky, iron wall sconces and floor-to-
ceiling torchlights, I expected Sir Lancelot to clank down the
hall in his shiny suit of armor.

Warren said that the majestic 1932 Tudor home took
four years to build; it has twenty-five rooms, with nine origi-

nal guest rooms. "Used to have ten guest rooms," Warren said. "The original owners used three. The rest housed servants."

This is a house that made me feel special. An exquisite touch is the library, crafted in English hand-hewn white pine, with a 5-foot-wide fireplace and a tremendous selection of classic books. A cozy spot is a Swedish pine–paneled living room with another fireplace, brass chandeliers, and leaded windows. Just down the hallway is a large screened porch with arched windows.

Many guest rooms have a view of Lake Superior. My favorite is the South Room, with its high walnut Victorian headboard and matching furnishings that are at least 150 years old. There's also a working fireplace, and I could hear the sound of crashing waves pound the beach.

Would you like to have the entire third floor of the fabulous mansion to yourself? That's what you get when you take the Anniversary Suite.

Nobody goes hungry here. Susan whips up a handsome breakfast of French toast, bacon, eggs, and sausage—and her special home-baked caramel rolls. Best bets for a Duluth dinner are at the Pickwick and Fitger's.

French doors off the Gallery lead to magnificent grounds fronting the lake. I walked down to the beach and skipped stones off the water.

How to get there: In Duluth, follow U.S. 61 (also called North Shore Drive and London Road). Follow this north and turn into the driveway leading to the mansion.

❧

B: An exceptional privacy-filled lakeside retreat.

The Rahilly House
Lake City, Minnesota
55041

Innkeepers: Dorene and Gary Fechtmeyer, owners; Denise and
   Mark Peters, managers
Address/Telephone: 304 South Oak Street; (612) 345-4664
Rooms: 7, with 1 suite; 1 with private bath.
Rates: $50 to $70 single, $60 to $80 double. Includes full country
   breakfast. No children under 12. Wheelchair access. No credit
   cards.
Open: All year.
Facilities & Activities: In beautiful Mississippi River bluff country.
   Lake City has one of the largest marinas on the river, with all
   kinds of boating and fishing. Nearby parks offer walking trails,
   cross-country and downhill skiing, biking, and tubing down
   the Zumbro River. Back-hills birdwatching paradise, with
   greatest number of bald-eagle aeries of any area in nation.
   Nearby golf course overlooking Lake Pepin.

   I stumbled onto The Rahilly House after trying to make
a U-turn and getting lost in a maze of streets. Thank good-
ness for this momentary lapse in my sense of direction.
   The handsome 1868 Greek Revival home with tall white
columns is an elegant ornament in this river town. It's

charming, luxurious, and yet cozy. I was impressed by shining oak floors, sparkling stained glass, and five marble fireplaces dotted throughout the house.

Denise showed me guest rooms that have true old-world charm, with beautiful antiques and down comforters. For example, the enchanting Russell Room has a large antique sleigh bed and brick fireplace. I imagined what it would be like to snuggle under the covers with a warm fire crackling on a fierce winter day.

But it's the Rahilly Room, named after the immigrant from Limerick who became a state senator, that has my favorite piece of inn furniture: a huge four-poster bed with hardwood canopy draped in linen—in true Empire style.

"I'm sure you'll like our parlor," Denise said. "It has a fireplace of African marble decorated with inlaid gold." I found it's also a great place to share a glass of wine and exchange tales of recent town-exploring adventures with other guests.

Denise serves breakfast in a sunny dining room that has elegant brass-and-crystal chandeliers and antique Queen Anne furniture. She opened up French doors, and we walked out onto a screened porch, a favorite lazing spot for summertime guests.

Her fresh country breakfast includes juice, home-baked breads and muffins, bacon, eggs, quiches, and soufflés. There are lots of good restaurants in town; Port of Call and Waterman's are two she recommends.

How to get there: U.S. 61 goes right into Lake City. From the south, go two blocks past the first set of stoplights and turn right on Marion. From there, it's two blocks to Oak and the inn.

B: Inn motto: *"Friends may we part and quickly meet again."*

Mrs. B's Historic Lanesboro Inn
Lanesboro, Minnesota
55949

Innkeepers: Jack and Nancy Bratrud
Address/Telephone: 101 Parkway; (507) 467–2154
Rooms: 9; all with private bath.
Rates: $35 single, $40 double. Includes full breakfast. Children OK.
  Well-behaved pets only. Wheelchair access. No credit cards.
Open: All year.
Facilities & Activities: Near bike and cross-country ski trails, antique shops, bluffs, golf, tennis, fishing. In heart of state hardwood forest.

Kirk, the innkeepers' son, is the chef. "I love to cook for guests," he said, as we walked to the inn's cozy dining room. "People come in here at first, frazzled, with little to say, and sit down at the table. But by the time dinner is almost finished, it's great to listen to all the laughter and noise. Sometimes they even burst into song."

You might, too, after sampling some of Kirk's five-course country dinners. Imagine homemade borscht, hardtack, mixed greens, six-grain bread, boned chicken stuffed with forest mushrooms, succotash, asparagus spears, cranberry-and-orange sauce—and lemon meringue pie. (You may be lucky enough to get one of Kirk's favorite desserts, bananas *Blagsvedt*.) And there are lots more inn specialties.

Historic Lanesboro is surrounded by high bluffs covered with tall hardwood trees. In fact, a 500-foot bluff, looming just beyond the inn, almost blocks the town's main street.

The 1872 inn has a big canopy shading tall arched merchant windows facing the street. Kirk says that anyone is welcome to play a tune on the sitting room's baby grand piano; there's also a big brick fireplace with comfy high-back chairs and sofa nearby.

The guest rooms are comfortable and cozy, with pine headboards and canopy beds, quilts, rose floral print wallpaper, writing desks, and other antique pine reproductions. Some of them have ☞ outside balconies, and it's fun to sit out on a ladder-back rocking chair and look out over the Root River behind the inn to the high bluffs beyond.

Kirk recommends a walk along a hiking trail that crosses the old bridge and faces the bluff. "You really get a feel for the bluff country," he said.

How to get there: Take Minnesota 16 to Lanesboro. In town, turn north on Parkway and proceed to the inn.

Pine Edge Inn
Little Falls, Minnesota
56345

Innkeeper: Kevin Mooney
Address/Telephone: 308 First Street; (612) 632–6681
Rooms: 60, with 1 suite; all with private bath.
Rates: $25.25 single, $29 double. Children under 12 free. Well-
   behaved pets OK.
Open: All year.
Facilities & Activities: Full-service restaurant with 3 dining rooms.
   Swimming pool. Nearby pan and sport fishing in Mississippi
   River. Mississippi River excursion boats. Golf course, hiking
   trails, snowmobiling, and skiing close by. Charles A. Lindbergh
   Home and Interpretive Center.

Sitting at a table in the Edge of the Ledge, the inn restaurant with two walls of windows overlooking the Mississippi River, I savored my home-baked apple pie.

"This is really good," I said to my waitress.

She smiled. "That's 'cause ☛ all the food here is made
from scratch."

This exemplifies the down-home flavor of the Pine Edge
Inn. The town is the birthplace of Charles Lindbergh; after

his historic transatlantic flight, a banquet was held here in his honor.

Kevin prides himself on old-fashioned hospitality. I could almost feel the coziness, especially in the simple comfort of the guest rooms. Ask for a room facing the river. I ☞ opened my window and heard the white-water gurgle of the Little Falls, just a stone's throw away. (Be sure to ask for a room at the original inn, not across the street at the newer motel unit.)

Pine Edge Inn food has been called "conversation-stopping good." Hearty meat-and-potato dishes are staples of the townspeople who often gather here for meals, but you can also try exotic entrées like ☞ veal bird with mushroom sauce, smoked beef tongue, and more. There are scrumptious fresh fruit pies for dessert.

Another favorite inn activity is sipping piping-hot morning coffee amid the clatter of coffee cups and early morning conversation, nibbling on a home-baked cinnamon roll, and reading the newspaper.

How to get there: Take U.S. 10 into Little Falls (which turns into First Street). This leads directly to the inn, located on the river side of the street.

Schumacher's
New Prague Hotel
New Prague, Minnesota
56071

Innkeeper: John Schumacher
Address/Telephone: 212 West Main Street; (612) 758–2133
Rooms: 12; all with private bath.
Rates: $48.50 to $63.50 Sunday through Thursday, $65 to $85 Friday through Saturday, double occupancy; $5 less for single occupancy. No children.
Open: All year.
Facilities & Activities: Golfing nearby. Minnesota River canoeing, fishing, 9 miles away.

I stepped into Schumacher's New Prague Hotel through a hand-stenciled door and thought I'd somehow been caught in a time warp, ending up in old-world Bavaria.

John is very proud of his beautiful inn, and rightly so. It looks similar to many European country hotels I've stayed at. A peaceful air of rich handiwork, fine craftsmanship, wonderful imported old-world antiques, and a deep commitment to dining excellence are what make Schumacher's one of the best there is.

Built in 1898, the hotel boasts an ornate European-style lobby, with pressed-tin ceilings, rich floral wallpaper, fine European antiques, and Oriental rugs that cover original maple hardwood floors. A wonderful front desk is original, too.

John commissioned renowned ☞ Bavarian folk artist Pipka to design the graceful stenciled scenes that enliven guest, lobby, and restaurant rooms.

Upstairs are twelve individually decorated guest rooms, named in German for the months of the year, and furnished with old-world trunks, chairs, beds, and wardrobes. More authentic touches include ☞ eiderdown-filled pillows and comforters, and 100 percent cotton bedding and tablecloths, which John purchased in Austria, Czechoslovakia, and West Germany.

August is my favorite, with its ☞ twin beds pushed together to make one king-sized bed (a typically European custom), primitive Bavarian folk art, and a red color theme carried out in stenciled hearts on the pine floor and on an ornately decorated wardrobe.

And *Mai* has, in addition to a high-canopied double bed reached by a small ladder, a hand-painted claw-footed bathtub. John thoughtfully places a complimentary bottle of imported German wine and two glasses in each room, just one of the many thoughtful touches.

Guess who's the chef? John is a classically trained cooking school graduate who specializes in excellent old-world cuisine—with a Czech flair. His ☞ extensive menu features more than fifty-five dinner entrées.

"What's your pleasure? I'll cook you a feast!" he said. A typical feast is *Schumachrovo posviceni* (flaming veal, pork, chicken, and Czech sausage served with dumplings, red cabbage, sauerkraut, and hot German potato salad).

How to get there: From Minneapolis, take U.S. 169 south to Minnesota 21 south and continue into New Prague. Turn left on Minnesota 19 (Main Street). The hotel is past the railroad tracks on the right side of the road.

B: A romantic "European" hideaway for really special celebrations, like saying, "I love you!"

The Archer House
Northfield, Minnesota
55057

Innkeeper: Dallas Haas
Address/Telephone: 212 Division Street; (507) 645–5661, toll free
    in Minnesota (800) 247–2235
Rooms: 28, with 9 suites; all with private bath.
Rates: $40 to $95. Continental breakfast available at extra charge.
    Children OK.
Open: All year.
Facilities & Activities: Tavern restaurant; ice-cream shop, book-
    store. Nearby, Carleton and St. Olaf colleges and Northfield
    Arts Guild offer programs of theater, art, concerts, films, and
    lectures. Hiking, biking, canoeing on Cannon River; tennis,
    swimming, cross-country skiing and ice skating (in season).
    September celebration of defeat of Jesse James with reenact-
    ment of James gang's attempted robbery of Historic First Na-
    tional Bank of Northfield; the bank museum is just down the
    street from the inn.

A real Wild West frontier hotel!
    The Archer House is just a short walk from the local
bank that the Jesse James gang attempted to rob in 1876.

Yep, the "Great Northfield Raid" was the desperado disaster that virtually ended Jesse's reign of terror on the frontier.

Dallas said that the fancy hotel, sporting grand French Second-Empire stylings like arched windows and a long front porch, was built one year after Jesse and his gang were defeated by the townspeople. "It was supposed to make the town seem more civilized," he said, taking it further away from the "cowboy image" fostered by the notoriety of gun battles in the street that took place during the attempted bank robbery.

Dallas has done a terrific job restoring it. He leaves doors to unoccupied rooms open so browsers can appreciate the turn-of-the-century charm inside. Each room is decorated in a style of its own, but always with ruggedly elegant country warmth. I loved the ☛ handcrafted pine furniture, handmade quilts, dust ruffles, tieback curtains, and embroidered samplers. Made me feel as though I were boarding in Old Tucson.

I stayed in the Manawa Room, decorated in Dutch country style: blue floors, stencils on the walls, a fine pine bed with a beautiful blue-and-white pointed-star quilt, and a needlepoint sampler. I'm sure my room's ☛ Dutch hex sign has brought me good luck.

The pace here is unhurried and casual, making it an ideal place to relax amid the homespun graciousness of this interesting and pretty Minnesota town. The hotel's dining room offers country breakfasts (ham and egg plates) and light lunches. Le Bistro Café downtown serves interesting country-French dinners.

How to get there: From the Twin Cities: Take I–35 south to the Northfield exit. Follow Highway 19 east to the first stoplight. Go east for two blocks. Turn left onto Division Street and go two blocks. The Archer House is on the left.

From Rochester, take Highway 52 north to Cannon Falls. Then take Highway 19 west 11 miles to Northfield. Go straight onto Division Street. The Archer House is on the right.

B: *Jesse's gang "robs" the local bank every September in a colorful festival celebrating the "Town That Defeated Jesse James."*

The Calumet Hotel
Pipestone, Minnesota
56164

Innkeeper: Lani Hale
Address/Telephone: Corner of Main and Hiawatha; (507) 825–4273
Rooms: 13 antique, 14 modern, with 1 suite; all with private bath.
Rates: Antique rooms: $35 to $75 single, $45 to $75 double. Children OK. Wheelchair access.
Open: All year.
Facilities & Activities: Two full-service dining rooms, bar. Part of Pipestone Historic District. Pipestone National Monument, Upper Midwest Indian Cultural Center nearby. Hole in the Wall ski area nearby.

The Calumet Hotel is located in the historic district of tiny Pipestone, a wisp of a town located in the heart of traditional lands home to the Dakota Yankton-Sioux nation. I drove just outside of town and stood gazing over the "grass prairies," still a massively empty, windy landscape—the beginning of the Great Plains.

Native Americans mined pipestone at ancient quarries

nearby. The "sacred" soft stone still is used for ceremonial pipes.

This pioneer legacy continues at the hotel, a massive pink-and-red quartzite building made of hand-chiseled, locally quarried stone, completed in 1888. Easily its most outstanding feature is a ☞ four-story exposed red-stone wall that overpowers the lobby.

Everything here seems larger than life. I walked up a ☞ magnificent four-story staircase of oak and maple to reach my room. A high skylight washed the stairs in warm sunlight. (I counted ninety-two steps. Don't worry, there's an elevator, too.)

My room was classically restored to Victorian elegance, with marble-topped dressers, a velvet-covered rocking chair, and two walnut beds sporting high headboards. Later, I found out that antique brokers were commissioned to seek out the nineteenth-century pieces. They ☞ searched old British estates, Colorado-gold-rush mansions, Carolina plantations, and historic New England homes to uncover the splendid period pieces.

All the rooms have names like Paradise Regained and Abigail's Dream. My favorite is the Choctaw Indian Walk, with a wall of exposed brick and Indian artifacts and designs.

Throughout the restored rooms I found fainting couches, chairs of golden oak built extra wide to accommodate ladies' Victorian-era bustles, rose silk-damask draperies, claw-footed dressers, and antique prints and photos. The hotel quickly became one of my favorites.

Food at the hotel's Farmer's Market restaurant rivals Granny's home cooking: wholesome meats and vegetables, baked goods hot from the oven, and delicious desserts.

How to get there: I–75 and Minnesota 30 and 23 lead into Pipestone, located in extreme southwestern Minnesota. Once in town, make way to East Main Street and continue to the corner of Hiawatha and the hotel.

🥛

B: *Pipestone National Monument (ancient Indian pipestone quarries a short drive away) is fascinating. I stayed there for hours.*

Pratt-Taber Inn
Red Wing, Minnesota
55066

Innkeepers: Darrel and Jan Molander and Chuck and Jane Walker
Address/Telephone: 706 West Fourth; (612) 388–5945
Rooms: 6, with 1 suite; 2 with private bath.
Rates: $49 to $130. Includes continental breakfast. Special mid-week and winter rates. Children OK.
Open: All year.
Facilities & Activities: Bikes available. Nearby are riverboat excursions on the Mississippi River, trolley-car rides, horse-and-buggy rides, cross-country and downhill skiing at Frontenac Ski Area and Welch Village (in season), 5 golf courses, bingo on Prairie Island Indian Reservation. Also, Red Wing offers antique shops, specialty shops, and art galleries.

Taped to the door was a note from Darrel and Jan asking guests to come inside and make themselves comfortable until they returned from an errand. So I turned the door handle of this elaborate Italianate mansion and walked into a world of old-time elegance.

The thirteen-room mansion, built in 1876, has been restored to a special magnificence in this historic river town crested by high bluffs of the Mississippi River. I was over-whelmed by the ☞ immense leaded-glass doors that open into a sitting room full of Victorian finery. Heavy floor-length balloon draperies cascade down tall windows, a handsome secretary almost reaches the high ceiling, and a high-back sofa sits on an elegant Oriental carpet.

I admired fine details like ☞ feather-painted slate fire-places and fancy gingerbread woodwork. Rich woods of but-ternut and walnut provide a graceful backdrop for ☞ early Renaissance Revival and country-Victorian furnishings that the innkeepers have spent years collecting.

One guest room has an antique Victorian dresser that stretches almost to the ceiling. Rich antique wall coverings also add to the period charm. Some rooms even have fire-places.

A light breakfast of juice, rolls, and coffee is usually taken in the Victorian dining room, but just a ☞ note on the kitchen table the night before will fetch you breakfast in bed. Don't pass up the sumptuous seafood or steak dinners served in the elegant Victorian dining room at the St. James Hotel in the heart of town.

I want you to try and spot the hidden Murphy bed in the library. No fair asking Jan for hints.

How to get there: Take U.S. 61 into Red Wing and proceed to Da-kota. Turn west; then turn north on West Fourth to the home.

ⵆ

B: *The inn makes a great first impression—and later surpasses it.*

St. James Hotel
Red Wing, Minnesota
55066

Innkeeper: E. E. Foster
Address/Telephone: 406 Main Street; (612) 388–2846
Rooms: 61; all with private bath.
Rates: $55 to $98.50. Children welcome. Wheelchair access.
Open: All year.
Facilities & Activities: Three dining areas, 13 specialty shops. Walking and driving tours of historic river-front town. Antique and specialty shops. Mississippi River water sports and activities nearby

E.E. told me that the St. James Hotel was one of the first fine Victorian hotels in the Midwest. It was built in 1875, and its elegance reflected Red Wing's prosperity as the world's largest wheat market at the time.

Now Red Wing is just an historic Mississippi river town. But the St. James's tradition of refined Victorian tastes continues.

☛ "Quiet elegance" is the phrase that best describes the guest rooms. Each is uniquely decorated; I especially like the ☛ fancily scrolled wall borders, so popular back in the hotel's heyday. In fact, they set the color tones for coordinated wallpapers and handmade quilts.

Authentic antiques and fine reproductions recreate a long-ago era of luxury. E.E. has a great collection of beds; massive four-poster beds, Jenny Lind spindles, shiny brass beds, and more. Unique gingerbread window treatments splash spiky shafts of sunlight into rooms.

In some rooms, a ☞ view of the Mississippi River and surrounding high bluffs is a big treat.

Of course, you'll be spoiled after just one day at the St. James. A complimentary chilled bottle of wine welcomes you to your room, and there'll be a steaming pot of coffee and morning paper delivered to your door.

I love all the choices for dining because there is something for every mood and taste: a light snack at the Veranda Café, with ☞ al fresco dining on a porch overlooking the Mississippi; a hearty sandwich at the Port of Call, decorated to recapture the warmth of the riverboat era; or the elegant Victorian Dining Room, boasting fine antique pieces from around the world—and exquisite dinner presentations like Filet of Canadian Walleye and Baron of Beef Garni.

Then it's up to Jimmy's, the hotel's English-style pub— a great way to end the day.

(*Note:* Ask for an historic room if that is your preference; there are several with modern décor.)

How to get there: Take U.S. 61 into Red Wing, where it becomes Main Street; the hotel's address is 406 Main Street.

Canterbury Inn
Rochester, Minnesota
55902

Innkeepers: Mary Martin and Jeffrey Van Sant
Address/Telephone: 723 Second Street S.W.; (507) 289–5553
Rooms: 4; all with private bath.
Rates: $55 single, $65 double. Includes full breakfast and "high
tea." No children.
Open: All year.
Facilities & Activities: Three blocks from the Mayo Clinic. Nearby:
Richard J. Dorer Memorial Hardwood State Forest.

Mary and Jeffrey are great ladies. And so is their Canterbury Inn, a beautiful 1890 Victorian with its multi-gabled roof, gingerbread adornments, stained glass, and elegant interior—not to mention the delicious breakfasts and intimate afternoon teas.

"We just love the teas," Jeffrey said. "It's a time when we can be more than hostesses. We take off our serving aprons and join in as one of the guests. We have so much fun."

"That's right," Mary added. "We just love to host people in our home. After all, we live here. We're proud of it."

As they should be. The home is graced with 🖝 oak, pine, and maple hardwoods, with magnificent golden-pine woodwork. A stained-glass window spills colors onto a grand staircase that leads to the upper-floor rooms.

The rooms are all bright and airy, with four-poster beds, bright quilts, Victorian dressers, hardwood floors, scatter rugs, and rocking chairs by tall windows. Cute and cozy.

Teatime means late-afternoon sherry, white wine, elegant hors d'oeuvres—and tea, of course. Expect lots of conversation from Mary and Jeffrey. Their outgoing personalities are one of the inn's most engaging touches.

Breakfast is the time Mary and Jeffrey really try to spoil you. When is the last time you had 🖝 Grand Marnier French Toast? With bacon, baked apples, gingerbread waffles, and exotic egg dishes, it's a real treat.

The innkeepers recommend the Broadstreet Café for fine dining. It's housed in a restored warehouse building and features gourmet-style food and desserts in an informal atmosphere. My dad tried the beef and onions braised in beer and cleaned his plate. I found the seafood quiche light and tasty.

And the Mississippi Pecan Pie was a winner, too!

How to get there: Take I–90 to either U.S. 52 or directly to U.S. 63, which goes into Rochester. Turn left on Second Street and go about eight blocks to the inn.

Palmer House Hotel
Sauk Centre, Minnesota
56378

Innkeepers: Al Tingley and Richard Schwartz
Address/Telephone: 500 Sinclair Lewis Avenue; (612) 352-3431
Rooms: 37; 4 with private bath.
Rates: $13.78 single, $19.08 double. Children and pets OK. No
    credit cards.
Open: All year.
Facilities & Activities: Full-service restaurant, with banquet hall
    and private dining areas. Nearby is boyhood home and mu-
    seum of author Sinclair Lewis. Walk to fishing on shores of
    Sauk Lake.

I met Al as he came out of the hotel kitchen. Of course,
that's the most likely spot to find him, as he's renowned for
preparing delicious nine-course meals for groups of two to
twenty on only a few days' notice.

"I love the place," Al said. "It's somewhere you can still
get a clean room and good food at reasonable prices." Then
there's all the history, too.

Sauk Centre is Sinclair Lewis's home town. Lewis
worked at the Palmer House during his spare time in high

school and was fired by his bosses for daydreaming and reading.

But he got even by writing his searing portrait of the archetypal small town in *Main Street,* wherein he immortalizes the hotel as the "Minniemashie House."

Al said that the 1901 hotel originally serviced drummers (traveling salesmen brought into town by twelve trains daily) who'd pay $3 for a room.

Everything in the guest rooms is original to the hotel, Al said. The rooms are clean and pleasant, with period pieces like hurricane lamps, Depression-era dressers, firm mattresses covered by chenille bedspreads, and wall sinks in rooms without bath.

Al ran his hand along one of the desks. "These were designed by the hotel's original owner so drummers could have a convenient place to write up their orders."

Al and Richard, friends since college days, have spent nearly half a million dollars in restoration work since they bought the place in 1974, saving it from the wrecker's ball. They've also found some hidden treasures along the way, like the ☛ seventeen Austrian stained- and rippled-glass windows they uncovered under temporary walls.

There are some funky excesses, like an ☛ autographed picture of actor Lorne Green in Room #2. "He came into town in 1963 during the height of his 'Bonanza' fame, so the hotel fashioned a room with plywood paneling and a big brass bed to resemble his 'Ponderosa' TV ranch home," Al chuckled. "We thought it was kind of funny, so we left it."

An old-fashioned dining room is the gathering place for town citizens and a den of local gossip. Food is small-town wholesome (meat loafs, casseroles, and the like) with some great homemade desserts along the way. Or Al will prepare one of his famous impromptu gourmet multi-course dinners for an intimate romantic meal in the hotel's "Minniemashie House" dining room.

Get him to talk about ☛ the ghost that stalks the second floor rooms. A number of guests claim to have seen or "felt" its presence.

How to get there: Take I–94 to U.S. 71. Go north into the city (the road turns into Original Main Street) to the hotel at the intersection of Lewis and Main.

Country Bed & Breakfast
Shafer, Minnesota
55074

Innkeepers: Lois and Budd Barott
Address/Telephone: 32030 Ranch Trail Road; (612) 257–4773
Rooms: 3; all with shared bath.
Rates: $31.80 to $58.30. Includes full country breakfast. Children and pets OK. No smoking. No credit cards.
Open: All year.
Facilities & Activities: Thirty-five quiet acres in the middle of peaceful agricultural lands. Spacious tree-shaded lawn. Maple groves. Walking in surrounding fields. Near to Ki-Chi-Saga Lake, the Sunrise and St. Croix rivers with riverboat cruises, tubing, canoeing, swimming, fishing. Two downhill ski resorts close by. Cross-country ski and nature trails at Wild River State Park. Also antique, pottery shops in area. Five miles west of historic Taylors Falls.

"I'm so tired from collecting sap, and I still have to boil it down today. Then I'll just go to sleep."

Poor Budd. I'd stopped midweek by his country spread and caught him in the middle of his busy chores. But that didn't stop him or Lois from showcasing their overwhelming country hospitality. ☛ After a few minutes with them, I felt as if I'd returned home after a long journey away from this pretty farmstead.

Both Lois and Budd showed me around the place. Lois pointed to the chickens running in frantic circles near their coop. "I'm so proud of my chickens," she said. "I got to have lots of them. You know, fresh eggs for breakfast."

Budd and I laughed. "Yeah, we give you an $18 breakfast here for nothing," he said, "and you can eat as much as you want."

This is no mere boast. Country breakfast features Swedish egg-coffee; eggs fried with ham, sausage, or bacon—Budd's specialty; Lois's buttermilk pancakes with homemade maple syrup from their groves out back; and raspberries and strawberries from Budd's organic garden. There's fresh honey, too—Budd's also a beekeeper. "If you leave here hungry, it's your own fault," he joked. The innkeepers suggest that guests take a short drive to Marine on St. Croix for delicious homemade dinners at Crabtree's Kitchen.

Their farmhouse is a quaint 1881 red-brick Victorian. Lois, who grew up here, pointed out original plank floors and a big wood-burning stove in a country kitchen. A comfortable sitting room has a sofa, chair, and TV.

Guest rooms upstairs are pictures of farm-country charm. Lois has covered plank floors with scatter rugs; she also uses some white wicker chairs and other country antiques, sheer white curtains on tall windows that flood rooms with sunlight, and pretty print wallpapers.

I lazed part of the day away on the front porch—Budd, my dad, and I just "stirring up the pot" with our stories. There's also a back deck where you can just sit and breathe the fresh country air.

This is the *perfect* place to retreat to country solitude. And you couldn't find two kinder hosts.

How to get there: Enter Shafer on U.S. 61. Then turn left on Ranch Trail Road and proceed to the inn.

B: *I already missed Budd and Lois five minutes after we left.*

The Lowell Inn
Stillwater, Minnesota
55082

Innkeepers: Arthur and Maureen Palmer
Address/Telephone: 102 North Street; (612) 439–1100
Rooms: 25, with 2 suites: all with private baths.
Rates: Rooms $69 to $99, suites $109 to $119. Children OK.
Open: All year.
Facilities & Activities: Full-service restaurant. Many quality antique, gift, and specialty shops nearby. Good town bakeries. Cave tours. Not far from the Mississippi River. The inn can arrange River Run excursions May to September. Winter cross-country skiing at O'Brien State Park. Downhill skiing at 3 resorts nearby.

I remember The Lowell Inn for its ☞ china cats.

That's right. I walked into my enormous French Provincial–style room only to find a little "kitty" curled up on the foot of my bed. Cats and kittens are in every guest room; Arthur and Maureen believe they add homey warmth to the elegant rooms.

It's not something I expected to find here. The inn, which opened on Christmas Day 1930, is built in a formal colonial-Williamsburg style. The huge veranda is supported by thirteen tall white pillars that represent the original thirteen colonies, and each bears a pole flying respective state flags.

Stepping inside, I saw an exquisite mixture of colonial and French Provincial antiques. Many of the inn's gorgeous collectibles are part of the private collection of Nelle Palmer, wife of the original owner.

The dining rooms are handsome, dotted with ☛ Dresden china, Capo di Monte porcelain, Sheffield silver, and more. The George Washington Room is adorned with hand-crested Irish linen, authentic Williamsburg ladder-back chairs, and portraits of George and Martha. Still another surprise is an indoor trout pool in the Garden Room. You can select your dinner by pointing to the fish of your choice. Huge polished agate tables accentuate the earthy quality of the room.

Easily my favorite is the Matterhorn Room, all done in deep, rich woods and authentic Swiss wood carvings. The inn's showpiece, as far as I'm concerned, is a ☛ life-sized eagle hand carved by a seventy-eight-year-old Swiss master wood carver.

Dinners here might begin with Swiss *escargots* (pure-white snails picked from vineyards in France and Switzerland), followed by a large chilled green salad with pickled relishes; and for an entrée, *Fondue Bourguignonne* (beef or shrimp individually seasoned with six different sauces).

The guest rooms are individually decorated in a combination of colonial and French Provincial styles, with soft colors, frills, mirrors, antiques, and goose-down comforters. A complimentary bottle of wine in my room was a welcome surprise.

How to get there: From Minneapolis–St. Paul, take State Road 36 east. It changes into Stillwater's Main Street. Turn left on Myrtle and go about a block to Second Street.

Historic
Taylors Falls Jail
Taylors Falls, Minnesota
55084

Innkeeper: Helen White
Address/Telephone: 102 Government Road; (612) 465–3112
Rooms: 1 guest house.
Rates: $110 for 3 days, 2 nights weekend/double occupancy; optional third night at no extra charge; 1 night Monday through Thursday, $55. Includes country breakfast. Children OK. No credit cards.
Open: All year.
Facilities & Activities: Part of the Angels Hills Historic District, a cluster of well-maintained and restored nineteenth-century buildings overlooking the St. Croix River. Just across the river in St. Croix Falls, Wisconsin, is the St. Croix National Scenic Riverway, with Visitor and Interpretive Center, and the falls. Also nearby: canoeing, fishing, other sports.

The minute I drove into Taylors Falls, I was hustled off to jail.

Fortunately for me, it was the Historic Taylors Falls Jail,

now a country inn located high on historic Angels Hill, overlooking the rushing St. Croix River.

Helen pulled on the ☞ original full-sized steel grate that covers the front door, and we went inside. She pointed out the bars on a second-story window. And I could count old stud marks that show how the sturdy building was divided into individual cells. But those were the only things that resembled a "hoosegow."

"If the jail looked then like it does today, you'd have people jockeying for a town-sponsored stay," Helen told me. There are pine floors throughout, with a ☞ wood-burning potbellied Montana Queen stove in a spacious living room, complete with a richly colored Navajo rug. There's a sofa bed to accommodate a second couple, too. Original ceiling two-by-fours were used to recreate the old jail ambience. A combination kitchen and dining room has all the modern conveniences.

The sleeping loft is reached by an attractive staircase. I liked the bright bed coverings; Helen said that they are all hand-quilted. And along with ☞ wall hangings, tapestry, stenciling, pottery, artwork, rush seating, and rag rugs that captivatingly decorate the jail, they are works of local craftspeople.

Breakfast food is provided for guests, so you may dine at your leisure. It includes locally produced cheeses (made five miles from here), and maple syrup bottled especially for the jail. The nearby Chisago House offers weekend smorgasbord dinner dining, while delicious deli sandwiches are served up at Sgt. Pickles Deli & Saloon.

How to get there: Take Minnesota 95 to Taylors Falls. At Angels Hill, go west one block to Government Road and the jail.

B: *What kind of criminals were jailed here? Here's a local newspaper report from June 30, 1876: "Archy Cummings of Dodge County came down on one of the drives, and after getting a little full, concluded he weighed about four tons, and very loudly proclaimed the fact that he could whip anybody in town. Marshal Peter Trump took the young man to the calaboose. Next morning he paid $10 and costs, $14 in all, for his drunk."*

The Anderson House
Wabasha, Minnesota
55981

Innkeepers: John, Jeanne, and Gayla Hall
Address/Telephone: 333 North Main Street; (612) 565–4524, toll free in Minnesota (800) 862–9702, toll free from outside Minnesota (800) 325–2270
Rooms: 52; 35 with private bath; 2 suites.
Rates: $29.50 to $49; suites $65.50 to $69. Traveler's special, Sunday through Thursday: dinner, bed, and breakfast, $29.95. Numerous packages. Children OK; pets OK in certain rooms. Wheelchair access.
Open: All year, except Christmas Day.
Facilities & Activities: Full-service dining rooms, ice-cream parlor. In winter, ice fishing, skating, boating. About 30 miles from 3 ski resorts. Right across the street from Mississippi River and fishing, boating. Also area antique shops.

The Anderson House has the most unusual special inn services I've ever run across!

☞ Hot bricks wrapped in cotton warm your feet after a long day's journey.

☞ Shoes will be shined free of charge if you leave them outside your door before retiring for the evening.

☞ Mustard plasters will be conjured up to treat stuffy congestion and chest colds.

☞ Ten cats are on daily call: you can rent one to help purr you to sleep and make you feel more at home.

☞ Pennsylvania-Dutch specialties like scrapple and *fastnachts,* a meat dish with tasty doughnuts, are served for breakfast.

Now have I got your attention?

It's the oldest operating hotel in Minnesota, never having closed its doors since opening day in 1856. The rambling red-brick inn, which takes up a block of the town's Main Street, traces its roots back to Pennsylvania-Dutch country. In fact, Grandma Ida Anderson, who ran the hotel at the turn of the century, earned her reputation for scrumptious meals conjured up in the hotel's kitchen. The tradition continues under her great-grandson, John.

John has delightfully remodeled all the guest rooms. Most have floral-print wallpaper, antique maple, oak, and walnut beds and dressers—and handmade quilts and bedspreads. John said those were made by two ladies from a nearby nursing home. Some rooms that share a bath have a sink. Other rooms will afford you a glimpse of the Mississippi River, just across the street.

A favorite of mine is a room with an enchanting Dutch sleigh bed and matching chest; both are hand-stenciled with flowery patterns and fine handiwork.

Get ready for a real dining treat. Unique inn offerings include cheese soup, chicken with Dutch dumplings, bacon-corn chowder, *kugelhopf, limpa,* pork tenderloin medallions cooked in sauerkraut, and Dutch beer—and if you're very lucky, sometimes sticky-sweet shoo-fly pie for dessert.

How to get there: U.S. 61 and Minnesota 60 go right through town. The inn is located right on North Main Street.

B: John's family marks the fourth generation of Anderson House ownership. That means a long-standing tradition of warm hospitality that's hard to beat.

The Hotel
Winona, Minnesota
55987

Innkeeper: Joanne Carlson
Address/Telephone: 129 West Third Street; (507) 452–5460
Rooms: 25, with 1 suite; all with private bath.
Rates: $27 to $48 single, $40 to $65 double. Includes continental
  breakfast. Various packages. Children OK. Well-behaved pets
  only.
Open: All year.
Facilities & Activities: Nearby are antique stores, Winona Knitting
  Mills, Bunnell House, Polish Heritage Museum, "Julius
  Wilke" riverboat museum. Also nearby are fishing, hunting,
  swimming and water sports, horseback riding, hang gliding,
  cross-country and downhill skiing, snowmobiling, ice skating,
  and ice fishing. Annual Victorian Fair in October.

"What do you make of that?" I asked my dad, pointing
to the ☛ two blue globes that appear in bas relief on the
stone façade above The Hotel's front door.

"This is the old Schlitz family's hotel. Maybe they're the
same symbols that used to appear on the beer cans," Dad
guessed. "Look pretty much the same."

That's what they turned out to be. The Hotel is the restored and renamed Schlitz Hotel. It had catered to an exclusive men-only clientele and was built in 1892 by Milwaukee's Schlitz brewing magnates. (The Milwaukee connection extends to the use of cream-colored Milwaukee brick in its construction.)

Not that much has changed from the hotel's turn-of-the-century décor. We walked down long corridors with exposed brick walls that had bright chandeliers lighting the way to the rooms. Our room had soft colors and Victorian appointments: wood-and-brass beds adorned by floral quilted bedspreads, scalloped lace curtains—simple, yet classic, like a step back to yesterday.

I ran my fingers along the beautiful old staircase banister leading to the upper-floor rooms. We think the hotel's most colorful touch is an ☞ antique opera house stage drop scene that covers an entire wall just above the staircase's second-floor landing. It depicts a turn-of-the-century roadster.

The wonderful antique furniture, pictures, and artifacts strewn about the hallways are on loan from the Winona Historical Society. Of course, we had to stop for a brew in the old barroom; it still has the ☞ original mahogany bar and hideaway booths.

Dinner at the hotel restaurant (I adore the huge brass chandeliers) means anything from wholesome meat and potatoes to stuffed sole Florentine. Special romantic dinners for two feature elegantly presented roast duckling with twice-baked or cheese-stuffed potatoes. A continental breakfast of juice, rolls, pastries, and coffee or tea comes with your room.

How to get there: Winona is on U.S. 61. The Hotel is in the heart of the downtown area, at the corner of Third and Johnson streets.

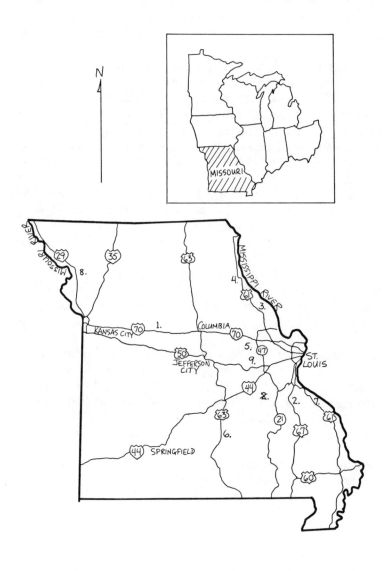

Missouri

Numbers on map refer to towns numbered below.

Borgman's
Bed and Breakfast
Arrow Rock, Missouri
65320

Innkeepers: Kathy and Helen Borgman
Address/Telephone: Van Buren Street; (816) 837–3350
Rooms: 4, sharing 3 baths.
Rates: $25 single, $30 double ($35 with two beds). Includes break-
   fast. Children OK. Smoking discouraged.
Open: All year.
Facilities & Activities: Near state historical sites, archeological
   digs, antique and specialty shops, and The Lyceum Theatre,
   one of Missouri's oldest repertory companies. Walking tours.
   Four miles from Kruger Winery.

Borgman's Bed and Breakfast has been called "one of
the most enjoyable inns in the state." After my visit to this
charming white clapboard home, I heartily agree.

Helen greeted me at the door of her little farmhouse,
built between 1855 and 1865 in this historic tiny town. It's
filled with country-style antiques and furnishings that put
even the most harried guests at ease.

Helen's daughter, Kathy, designed the ☞ stenciled wall
borders that adorn each of the guest-room ceilings. And the

beautiful ☞ country quilts that add splashes of colors to the beds were handmade by Helen, of course!

Relaxation is the key here. I just sat on the porch, in the shade of tall trees, feeling the cool summer breeze. Helen wound up the old Victrola for a song. It's also fun to stop by the kitchen to visit with Helen when she's making her famous sticky buns fresh each morning for breakfast treats. She also offers homemade breads, cereal, fruits, and beverages.

As Helen and I walked to the upstairs guest rooms, she told me that the plank floors throughout the house are original. I could feel the country comfort soaking into my city bones when I saw tall Victorian headboards, exposed chimney brick, hurricane-style lamps, lacy window curtains, and rocking chairs in the handsome rooms. The only first-floor guest room has the original plank floor, a four-poster bed adorned with one of Helen's bright quilts, and another antique rocker. All the rooms are bright, cheery, and peaceful.

Kathy works at the Arrow Rock information center and can tell you all about the wonderful history and attractions the village offers. She'll also recommend restaurants that serve wholesome down-home dinner fare.

Area history is fascinating. Lewis and Clark noted the region during their historic explorations. Indians used local outcroppings of flint to point their arrows—hence the town name. Three forts were once located in the area; one was used during the War of 1812. A portion of the town was burned down during the Civil War.

In town, I toured a wonderful ☞ "pioneer" Main Street, lined with historic buildings that still have woodenboard sidewalks and rocky boulders forming crude street gutters. A guided historic walking tour is offered from April through October (sometimes on weekends only, so check ahead).

How to get there: From Kansas City or St. Louis, take I–70 to Route 41. Go north to Arrow Rock and turn right on Van Buren (the first road into Arrow Rock) to the inn about two blocks up the street.

B: *Being here is like visiting Grandma's home in the country.*

The Lamplight Inn
Bed and Breakfast
Guest House
Bonne Terre, Missouri
63628

Innkeepers: Carrick and Mary Berry, owners; Krista and Jorgen
Wibskov, managers
Address/Telephone: 207 East School Street; (314) 358–4222 or
358–3332
Rooms: 4; 2 with private bath.
Rates: $30 single, $35 double. Includes full breakfast. Children and
pets OK.
Open: All year.
Facilities & Activities: Gourmet dining across the street at The
Lamplight Inn Restaurant. Short walk to tours of Bonne Terre
mine, a national historic site. An hour's drive from Ste. Gene-
vieve, a French colonial fur-trading center in the 1700s.

Krista met Jorgen while she was attending college in
Denmark. Later, they moved back here (it's Krista's home
town) to take charge of the family restaurant that has gotten
rave reviews and won many awards for dining excellence.

Because so many people travel long distances to enjoy The Lamplight Inn's delicious food, Krista thought it would be a good idea to offer travelers an equally charming place to stay overnight.

The result is what she informally calls the "Blue House," a charming home that's part of this old lead mining town's rich legacy. "This home served as a boarding house for the [mining company's] bachelor engineers," Krista said. "So that's probably one of the reasons it's still pretty much in mint shape."

Some of the wonderful Victorian touches include steeply pitched gables and a marvelous 🖝 wraparound porch that catches cooling breezes.

Krista has decorated the home with cozy and comfortable antiques and warm floral wallpapers that add to the inn's friendly feeling. A fire in the charming brick fireplace in the parlor is welcome on chilly nights—a terrific place to warm up and read a good book.

The 🖝 Oak Room is the handsomest of the inn's guest retreats. Soothing shades of soft red are offset by the room's attractive antique oak furniture, and six large windows adorned with lace curtains shoot arrows of sunlight into the room.

Inn breakfasts are tasty, with eggs and breakfast meats among the choices. Of course, who can pass up homemade breads with delicious jams? And freshly ground, specially blended coffee. I also dare you to resist 🖝 Krista's freshly baked sticky buns.

Krista was graduated from the Cordon Bleu cooking school in London and has won cooking awards from the Missouri Restaurant Association. That's why you cannot pass up a meal at The Lamplight Inn Restaurant, just across the street from the Blue House. The inn specialty is 🖝 pepper steak flambéed in brandy sauce at the table. Other gourmet choices include filet of Louisiana sole prepared Cajun style and beef tips *à la Bourguignonne*.

How to get there: From St. Louis, take I–55 south and continue south on U.S. 67. Turn west on Route 47; then turn left on Allen Street in Bonne Terre. Take a quick right on Main; then an immediate left on East School Street to the inn.

Mansion Hill Country Inn
Bonne Terre, Missouri
63628

Innkeepers: Doug and Cathy Goergens
Address/Telephone: Mansion Hill Drive; (314) 358–5311
Rooms: 10; most with private bath.
Rates: $50 single, $60 double. Two-night minimum on weekends.
   Includes continental breakfast. Special packages can include
   SCUBA diving. Children not encouraged.
Open: All year.
Facilities & Activities: Bar, gift shop. Situated on 130-acre estate,
   view of Ozark Mountain foothills; cross-country skiing, nature
   trails, fishing; horse-drawn carriage tours of the mining town.
   Short ride to Bonne Terre mine, with land tours at this Na-
   tional Historic Site. Also world-class SCUBA diving at the mine.

   Cathy always dreamed of owning a country inn. Little
did she imagine that it would be a ☛ thirty-two-room mansion on a 130-acre estate on the highest point in historic
Bonne Terre.
   But first, sit still—you have to know some history. This
old mining town was once the richest lead district in the
country. When mining ceased and water pumps were shut

down, the 200-foot-deep mine shafts filled with water. So Cathy and Doug, in a stroke of genius, created a world-class SCUBA-diving center in the old Bonne Terre mine, with more than seventeen miles of dive trails.

Now both divers and dedicated inn hoppers have an equally impressive place to stay overnight. The early-1900s mansion, built as a home for the president of the St. Joe Lead Company, reflects the gracious living and prosperity of those lead-boom days

I walked into a ☞ foyer gleaming with polished hardwood everywhere. Wandering into the library, with its massive brick fireplace, heavy-beamed ceiling, stately columns, and decidedly nautical themes (with model sailing ships and other waterabilia), I eavesdropped as a group of divers planned their next mine dive.

Doug told me that he had done most of the inn's heavy-duty interior restoration, while Cathy spent hundreds of hours coordinating inn décor and searching out special antique items that bring the mansion to life. It shows.

We walked through French doors onto an enclosed porch overlooking an ☞ impressive courtyard, garden, and fountain on the first terrace level. The second level was designed for world-class lawn croquet, Doug told me. You also can ☞ see miles of surrounding Ozark Mountain foothills.

The guest rooms have a view of the surrounding estate grounds and are decorated in period pieces and reproductions, with four-poster beds among the furnishings. Cathy made many of the inn's floral-styled draperies, valances, and other appointments.

Dining here is another treat; Doug has ☞ fresh fish flown in twice weekly. Beef Wellington is an inn specialty, and so are calf sweetbreads and veal *piccata;* for dessert, the Key lime pie is delicious.

In a dashing touch of weekends-only showmanship, Doug has the inn's ☞ elaborate horse-drawn carriage bring guests from the parking lot to the front door.

How to get there: From St. Louis, take I–55 south to U.S. 67. Continue south to Route 47. Go west into Bonne Terre. At Summit, turn left. At the top of the hill, turn left into a driveway marked by estate posts and inn signs. Proceed up the long road to the inn.

Falicon Inn
Clarksville, Missouri
63336

Innkeepers: Carl and Karen Schulze
Address/Telephone: One Grandview Heights, St. Louis, Missouri
    63131 (mailing address only); (314) 965–4328
Rooms: 3; 1 with private bath.
Rates: $60 to $70. Includes breakfast. Children and pets not en-
    couraged. Wheelchair access. No credit cards.
Open: All year.
Facilities & Activities: Parlor, library, dining room, long veranda,
    estate grounds. Short ride to downtown Clarksville and antique
    shops. Near Sky Ride, where you can see 80-mile view of Mis-
    sissippi River Valley.

Coming here is like stepping into the Old South—and a
real adventure. I drove up to the old plantation entrance
along a twisting back road, with ☞ high bluffs and rolling
hills that provide some of the best views of the Mississippi
River Valley. Finally I reached a dirt path that dives, snakes,
and curves past tall trees and brush.

Then I emerged from the foliage—and the Falicon Inn
overwhelmed me. It's the picture of a Southern gentleman's

plantation farm, a massive thirty-room antebellum mansion with tall white columns and a sweeping veranda.

Karen told me that parts of the home date from before the Civil War; other major renovations took place around the turn of the century. She pointed out the ☛ old ice house, playhouse, wash house, cottage for greenhouse workers, and carriage house that still stand on the grounds.

You're in for a treat: Karen and Carl specialize in Old South hospitality in a lavish setting. Some of the ☛ huge wall mirrors are from the old historic Clarksville Opera House. The dining room glistens with fine mahogany hardwood everywhere. And that wallpaper I was eyeing? Karen said that it was painted with ☛ English gold leaf.

The library is quite handsome, too, done in heavy oak, with tapestry draperies, hardwood floors, and a marble fireplace.

I walked up a long flight of stairs to reach the second-floor guest rooms. My favorite room has a fireplace and a tall canopy bed. Other rooms feature some period antiques; all are comfortable.

Karen serves up a full plantation-style breakfast. Her French toast is light and fluffy; then there's fruit, bacon and sausage, juice, and other beverages. She'll arrange special dinners—intimate feasts in the antique-laden dining room. Stuffed chicken breast, lamb, and a shrimp *de Jonghe* are some of the inn specialties. It's BYOB for wines and liquors.

And don't be startled by that "monster" lurking about the grounds; it's not the Hound of the Baskervilles. It's just Tramp, the inn's English sheepdog, who doubles as a living doorbell.

How to get there: From St. Louis, take I–70 west to Route 79 north into Clarksville. At County W, turn left and follow it for about 3½ miles until you reach the inn road.

The Fifth Street Mansion
Bed and Breakfast
Hannibal, Missouri
63401

Innkeepers: Lance Zedric and Tom Meiron
Address/Telephone: 213 South Fifth Street; (314) 221–0445
Rooms: 7, with 1 suite; 2 with private bath, others share three
   baths.
Rates: $35 single, $40 double, $55 suite. Includes continental
   breakfast. Children and pets OK.
Open: All year.
Facilities & Activities: Near Mark Twain Boyhood Home and Mu-
   seum, and other Mark Twain historical sites and attractions.
   Short drive to Rockcliffe Mansion, Gerth Mansion, Mark Twain
   Cave, Mississippi Riverboat rides, Samuel Langhorne Clemens
   Amphitheater, and city tours.

Hannibal is the town where Mark Twain spent his boyhood. You can visit the cave where Tom Sawyer and Huck
Finn found the gold hidden by robbers, or you can take a riverboat ride on the wide Mississippi River; Lance will recommend all the "can't miss" spots of this historic river town.

But after a day's wanderings, it's nice to kick back at

this 1857 Italianate "winter townhouse" that boasts twenty-three rooms. Samuel Clemens often visited this house, located on what used to be called "Millionaire's Row," the name given to a string of fine antebellum houses once lining the block.

Lance showed me some fine Victorian touches: ☞ eight fireplaces crafted in tile, mosaic, and hand-carved woods; and a grand Tiffany-style glass window in the entryway.

But he's most proud of a ☞ striking 8-foot-tall by 6-foot-wide stained-glass masterpiece adorning the first-floor staircase landing, added to the home in 1890.

A sitting room and parlor, with 12-foot ceilings, original brass chandeliers, and period furnishings, offer good spots for you to talk about your sightseeing discoveries with other guests. I especially like the library and its fine hand-grained wainscoting and leaded-glass window exhibiting the family crest of the original owner.

Lance and I walked up a long flight of stairs—past that magnificent stained-glass window—to reach the second-floor guest rooms. All the rooms have tall Victorian windows, floral-print wallpapers, and some period furnishings. They exhibit a comfortable, lived-in look. My favorite has a four-poster bed (circa 1870).

In the morning, breakfast fare is a light treat, with fresh fruit, English muffins, hot breads and rolls, juice, and other beverages served in the main dining room. Lance suggests dinner at the Missouri Territory restaurant, located in the state's oldest surviving Federal building; it serves great steak dinners.

Visit Hannibal during Fourth of July week, and you'll help celebrate National Tom Sawyer Days, with events like fence painting, frog jumping, and a Tom-and-Becky Pageant. In November, the Autumn Folklike Festival celebrates area history with period costumes, homemade cooking, and a giant arts-and-crafts fair.

How to get there: From St. Louis, go north on Route 79 into Hannibal. Turn west on Broadway; then turn north on South Fifth Street to the inn.

William Klinger Inn
Hermann, Missouri
65041

Innkeepers: Nancy and John Bartel
Address/Telephone: 108 East Second Street; (314) 486–5930
Rooms: 7, with 2 suites; all with private bath.
Rates: $70 to $90. Includes hearty breakfast. Children discouraged.
No credit cards.
Open: All year.
Facilities & Activities: Special mystery weekends. Located in an
historic German settlement amid rolling hills and wineries of
Missouri Wine Country, alongside the Missouri River. Several
historic museums and sites, preserved architecture, specialty
stores, and antique shops. Annual town events include *Mai-
fest, Oktoberfest, Volksmarsch, Wurstfest.*

"I love old Victorian homes, but so many are dark and
dreary," Nancy told me. "I wanted to make this one bright
and happy, while still focusing on Victorian elegance."

That's exactly why I adore the William Klinger Inn. It's
an extremely cheerful place, not only because of its décor but
also because of the enthusiasm and bubbliness Nancy brings
to her elegant home.

The 1878 Queen Anne townhouse, built by local mill

owner William Klinger for his family, is an imposing building on a quiet residential street.

The beautiful green-and-white marble tile, Nancy told me, pointing to the rich foyer floor, is original to the home and quite unusual. The tall coatrack bench also is a Klinger original, as is the colorful stained-glass window above it. The coatrack bench is one of Nancy's favorite inn pieces. She marveled that it was especially made to fit the contour of the hallway walls.

But most spectacular is an elaborate staircase leading to the upper-floor rooms, magnificently hand-carved in rich cherry, with tall columns the epitome of elegance.

The parlor also is elaborate, dominated by a fireplace with a finely hand-carved cherry mantel. "It took three weeks to strip the paint off this masterpiece," Nancy said, shaking her head, "and lots of elbow grease."

The only guest bedroom on the first floor is decorated in white and shades of blue, with an iron-rail bed, balloon draperies, and a hardwood floor.

The second-floor Klinger Suite, done in Williamsburg blue, with a blue tile fireplace, tall windows with balloon draperies, high walnut Victorian bedboard and dressers, and period prints on the walls, is a guest favorite. But I especially liked the Kallmeyer Suite, with its tall Victorian four-poster canopy bed.

The third floor has a small sitting area, and the rooms are named for their different views. The Courthouse Room overlooks that historic building; River View is a great room, with a four-poster bed, huge antique armoire, and a view of greenery, hills, and the river.

Nancy's special breakfasts include hearty sausage casseroles, home-baked breads and muffins, sugar twists, and more. She'll be happy to recommend one of the town's many ethnic restaurants—most of them serving German fare—for dinner treats.

How to get there: From St. Louis or Kansas City, take I–70 to Route 19 and go south into Hermann. Turn left on First Street, right on Market Street, and left on East Second Street to the inn.

Wilderness Lodge
Lesterville, Missouri
63654

Innkeeper: Helen Powers
Address/Telephone: Box 90; (314) 637–2295, toll free from St. Louis 296–2011
Rooms: 40 units: riverside suites, 4 cottages, 1 summer house; all with private bath.
Rates: $49.50 per person per night for rooms, cottages, and summer house; children 5–12, $37; children under 5 free. $61 per person per night for riverside suites; children 5–12, $48; children under 5 free. Two-night minimum required. Special package rates. All rates include family-style dinner and breakfast. Children welcome; special kids' activity schedule.
Open: May 1 through November 30.
Facilities & Activities: Dining room, bar. Archery, shuffleboard, volleyball, horseshoes, walking trails, tennis courts, platform tennis. Also children's playground, swimming pool, hot tub (cold weather only), hayrides, canoeing, tube floats. Horseback riding nearby.

I drove deep into the beautiful Ozark Mountain foothills to find this woodsy retreat. Located on 1,200 rolling acres near the bank of the crystal-clear Black River, the Wilderness

Lodge offers some of the best country-style fun imaginable.

A group of canoers were excitedly telling their parents about the afternoon's adventures as I entered the Main Lodge, the oldest and largest building on the property. The heavy log-beam construction and tan pitch made me feel like a pioneer in the wilderness.

"I like all the stuff for kids," one little guy told me as he headed for the lodge's swimming pool. "I can do stuff all day." That's because the lodge specializes in ☛ daily children's activities that include everything from canoe trips to hikes in the forest. In fact, each day an activity sheet is tacked onto an outdoor bulletin board to clue youngsters in to the day's fun.

The lodge's rough-hewn country-style furniture is just what you'd expect. Especially interesting are ☛ American Indian–style rugs displayed on the walls, animal trophies, and the obligatory rifle hanging above a manteled hearth.

Later, I sat in an open dining room with a giant picture window looking out over the grounds, watching more kids frolic in the pool. A game room, just off to the side, has card and game tables for all kinds of family fun. For romantics, the lodge has a large fireplace room for snuggling on chilly evenings.

Family-style breakfasts and dinners are lodge specialties. Morning menus include eggs, pancakes, and beverages; dinner platters are heaped high with good country cooking like fried chicken that's "finger-lickin' good," fresh bread, and sweet pastries. After dinner you might sidle up to the bar for a nightcap.

I've never seen guest cabins so complement the beautiful Ozark countryside. Especially attractive is the use of ☛ native rock, peeled logs, pine siding, and porches built right into the landscape. Country-antique furniture and Indian artifacts add to the woodsy ambience; many rooms feature large fireplaces and high loft ceilings.

How to get there: From St. Louis, take I–270 south to Route 21 and continue south to Glover. Then head west on Route 21/49/72. Near Arcadia, take Route 21 south, then west for about 22 miles to Peola Road. Turn left and continue down the dirt and gravel path, following the signs to the lodge.

The Inn
St. Gemme Beauvais
Ste. Genevieve, Missouri
63670

Innkeepers: Frankye and Norbert Donze
Address/Telephone: 78 North Main Street (mailing address: Box
  231); (314) 883–5744
Rooms: 7; all with private bath.
Rates: $35 single, $45 double; $6 per child. Includes breakfast.
Open: All year.
Facilities & Activities: Dining room at inn. Near antique shops,
  galleries, and museums (many specializing in pre–Civil War
  pieces). Historical town architecture includes some of the best
  examples of French Colonial homes in the United States, including vertical-log homes. Annual Jour de Fête second full
  weekend of August.

I will come back time and time again to The Inn St.
Gemme Beauvais. This 1847 three-story, red-brick building is
located in a town that's been called "the finest surviving example of French Colonial architecture in the country," with

more than fifty historic buildings dating back to the 1700s when the fur traders settled here.

Not only that—Frankye and Norbert are as warm and friendly as this French-flavored village—and so is their wonderful inn.

Walls here are pioneer-tough—18 inches thick—and they're only one of the inn's unique features. In the foyer, I walked under an ☞ historic chandelier, dating from the early 1800s, that casts an amber glow over the hallway. Just to the right of the door is the inn desk, an old rolltop where you often can find Frankye ready with a touring suggestion and a welcoming smile.

The guest rooms are upstairs and are decorated in a mixture of Victorian furnishings and other antiques—nothing fancy, but comfortable and cozy.

Frankye serves a ☞ French feast for breakfast, with hand-filled ham crêpes an inn specialty. There are also tasty omelets, delicious homemade nut bread with honey butter, fresh (in season) fruit cup, blueberry muffins, and more.

Another "can't miss" is the inn's French luncheon, served every afternoon except Sunday. I found the *quiche Lorraine* delicate and tasty. And I had still more crêpes, two vegetables, a large chef's salad, and milk for only $5. For dinner, the innkeepers will suggest a spot to match your tastes.

Eating in the historic dining room is a treat in itself. It's cozy and quaint with white walls, a white marble fireplace, and antique tables and chairs. I also felt a bit larger than life as I walked around this room. That's because its scaled-down dimensions are typical of the town's historic French-styled homes.

Just a short walk away are all the town's fabulous architectural attractions. Especially interesting is the 1770 Bolduc House, a vertical-log "fort" regarded as the most authentically restored Colonial Creole house in the country.

This is also a great town for antique hunting; my favorite place is the Maison Aurélie, housed in the oldest brick building west of the Mississippi River.

How to get there: From St. Louis, take I–55 south to Route 32. Turn east and continue into Ste. Genevieve. Turn right on Market Street and continue for about three blocks to Main Street. Turn left on Main Street and continue to the inn.

Schuster-Rader Mansion
St. Joseph, Missouri
64501

Innkeepers: Charles and Joetta Rader
Address/Telephone: 703 Hall Street; (816) 279–9464
Rooms: 5, with 3 suites; 1 with private bath.
Rates: $55 single, $65 double. Includes continental-plus breakfast.
No children. No credit cards.
Open: All year.
Facilities & Activities: Home tours to public. Festivities with special themes: chamber music, vintage clothing, and the like. Located in Hall Street Historic District, where other fine mansions still stand. Short drive to Pony Express Museum, Pony Express statue, Patee House Museum (Pony Express headquarters in 1860), Jesse James's home.

"Magnificent" is the only word to describe this 1881 Italianate mansion resting atop a high hill on a quiet street in St. "Joe." The ☞ mosaic tile floors are exquisite; the tiles are laid out in a pattern of fan-shaped waves, like the streets of Rome, with a Roman wreath in the middle of the design.

Walking into the ☞ grand foyer made me feel like a

king; it's thirty-five feet long, with a walnut double-pillared archway separating the hallway from other rooms.

Every bay window has an ornate arch. The library's beautiful walnut mantel is decorated with Italian marble depicting scenes from Shakespearean plays. Joetta pointed to the draperies hanging in the library. Louis Comfort Tiffany designed them, she told me.

I thought that the unusual chandelier hanging in the parlor was exquisite; it's a giant teardrop made by Waterford.

"This house is 100 percent pure Victorian," Joetta said. "It's had only four owners, and nothing has been altered, except for the bathrooms. It's like stepping back into time." (Especially when Joetta and Charlie greet visitors dressed up in vintage Victorian clothes!)

How can I describe my reactions to the guest rooms? The ☛ Schuster Suite is twenty-eight feet long, with a massive canopied bed crowned by a silk rosette; yet I found it a warm, inviting room. It also has an 1830s dresser and Oriental rugs on the floor.

Another suite has a sitting porch furnished with fine wicker pieces, while the Yellow Room has an 1870s bedframe. I challenge you to find the ☛ secret velvet-lined jewel box. A hint: Look at the footboard.

Other rooms feature masterful pre–Civil War furnishings, brass and iron beds, balloon draperies, and other special touches.

Joetta's ☛ breakfasts are mouth-watering: Homemade pecan waffles are especially tasty, along with crêpes, breakfast casseroles, and fresh breads. She whips up all these treats on a 105-year-old stove; that's a real labor of love.

How to get there: From Kansas City, take I–29 north to St. Joseph and get off at the Edmond Street Central Business District exit. Then go up to 8th Street and turn left. Proceed to Hall Street and look for the hill-rise home with the massive belvedere.

⧗

B: *The mansion is the finest example of Victorian architecture in the state, according to the Missouri Department of Natural Resources.*

The Schwegmann House
Washington, Missouri
63090

Innkeeper: Cathy French
Address/Telephone: 438 West Front Street; (314) 239–5025
Rooms: 9; all with private bath.
Rates: $45 single, $55 double. Includes breakfast. Children OK.
Open: All year.
Facilities & Activities: Guest parlors, formal gardens. Across the street from Missouri River. In historic Washington, near historic river-front district and preserved 1800s architecture. Also near restaurants and antique and specialty shops. In the heart of Missouri's Wine Country; short drive to winery tours.

Cathy has captured all the warmth and old-world hospitality of this historic German-influenced Missouri River town in her charming inn. I found it exciting to look out my window and see the waters of the "Big Muddy" and listen to the distant bellow of boat traffic on the river.

This stately pre–Civil War Georgian-style home was buzzing with activity upon my arrival. A family with three tow-headed kids was in the parlor looking over the dinner menus from area restaurants that Cathy provides for guests.

They couldn't decide if they wanted to "dude up" for supper or grab a hamburger and picnic next to the river.

Another young couple had bicycled to area wineries (this is the heart of Missouri wine country), and was showing off some of the bottles they'd purchased. They promised me samples later that evening. That's just typical of the inn's friendly atmosphere.

Most of the guest rooms are furnished with fine antiques and fun country accents. Some have river views; all have cute names. My favorites:

The Primitive Room, with its ☞ long church bench adorned with a cloth goose decoy, high-back rocking chair, marble-topped lamp stand, tall armoire, and calico curtains on the window. I especially liked the hand-stitched star quilt on the bed.

The Eyelet Room, ☞ generously decorated with shockingly white lace. White eyelet curtains brighten three tall windows and sprinkle sunlight in all directions. A padded rocking chair is absolutely required for gazing out at the river. There's also a marble-topped dresser, writing desk, and a colorful hand-stitched quilt on the bed.

Cathy's breakfasts are a treat. There are freshly baked croissants and a plate of imported and domestic cheeses. But save some room for homemade bread and thick fruity jams and some fresh fruit to satisfy a morning sweet tooth.

Especially interesting are the historic town's many antique shops and ☞ fine restaurants. The Old Dutch Restaurant and Bar serves terrific home-style lunches—and great pies when the owner's daughter is in town. At the East End Tavern, you can grab a tasty burger while listening to colorful talk about "Mizzou's" college football teams. The Landing is an informal dinner spot for families, with pizza and great burgers that are favorites. Then there's Elijah McLean's, fine dining in a restored home overlooking the Missouri River—choices include sautéed veal, swordfish, and roast duck.

How to get there: From St. Louis, take I–44 southwest to Route 100 and go west until you reach Washington. Turn north on Jefferson, then turn west on Front Street (along the river). The inn is at the corner of Front and Olive.

Zachariah Foss
Guest House
Washington, Missouri
63090

Innkeepers: Joy and Sunny Drewel
Address/Telephone: 4 Lafayette Street; (314) 239–6499 or (314) 938–4966
Rooms: Seven-room historic house (rent entire house).
Rates: $95 per night, double occupancy. Each additional person $10 per night. Includes breakfast. No children under 12.
Open: All year.
Facilities & Activities: Historic river town with antique shops, specialty stores, and excellent restaurants a short walk down the street. In the heart of Missouri wine country; several wineries nearby.

I arrived at the Zachariah Foss Guest House just as a storm was sweeping into town. Standing on the high porch just across the street from the river, I saw gray billowy clouds, channeling down the Missouri. The breeze stiffened; the air suddenly became chilly and damp; thunder began to rumble.

It was beautiful, this spring storm, and as I stood watching the weather follow the bend of the river, heading right toward me, I thought that I wouldn't want to be in any other place at this precise moment. Not until raindrops splattered against my face was the reverie broken.

That's just the kind of magic Joy and Sunny's guest house weaves among its visitors. And they've lovingly restored this 1846 Federal-style home (the ☞ oldest frame house in this historic building–rich town) into a real down-home showplace.

Joy and Sunny welcome inn guests with a ☞ chilled bottle of Missouri wine (the region is called the "Rhine" of Missouri). One way to soothe traveling aches and tensions immediately is to enjoy the local vintage while soaking in a hot tub. In this case, there are ☞ "His & Hers" claw-footed bathtubs only an arm's length apart.

Another way to relax is to just plain stretch out on a high four-poster bed; but you'll need a footstool to climb to the top!

It's fun to play board games in the parlor on the antique gaming table. But my favorite pastime is sitting in a ladder-back rocking chair out on the second-story porch and ☞ watching wide barges glide down the Missouri.

Juice, eggs, bacon, rolls, and jams are left in the refrigerator to fix whenever you're ready for breakfast. And you'll get bicycles to tour area wineries that begin just across the river; the bicycles have large baskets so that you can carry your favorite wine back to the inn. Elijah McLean's restaurant is just a short walk down the street; it's one of the town's finest and most romantic dining spots. Or you can take inn coupons to Cowan's Café, just down the street, and redeem them for a down-home breakfast of biscuits and gravy—and more.

How to get there: From St. Louis, take I–44 west to Route 100; then go west on 100 to Washington Street. Turn right at Jefferson Street, follow to the river front, or Front Street. Turn left and go to Lafayette and the inn. From east or west on I–70, take Route 47 south to Washington. Turn right at Third Street to Jefferson; then turn right on Jefferson to Front. Turn left on Front to Lafayette and the inn.

B: *Be sure to visit the cheery country antique stove located in the home's old stone cellar.*

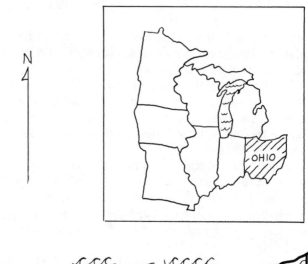

Ohio

Numbers on map refer to towns numbered below.

The Frederick Fitting House
Bellville, Ohio
44813

Innkeepers: Jo and Rick Sowash
Address/Telephone: 72 Fitting Avenue; (419) 886–4283
Rooms: 3; all share 1 large bath.
Rates: $35 single, $40 double. Includes continental-plus breakfast.
  Children and pets OK. No credit cards. No smoking in the
  house.
Open: All year.
Facilities & Activities: Golf course, tennis courts nearby. Little
  shops and jogging trails in all directions. Canoeing and skiing
  (in season) within a few minutes' drive. Two state parks a
  short drive away. The Renaissance Theatre, the Mansfield Art
  Center, and the Kenyon Festival Theatre within a half-hour's
  drive. Mid-Ohio Raceway in Lexington is site of major sports
  car races.

Baby Kate discovered The Frederick Fitting House. It
was time for my two-month-old daughter's midday feeding,
so I drove down a quiet side street on this hot spring day
looking for a parking spot bathed in shade. We stopped in

front of a beautiful 1863 Italianate home and immediately were drawn inside.

It's absolutely beautiful, completely furnished in 🖝 American folk art and Ohio antiques; many are family heirlooms with interesting stories behind them, so be sure to get Jo and Rick to weave their magic tales.

The sight of the dining room almost took my breath away. Jo's 🖝 wonderful stencilwork is apparent everywhere; it covers even the original yellow-pine plank floor.

Jo's breakfasts are served on a big square table that invites conversation. (In summer, she serves breakfast outside in the gazebo.) Specialties include crêpes, home-baked breads, and Dutch pastries, served along with Richland County honey, fresh fruit, and juice. There's even a choice of specially blended coffee and herbal teas.

Jo and Rick also will arrange for country-gourmet dinners at the inn—anything from wholesome farm-food meals to French cuisine. They recommend the nearby San-Dar restaurant for smorgasbord-style dining.

Walking up a 🖝 magnificent, freestanding spiral staircase of walnut, butternut, and oak, I found three charming guest rooms. The Colonial Room, with a canopy bed covered in lace, is perfect for romantics. Especially noteworthy among its many fine antique furnishings is a primitive pioneer coverlet.

But my favorite is the 🖝 Shaker Room, with its simple twin beds, antique writing desk, straight-back rocking chair, and wall pegs from which hang antique Shaker work utensils.

How to get there: Bellville is directly between Cleveland and Columbus. Leave I–71 at exit 165 and proceed east on State Route 97 into the village. Turn left onto Fitting Avenue. The inn is the last home on the left at the intersection of Fitting Avenue and Ogle Street.

B: *During the holiday season, the inn's two 10-foot Christmas trees are decorated with handcrafted ornaments, and luminaries glow along the outside walkway.*

Roscoe Village Inn
Coshocton, Ohio
43812

Innkeeper: Carol Ludholtz
Address/Telephone: 200 North Whitewoman Street; (614) 622–2222
Rooms: 50; all with private bath.
Rates: $60 to $65. Several seasonal weekend packages. Well-behaved children only. Wheelchair access.
Open: All year.
Facilities & Activities: Roscoe Village canal-era town. Amish country nearby. Pro-football Hall of Fame in Canton. Scenic countryside of Ohio River Valley.

Inn services director Carol Aoun met me in the Roscoe Village Inn's King Charlie's Tavern. "It's named after Charlie, the first white settler in these parts," she said. "Legend has it that an heir to the throne of England stopped in the village tavern on his way across the country and made quite a fuss about how towns were so much more interesting in Europe.

"Charlie made things a lot more interesting for him

right then and there. He hiked him up by the seat of his pants and threw him out the door."

Carol explained that the inn's choppy brick exterior design borrows heavily from other canal-era structures in town. Inside, the second-floor parlor is a favorite with guests. It's easy to see why: It has ☞ exposed wood beams, a huge fireplace fronted by high-back sofas, a beautiful wrought-iron chandelier, and tall windows. Carol added that the wonderful crafts sprinkled throughout the inn (including breathtaking hand-stitched quilts) are ☞ native Ohio folk art reflecting the village's canal-era heritage.

Rooms have sturdy, handcrafted wood furniture, and I wasn't surprised when Carol said that it was ☞ made by Amish craftsmen in nearby Holmes County. Four-poster beds, high-back chairs, and more tall windows add to the charm.

A full-service dining room offers meals to guests. Carol urges you to try the inn's traditional dinner specialty: *émincé* of beef tenderloin à la Stroganoff (sautéed with mushrooms, onions, and sour cream). Breakfasts offer terrific choices as well, including another inn specialty: waffles made with stone-ground whole-wheat flour, served along with farm-fresh eggs, honey, sweet butter, and a beverage—for only $2.95!

Later I walked along the historic Ohio & Erie towpath north from the village to where the *Monticello II*, a reconstructed canal boat, floats passengers to Mudport Basin.

How to get there: From Cleveland to the north, take I–77 south to exit 65. Follow Route 36/16 west into Coshocton. Turn west on Ohio 541, then north on Whitewoman Street to the inn. From Columbus and Indianapolis to the southwest, take I–70 and exit north on Route 60. Then turn east on Route 16 and follow into Coshocton. Next follow directions listed above.

B: Don't miss all the antique and specialty stores along White-woman Street, which gets its name from the Walhonding River—walhonding is the Delaware Indian word for "white woman."

The Buxton Inn
Granville, Ohio
43023

Innkeepers: Audrey and Orville Orr, owners; Cecil Snow, manager
Address/Telephone: 313 East Broadway; (614) 587–0001
Rooms: 3, with 2 suites; all with private bath.
Rates: $40 to $50 single, $45 to $55 double. Children OK. Wheel-
chair access.
Open: All year.
Facilities & Activities: Nine dining rooms; bar. Antique galleries,
specialty stores, historic town sites, and museums nearby. Also
near Ye Olde Mill of 1817 and Hopewell Indians' Newark
earthworks.

Cecil and I sat in the charming basement dining room
of The Buxton Inn, built in 1812 as a tavern by a pioneer
from Granville, Massachusetts. "Stagecoach drivers would
stop at the tavern during their journey across the frontier and
would sleep down here on beds of straw," he said. He pointed
out original rough-hewn beams and stone walls that are still
sturdy after all these years. And I saw the great open hearth
where the drivers cooked their meals.

And did you know that President William Henry Harrison supposedly rode a horse up the inn stairs to the second-floor ballroom during some spirited nighttime revelry?

The Buxton is Ohio's oldest continuously operating inn, and it's a treasure. Look closely and you'll see that the pegged walnut floors were laid with hand-forged nails. "Those windows were laid into foot-thick walls for protection from Indians," Cecil added. Black-walnut beams and timbers frame walls and ceilings; fireplaces are scattered throughout the house.

Cecil suggests that you make lodging reservations well in advance; the inn has only three guest rooms. The Victorian and Eastlake rooms are two-room suites. One features nineteenth-century Eastlake antiques; the other boasts elegant Victorian beds, an exquisite settee, and an antique crystal chandelier. The Empire Room is my favorite because of its large sleigh beds and fine silver chandelier.

Because the inn has limited guest space, its outstanding reputation rests largely on its delicious dining fare. Wholesome breakfasts feature farm-fresh eggs, sausage, and flapjacks. Lunch specialties lean toward "colonial style" fare: old-fashioned beef potpie topped with a flaky crust; and Osie Robinson's chicken supreme—a puff pastry filled with chicken in mushroom and pimento sauce.

Loosen up your belt before you get to the dinner table. Inn favorites include French pepper steak with brandy, Louisiana chicken with artichoke hearts, and calf sweetbreads with Burgundy-mushroom sauce.

Cecil even makes dessert a difficult decision. Shall I choose Daisy Hunter's hot walnut-fudge cake à la mode, gingerbread with hot lemon sauce, homemade pecan pie topped with whipped cream, or "olde tyme" vanilla-velvet ice cream?

How to get there: From Columbus, take I–70 to Ohio 37. Then go north to Ohio 661 and proceed into Granville. From Cleveland, take I–71 to Route 13 through Mansfield. Go south on Route 13 until you reach Ohio 661 just outside Mansfield. Head south on Ohio 661 into Granville and the inn.

B: Ask Cecil about the inn ghost who was once a light-opera star.

The Granville Inn
Granville, Ohio
43023

Innkeeper: Jennifer Utrevis, manager
Address/Telephone: 314 East Broadway; (614) 587–3333
Rooms: 27, with 2 suites; all with private bath.
Rates: $47 single, $52 double. Includes continental breakfast. Two-night minimum on selected April and October weekends. Children OK.
Open: All year.
Facilities & Activities: Dining rooms, sitting rooms, library, game room, wide veranda patio. Antique galleries and specialty stores in downtown Granville. Hopewell Indians' Newark earthworks and other historic museums and sites in Newark. Buckeye Lake State Park a short drive away.

Sitting on the 🖝 canopied flagstone terrace at The Granville Inn, sipping a gin and tonic and looking over the manicured grounds makes me feel like landed English gentry—not surprising, as this 1924 mansion was built to resemble an English country house.

The 🖝 fine oak paneling, leaded-glass windows, and brass chandeliers are outstanding. Well-polished wood floors are covered with rich Oriental rugs in the lobby. Of course, there's a large stone fireplace flanked by high-back chairs.

Perhaps the most important ingredient of the inn's English flavor is its excellent dining. Specialties like roast prime rib with Yorkshire pudding or flounder topped with crabmeat, bay shrimp, herb sauce, cheese, and toasted almonds are quite appropriate even for Prince Charles and Princess Diana. I say, is that who that couple is next to the . . . ?

My wife especially liked an appetizer called ☞ "Angels on Horseback." It's an authentic English recipe of fresh oysters wrapped in bacon, baked in lemon butter, and served on hot toast triangles. I think you'll like it, too.

The guest rooms are so comfortable, with their plump comforters and varied color schemes. Here's a bit of royal service: A continental breakfast of juice, coffee, and rolls is ☞ brought to your room each morning. What a nice way to start the day.

I loved wandering through all the quaint stores that line the town's streets. And strolling down the tree-lined street after a sumptuous dinner is a nice way to spend the evening.

Summer also brings great antiquing in shops tucked along little roads of the hilly countryside.

How to get there: The inn is located just off Route 16, about 25 miles east of Columbus and 5 miles west of Newark. From Columbus, take I–70 east to Route 37 north. From Westerville, take Route 161 east. Either way, exit at the Granville signs, Route 16/661, and continue into town, where the road's name changes to Broadway.

B: *The heart of downtown Granville is often called Central Ohio's "New England village."*

The Golden Lamb
Lebanon, Ohio
45036

Innkeeper: Jackson B. Reynolds
Address/Telephone: 27 South Broadway; (513) 932–5065
Rooms: 19, with 1 suite; 2 rooms share bath.
Rates: $48 single, $55 to $65 double. Well-behaved children OK.
   Wheelchair access in restaurant only.
Open: All year.
Facilities & Activities: Nine dining areas and bar. Upstairs museum with Shaker furniture collection. Waynesville, 9 miles north, has more than 40 antique shops and malls. King's Island amusement park a few miles south. Jack Nicklaus Golf Center nearby.

Early-1800s stagecoach drivers and travelers (many of whom couldn't read) were simply told to drive to the sign of The Golden Lamb for a warm bed and a good meal. I saw the large wooden sign depicting a golden lamb still hanging in front of this charming and historic inn.

"It's a real friendly place," Jackson said, "the kind of place people like to come back to again and again."

I heartily agree with him. From its beginning in 1803,

The Golden Lamb has offered warm hospitality to its guests. Samuel L. Clemens paced through its hallways while in rehearsal for a performance at the Lebanon Opera House. Charles Dickens eloquently complained about the "lack of spirits" at the then-temperance hotel, circa 1842. Benjamin Harrison, U.S. Grant, and eight other presidents stayed here.

The inn is famous for both its country-style cooking and antique-laden guest rooms named for illustrious visitors. I walked up creaking stairs and along squeaking hallway floorboards to marvel at the antique furniture gracing the second- and third-floor rooms.

Anyone can do the same; Jackson ☛ keeps the doors to all unoccupied rooms open. "We want people just coming to dinner to enjoy the antique collection of our inn, too," he said. "We encourage them to walk through the halls and look inside."

I couldn't resist bouncing up and down on the ☛ replica of the massive Lincoln bed in the Charles Dickens Room, resplendent in its Victorian finery. Another favorite was the huge four-poster Boyd bed in the DeWitt Clinton Room.

All the rooms are spacious. Besides a rocking chair, a tall secretary stuffed with books, and other antique furnishings, mine had two four-poster beds; that gave my two-month-old daughter, Kate, lots of space for stretching out to celebrate her first overnight stay in a country inn.

My family dined in the Shaker Room, with wall pegs holding all kinds of antique kitchen gadgets, pots, and pans. I thought that the ☛ roast Butler County turkey with dressing and giblet gravy was almost like Mom's—a special treat. My wife was delighted by another inn favorite, pan-fried Kentucky ham (specially cured and aged) steak glazed with bourbon. Baby Kate was fed well, too—with all the cooing and attention she received from the friendly waitresses.

The inn's ☛ collection of authentic antique Shaker furniture is said to be one of the largest private holdings of its kind. On the fourth floor are glass-enclosed display rooms featuring many fine Shaker pieces.

How to get there: Lebanon is on Route 63, between Cincinnati and Dayton. Get off I–71 or I–75 at Lebanon exits and proceed on Route 63 into the downtown area. (Route 63 becomes Broadway in Lebanon.)

The Old Stone House
Marblehead, Ohio
43440

Innkeepers: Don and Nilene Cranmer
Address/Telephone: 133 Clemons Street; (419) 798–5922
Rooms: 12; 6 with private bath.
Rates: $35 double occupancy, winter, $45 summer; $65 four people, winter, $75 summer. Includes breakfast. Children OK.
Open: All year.
Facilities & Activities: Antique shop in summer kitchen. Fishing off front patio; fish-cleaning facilities available. Lake charter fishing and pleasure cruising arranged. Swimming in front of the house. Near ferry to the islands, Cedar Point amusement park, Marblehead lighthouse, African Safari Wildlife Park, area winery tours.

I walked into The Old Stone House on the Lake Erie shoreline just as Nilene was retouching the Williamsburg-blue trim that brightens her inn. "If you just had come a half-hour ago, you could have seen the lake view from the Captain's Tower," she said. "But I just did the stairs."

It didn't matter. The Old Stone House 🖙 sits right on the edge of the water, with an unlimited horizon. I saw a terrific sunset from the patio.

The 1861 Federal-style, four-story inn gets its name from the heavy stone used to build it. The stone was mined from an historic local quarry belonging to the house's original owner.

Nilene showed me thirty-five rambling rooms, with twelve on the second and third floors open to guests. The ☛ pretty country stenciling on the walls was done by Nilene herself. The rooms' tall windows are set into thick walls, insulation against fierce winter lake storms. Antique furnishings include iron-rail beds covered with bright quilts.

The third-floor rooms have original poplar plank floors covered by braided rugs and are furnished with more antique pieces. The windows here are small and multi-paned, opening inward. Nilene pulled on them, and we were immediately refreshed by a cool lake breeze.

The ☛ Captain's Tower, on the fourth floor, is the home's original enclosed widow's walk—and a guest favorite. Walls of windows provide a panoramic lake view. There also are 15-foot-high ceilings, poplar plank floors, and a comfy rocking chair.

Don, a charter fishing captain, arranges angling trips out on the lake, but Nilene said that I could fish the lazy way, as well. "You'll catch white bass and catfish right off the patio."

A country breakfast includes fresh muffins, fruit salad, dry cereal, and beverages. Two ☛ charming breakfast rooms have long windows looking out over the lake. One has round oak tables and chairs, with homespun tablecloths and quaint oil lamps; the other has bright wall stencils and country antique furniture, some still with the original red paint. There are some fine seafood restaurants in and around town; the innkeepers will recommend one just right for you.

How to get there: From Port Clinton, take Route 163 east to Marblehead. At Clemons Street, which is very tiny and narrow, turn left to the lakeshore and the inn. From Sandusky, take U.S. 6 west to Route 269. Go north to Route 163 and turn east. Continue to Clemons Street and turn left, continuing to the inn.

The Inn at Honey Run
Millersburg, Ohio
44654

Innkeeper: Marge Stock
Address/Telephone: 6920 County Road 203; (216) 674–0011, toll
free in Ohio (800) 468–6639
Rooms: 25, with 2 suites; all with private bath.
Rates: $55 to $150. Two-night minimum Friday and Saturday. In-
cludes full breakfast. Children OK.
Open: All year.
Facilities & Activities: Full-service dining room (closed Sundays).
Meeting room hosts movies on weekends, library, game room,
gift shop. Near Holmes County antique and specialty stores,
cheese factories, quilt shops. Nine-hole golf course nearby.
Short drive to Roscoe Village canal-era town and Warther
Wood Carving Museum.

"Just look at that," Marge said, pointing to a black
Amish carriage clip-clopping down a winding country road
just below a room deck of The Inn at Honey Run. "That's
why I love spring, fall, and winter here. You can still see
sights like that through the trees. It takes you back to the
1800s."

I had driven down a hilly, twisting road that I thought

would never end to get here. "We're hard to find," Marge admitted. Her graceful ☛ inn is situated on sixty hilly, wooded acres in the middle of Ohio Amish country. Its wood and stone construction blends magnificently with the gorgeous landscape. And its contemporary décor, complemented by Amish and Shaker touches, conjures up a masterful mix of past and present not often seen in country inns.

☛ "Birding here is great," Marge said, as she pointed to countless feeders surrounding the inn. "Visitors have recorded about thirty different species."

I was anxious to see the rooms, and I wasn't disappointed. They're done in a potpourri of styles: early American; contemporary with slanted ceilings and skylights; and Shaker—my favorite—with many pegs on the walls to hang everything from clothes to furniture.

Marge uses Holmes County folk art to highlight each room; handmade quilts adorn walls and beds (which are extra long); and there are comfy chairs with reading lamps.

"I love books," Marge said, "so I made certain each room has a reading light and a chair that rocks or swivels, where you can put your feet up on the windowsill and read, or just stare out at the birds."

Inn food is made "from scratch," with pan-fried trout from Holmes County waters a dinner specialty. Marge's full country breakfast features juice, eggs and bacon, French toast with real maple syrup, and homemade breads.

How to get there: From Millersburg it is 3.3 miles to the inn. Go east on East Jackson Street in Millersburg (Routes 39 and 62). Pass the courthouse and gas station on the right. At the next corner, turn left onto Route 241, which makes several turns as it twists out of town. Nearly 2 miles down the road, while proceeding down a long, steep hill, you'll cross a bridge over Honey Run. Turn right immediately around another small hill onto County Road 203, which is not well marked. After 1 mile, turn right at the small inn sign. Go up the hill to the inn.

From Berlin, go west on U.S. 62 and Ohio 39. After crossing a small bridge, immediately turn right on County Road 201. Just over a mile down the road, note the crossroad sign on the right and the house on the left. Turn left immediately onto County Road 203. Proceed almost 3 miles to the inn sign on the left. Turn left to the inn.

Punderson Manor House
Newbury, Ohio
44065

Innkeeper: Joseph Artino
Address/Telephone: 11755 Kinsman Road; (216) 564–9144
Rooms: 29, with 2 suites; all with private bath.
Rates: $44 single, $49 double, $56 suite. Children welcome.
Open: All year.
Facilities & Activities: Located in Punderson State Park, with spectacular scenery, lake and water sports, fishing, and hiking and nature trails. Also cross-country ski trails (rentals available), tobogganing, sledding, ice skating; downhill skiing at Alpine Valley, 10-minute drive away. Golf and tennis nearby.

"This inn was originally started as a private summer house, if you can imagine that," said Kathy Bell, whom I had met in the grand lobby of this sprawling Tudor-style inn right on the lake in Punderson State Park. (She was taking over for Joseph, who was away on vacation.) "Then the Depression hit, and it never got finished."

Not until 1948, anyway, when the Ohio Division of Wildlife bought the land and huge Punderson Lake for hunting and fishing and decided to convert the magnificent home into a state park guest house. I think we're all pretty lucky.

Punderson Manor House is nothing like a typical state park lodge. There are no log timbers, country-style furniture, or Indian artifacts. Instead, I found some rather exquisite, antique-style guest rooms.

Be sure to request one of the ☞ seven rooms located in the historic wing of the home. These rooms still convey the richness and charm of the original summer retreat. They're on the small side, but many have fascinating nooks and crannies.

I also saw many of the home's original extra touches. There are ☞ arched hallways, brass and canopied beds, even exquisite displays of rosettes of flowers and griffins set in plaster along the walls.

Three dining rooms serve up delicious Midwestern fare, with prime rib a house specialty. Sunday brunch also is quite popular.

☞ Vaulted cathedral ceilings, a massive stone hearth, and much cherry and oak paneling in the lobby and parlor— all calling to mind a true English manor estate—further show what this "home" was meant to be.

How to get there: Punderson State Park, near Newbury, can be reached from the north or south on Route 44. Turn off Route 44 at Route 87 and go west. The park is about 1 mile up the road; then follow the signs to the Punderson Manor House.

Ohio State Park Lodges

For some people, lodges more than fulfill their definition of a country inn. They're unique structures surrounded by spectacular scenery; they provide all kinds of outdoor recreation; and they won't bust the pocketbook.

Ohio state park lodges provide a wide selection of "country" accommodations that are downright down-home. You'll also find seclusion, relaxation, and decent dining.

There are six of these lodges, and each has something to recommend it. (I've given Punderson State Park's Manor House a separate listing because of its unique history.)

a. Salt Fork State Park Lodge

Powerboaters and waterskiers skim across a 3,000-acre lake. This is a muscle-boat paradise because there are no horsepower restrictions. There are cabins, indoor and outdoor pools, boat tours, and riding stables nearby. (Salt Fork State Park Lodge, State Route 22 East, P.O. Box 7, Cambridge, Ohio 43725; [614] 439–2751.)

b. Hueston Woods State Park Lodge

The massive A-frame lodge at Hueston Woods, in the heart of historic Indian country, has a spectacular one-hundred-foot-high sandstone fireplace. Amenities include indoor and outdoor pools, excursion-boat tours, and an eighteen-hole golf course. (Hueston Woods State Park Lodge, R.F.D. 1, College Corner, Ohio 45003; [513] 523–6381.)

c. Shawnee State Park Lodge

In Shawnee State Park, tributaries of the Ohio River create miles of meandering streams for canoeing. The guest rooms in the lodge are paneled in knotty pine. There's also a putting green, an eighteen-hole golf course, and riding stables. (Shawnee State Park Lodge, P.O. Box 98, Friendship, Ohio 45630; [614] 858–6621.)

d. Burr Oak State Park Lodge

This lodge, in the abundant wildlife region of southeastern Ohio, features two levels of cedar decks. It also has an indoor–outdoor swimming pool, tennis, golf nearby, and a private beach on the crystal-clear waters of Burr Oak Lake. (Burr Oak State Park Lodge, R.F.D. 2, P.O. Box 159, Glouster, Ohio 45732; [614] 767–2112.)

e. Deer Creek State Park Lodge

Central Ohio boasts the state's newest park lodge, Deer Creek. The balconies off the guest rooms overlook the 1,277-acre lake, the park, or the pool. Fun includes swimming pools, an exercise room, whirlpool, four lighted tennis courts, and an eighteen-hole golf course. (Deer Creek State Park Lodge, P.O. Box 153, Mt. Sterling, Ohio 43143; [614] 869–2020.)

The Wooster Inn
Wooster, Ohio
44691

Innkeeper: Willy Bergmann, manager
Address/Telephone: Wayne Avenue and Gasche Street; (216) 264–2341, toll free in Ohio (800) 362–7386, toll free from outside Ohio (800) 321–9885
Rooms: 16, with 2 suites; all with private bath.
Rates: $39 to $60 single, $51 to $72 double. Includes breakfast, served in dining room off regular menu. Special weekend packages available. Children and pets OK.
Open: All year, except Christmas Day.
Facilities & Activities: Outside patio. Access to many Wooster College activities and sports facilities. Ohio Light Opera on special weekends.

Imagine an evening of 🖅 professional light opera, maybe Offenbach's *La Belle Hélène*—which might be described as a Woody Allen–type version of "Dynasty" with ravishing waltzes—and you'll get the idea of this production's flair. Followed by a scrumptious meal featuring champagne and a juicy steak served in a colonial-style dining room.

That's just some of the fun you'll have at the wonderful

Wooster Inn. Owned and operated by the College of Wooster, and located right on its beautiful campus, the inn is surrounded by tall trees and green fields. In fact, I watched a little action on the college's golf course right from the dining room window.

The inn has an English-country feel to it. The lobby is spacious and casually gracious, with a large sitting area of high-back chairs and sofas. A stately grandfather's clock softly chimes on the hour. French doors open onto the colonial-style dining room and terrace, which overlook the aforementioned links.

Guests may also 🖙 use many of the athletic facilities of the college. That means a 25-yard lap pool, tennis courts, a weight room, and a golf course just out the back door. You can even use the library.

Guest rooms are cheery, with multi-paned windows, flowered wallpaper, oak and cherry furniture, quaint bedspreads, and high-back chairs. Be sure to make reservations well in advance. College guests (and many visiting moms and dads) adore the inn.

You can choose anything from the regular breakfast menu in the morning. Inn specialties include blueberry pancakes with Ohio maple syrup. Dinner offers a wide selection of choices, including beef tenderloin in Burgundy wine and pepper sauce, sunny-basted pork chops with rosemary, fresh rainbow trout, and veal cutlets.

On the Fourth of July, the inn has a huge barbecue of chicken and ribs. There's a brass quartet playing music outside, and you've got the best view in town of nighttime fireworks.

How to get there: Five principal highways run through Wooster: U.S. 30 and 250, and State Routes 3, 585, and 83. From Cleveland, exit the 250 bypass at Burbank Road and continue south to Wayne Avenue. Turn east on Wayne to the inn.

The Cider Mill
Zoar, Ohio
44697

Innkeepers: Ralph and Judy Kraus
Address/Telephone: Second Street (mailing address: P.O. Box 441); (216) 874-3133
Rooms: 2; with shared bath.
Rates: $40 single, $45 double. Two-night minimum during fall Harvest Festival. Children 6 and over OK. Pets OK.
Open: All year.
Facilities & Activities: Zoar Historic Village tours. Antique and specialty stores. Near canoe livery and river trips, scenic bike paths along old Ohio-Erie Canal, fishing holes, "Trumpet in the Land" outdoor drama, National Football League Hall of Fame, Ohio Amish Country.

A rooster crowed about six times in a row. "School kids are on a tour of the village today," Judy said, "and with all the attention, he's just going crazy."

I was looking out the third-story window of Judy's restored mill building alongside tiny Goose Run Creek. The mill, which was built in 1863, served as a steam-powered mill for Zoar Village pioneers. At that time, Zoar Village was the nation's most successful religious communal settlement. Its quiet charm and serenity lured even President William McKinley here; Zoar was his summer retreat.

Well, the renovated mill lured me to this little village listed in the National Register of Historic Places. Judy's country-style antique-and-specialty store occupies the first floor. We climbed a ☛ three-story custom-made spiral staircase to reach her beautiful guest rooms. They have original cross beams, slanted ceilings, four-poster and brass beds, and other antique furnishings.

A comfortable second-level family room has a large stone hearth; a fire would feel good here on chilly Ohio nights. The sitting room is more formal, with a ☛ collection of Victorian high-back chairs, a divan, and other antique finery that Judy and Ralph have been searching out over the years. A warming touch is added by an exposed brick wall that's more than a century old.

Judy presents guests with complimentary glasses of wine or cups of tea upon arrival, and she and Ralph will be happy to tell you everything about the historic village's seven-building museum complex that lies along tiny, narrow streets. They'll also be glad to make reservations at recommended village restaurants serving everything from honest-to-goodness down-home family-style cooking to gourmet meals.

Inn breakfasts, served in a bright country kitchen, are sumptuous feasts of omelets, sausage casseroles, homemade breads and rolls, and more.

How to get there: Take I–77 to exit 93. Then it's 3 miles to Zoar on State Route 212, following the signs. In the village, turn left on Second Street, right past the old Zoar Hotel. The Cider Mill is just down the street on the right.

ᕱ

B: *Don't forget to say hello to Buddy the Cat, the mill's unofficial mascot. On my visit, he greeted me at the mill door.*

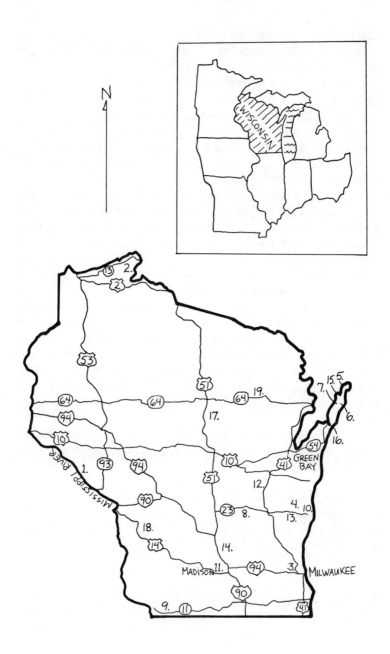

Wisconsin

Numbers on map refer to towns numbered below.

Laue House
Alma, Wisconsin
54610

Innkeepers: Jan and Jerry Schreiber
Address/Telephone: 1111 South Main Street; (608) 685–4923
Rooms: 7, sharing 2 baths.
Rates: $16 single, $22 to $30 double. Includes continental breakfast. Children and pets OK. No credit cards.
Open: March to December.
Facilities & Activities: Canoes to rent. Fish-cleaning shed. Alma is a slice of small-town Americana, with Friday-night fish fries, old-time evening dance socials. All kinds of Mississippi River water activities.

Jerry was sitting on his front porch that looks out over the Mississippi River, soaking up some afternoon sun with his pooch. "You try the river, yet?" he asked me.

The river is very important to Jerry and Jan because they're commercial fishermen, so it's not surprising that they often host other fishermen at the Laue House. And fishermen love staying here, especially since the innkeepers also know many of the best fishing holes on the Mississippi and will share their secrets with guests. Behind the inn, there's even a fully equipped cleaning shed.

This 1863 home offers seven guest rooms eclectically decorated with antiques and other types of furnishings. Jerry has installed corner sinks in most of the rooms for quick wash-ups. The Blue Room is his favorite because it gets the day's first sunshine.

The Big Room has windows overlooking the Mississippi. "And we've got one of the best deals around," Jerry said. "The ☞ Small Room, with a view of the river, sleeps one weary traveler for only $12, and that includes a regular inn breakfast of English muffins, juice, and coffee." The inn-keepers will direct you to area restaurants; many feature Friday-night fish fries, a local specialty.

The inn is very casual, and you might fill out your own registration card if Jerry and Jan are out fishing the river. There's a ☞ free boat launching across the street, along with rentals, in case you want to do the same.

How to get there: From the Twin Cities, take U.S. 61 south to U.S. 10. Go east to U.S. 63 and turn south. At Wisconsin 35, turn east and follow it into Alma. Route 35 becomes Main Street once in town.

⧗

B: *In nearby Stockholm, there's a little Amish quilt shop that's one of the finest I've seen outside of Lancaster, Pennsylvania. Just drive into town—you can't miss it.*

Cooper Hill House
Bayfield, Wisconsin
54814

Innkeepers: Sheree and Phil Peterson
Address/Telephone: 33 South Sixth Street (mailing address: P.O.
  Box 5); (715) 779–5060
Rooms: 4; all with private bath.
Rates: $41 to $44 single, $44 to $49 double. Includes breakfast.
  Children OK.
Open: May through October.
Facilities & Activities: Near car ferry service to historic Madeline
  Island, an old fur-trading post, and Big Bay State Park. Sport
  and charter fishing on Lake Superior, pleasure boat rentals.
  Orchards close by. Winter features 50 miles of groomed cross-
  country trails.

"We're on the comfortable side here," Sheree said.
"Guests can be very relaxed and not have to worry about
breaking things."

I'm glad she said that because I sometimes worry about
fragile antiques contending with my 6-foot-2-inch frame. But
at the Cooper Hill House, Sheree made me feel right at
home.

The 1888 house is on a street up a high hill from the

dock leading to the spectacular Apostle Islands National Lakeshore and historic Madeline Island, an old fur-trading post. Cooper Hill itself—named for one of the home's early families—also is well remembered because it was a favorite winter slide at the turn of the century. A few Bayfield residents still recall barreling down the hill toward the frozen lake on makeshift bobsleds when they were kids.

Sheree's four guest rooms are furnished in country-antique period furniture; I particularly like the ☞ beautiful antique quilts on the beds.

The inn's cozy sitting room is a favorite guest spot for sharing Madeline Island adventures or tales of the "big fish" that got away during a charter excursion out on Lake Superior's waters. It's also great to sprawl out in one of the comfy parlor chairs after a long winter's day of cross-country skiing along the area's wooded trails.

You're in for a breakfast treat of Sheree's ☞ delicious homemade bread and rolls, fresh fruits, a selection of teas, and specially blended coffee. Downtown restaurants like Greunke's Inn, The Pier, and the Bayfield Inn usually feature fresh Lake Superior whitefish and lake trout on their dinner menus. The Rittenhouse Inn offers multi-course gourmet meals in elegant Victorian surroundings.

A ☞ local delicacy is whitefish livers. They're a favorite of mine and alone are worth the trip up to this quaint old-time fishing village.

How to get there: Wisconsin 13 brings you into Bayfield. Follow the highway signs to the inn, which is on the left side of the road.

B: *Be sure to discover the many historic buildings in the sixty-block historic district of this interesting village. I enjoyed watching coopers fashioning barrels by hand in the historic barrel factory down by the lakeshore.*

Greunke's Inn
Bayfield, Wisconsin
54814

Innkeepers: Judith Lokken-Strom and Alan White
Address/Telephone: 17 Rittenhouse Avenue; (715) 779–5480
Rooms: 7; 2 with private half-bath; studio apartment with private
   bath.
Rates: Mid-April to Memorial Day weekend, $25 to $35; Memorial
   Day weekend to mid-October, $35 to $45; studio apartment,
   $65. Children and pets OK. Wheelchair access.
Open: Mid-April to mid-October.
Facilities & Activities: Dining room, bar. Across the street from
   ferry boat to Apostle Islands National Lakeshore and historic
   Madeline Island. Short walk to Bayfield specialty stores and
   historic architecture.

   I am compelled to stop at Greunke's for a beer every
time I visit this historic fishing village on the spectacular
shore of Lake Superior. The inn's bar, steeped in nostalgia, is
pure kitsch.
   There are ☛ old beverage trays displayed on the walls,
all kinds of antique beer signs, an ugly green malt mixer
(circa 1950) that whips up some great chocolate shakes, and

mounted fish trophies attributed to long-forgotten fishermen. I love to play vintage rock 'n' roll on the colorful juke box.

The yesteryear, small-town atmosphere of Bayfield is apparent in the guest rooms, which are styled with an eclectic mix of antique and contemporary furniture. The ☛ Swedish wall phone at the top of the inn stairway is a Greunke favorite.

Alan opens the inn dining room at 6 A.M. to feed a stick-to-your-ribs breakfast to all comers. Many are fishermen who challenge the sometimes nasty waters of Lake Superior to catch a local favorite—whitefish. In fact, an inn dinner specialty is ☛ whitefish livers, a real treat, especially for first-timers. Also offered is fresh lake trout cooked in butter and sesame seed breading, fresh whitefish, and more.

Judith and Alan have another inn, the Chez Joliet, just at the bend of the road past the docks on Highway 13. Its huge picture window overlooks Lake Superior's rugged waters.

How to get there: Take Wisconsin 13 (which becomes Rittenhouse Avenue) into Bayfield. Follow Rittenhouse toward the village's ferry docks in the heart of town. The inn is just across the street from the docks.

Le Château Boutin
Bayfield, Wisconsin
54814

Innkeepers: Jerry and Mary Phillips
Address/Telephone: 7 Rice Avenue; (715) 779–5111
Rooms: 6, with 2 suites; all with private bath.
Rates: $68 to $95. Includes continental breakfast. Children not encouraged.
Open: May through October and weekends November through December and February through April. Closed January.
Facilities & Activities: Historic fishing village on shore of Lake Superior. Sailing, touring, hiking, exploring Apostle Islands National Lakeshore, visiting Madeline Island and its fur-trading museum. Cross-country skiing (in season).

Jerry said that this massive sixteen-room Queen Anne mansion, completed in 1908, was home to Bayfield's first millionaire. I could see he wasn't ashamed to show off his money.

What a truly superb inn. I entered through heavy leaded-glass doors, stepping onto plank floors. To the left, the Music Room has 🐾 rare myrtle woodwork, Tiffany-style lamps, a lot of brass, silver plating, and original stained glass.

Several Art Nouveau pieces (Jerry's favorites) highlight the room: a 🖝 fabulous stone-and-tile fireplace and some unusual light fixtures. Of course, there's also a baby grand piano.

The dining room is formally gracious, with gorgeous leaded glass and fine hand-carved woodwork. The huge dining room table is original to the home.

What a treat to look out the tall windows of my bedroom and see the choppy waters of Lake Superior; in fact, 🖝 most guest rooms have lake views. The unique woodwork of tiger birch and maple is a handsome complement to the Tiffany-style stained-glass and leaded windows.

My favorite room is an ornate master suite with a second-floor balcony. I wanted to build a roaring fire in the hearth, crawl inside the bed with its shiny brass headboard, and pull the covers up to my chin. After all, whipping breezes off the lake had added quite a chill to the spring day.

A light continental breakfast is served in the dining room at your leisure. Jerry's Old Rittenhouse Inn (just a short drive away) serves fantastic six-course gourmet dinners in an elegant Victorian setting; dishes include grilled steak sautéed in Burgundy wine, butter, and garlic; steak stuffed with oysters; and the fresh fish catch of the day. Or you can try area restaurants (like the Bayfield Inn, Greunke's, or The Pier) for some Lake Superior whitefish.

And I never pass up a chance to delight in a local specialty—whitefish livers.

How to get there: From Duluth, take U.S. 53 south through that city to the bridge leading to Superior, Wisconsin. Pick up State Route 2 and go east. Near Ashland, turn north on State Route 13 and drive through Bayfield. Near the lakeshore, just around a bend in the road, turn left on Rice Avenue to the inn

B: *Builder Frank Boutin was a turn-of-the-century lumber baron. That's why there are so many exotic woods in this lovely inn.*

Old Rittenhouse Inn

Bayfield, Wisconsin

54814

Innkeepers: Jerry and Mary Phillips

Address/Telephone: 301 Rittenhouse Avenue (mailing address: Box 584); (715) 779–5765

Rooms: 9; all with private bath, many with fireplace.

Rates: $58 to $88. Includes breakfast. Children OK. Wheelchair access.

Open: All year.

Facilities & Activities: Three romantic dining rooms. Recreational activities of all kinds available: fishing, sailing, Apostle Islands National Lakeshore; fur-trading museum and other attractions on Madeline Island; canoeing on Brule River; annual festivals; cross-country skiing (in season).

I sat in an elegant Victorian dining room in the early morning as an immaculately dressed Jerry, resplendent in a black velvet vest—with a long gold watch fob and a wide bow tie—served me an exquisite breakfast.

After sipping ☞ freshly pressed apple cider, I started on brandied peaches and blueberries in sour cream. Next came delicious New Orleans–style cinnamon French toast and a tall glass of milk.

The sound of soft classical music wafted through the room, which was bathed in rich Victorian-print wallpaper, with brass chandeliers, and antique oak and mahogany tables and chairs. I pulled my seat closer to the roaring fire in the hearth.

"I think it's important that the feeling inside a home fit the personality of the house," Jerry said as we talked about what made a good country inn, "and it must deliver personal service that makes it a special place to stay."

The Old Rittenhouse Inn scores well on both points. It's an opulent 1890 Victorian red-brick and wood-shingle mansion, with a long wraparound veranda and gabled roof. Elegant dining rooms and sitting areas are done in formal prints, with fine Victorian furnishings and all kinds of period lamps.

Jerry's guest rooms are immaculate; many have four-poster beds, marble-topped dressers and vanities, and some have fireplaces to take the chill off cold winter days. Several boast tall windows looking out toward blustery Lake Superior.

The new rooms are incredibly spacious; I don't think it would be an exaggeration to say that they're the ☞ largest rooms I've ever seen in a country inn. Big brass, iron-rail, and walnut beds are inviting. Then there are pretty stained-glass windows depicting Bayfield lakeshore scenes. All the new rooms have their own fireplaces.

The inn also offers ☞ delicious multi-course gourmet meals. Here Mary is the genius. Her specialties include steak *Bercy* stuffed with oysters, fresh trout poached in champagne, and pork ragout. Homemade breads are served steaming in heaping baskets. Save room for incredible dessert treats.

How to get there: From Minneapolis–St. Paul, take I–94 east to U.S. 63. Take 63 north to State Route 2 and go east to Route 13. Take 13 north to Bayfield. The inn is on the corner of Rittenhouse and 3rd.

B: *A romantic inn along the spectacular shoreline of Lake Superior with historic islands nearby to explore—an almost perfect destination.*

Stagecoach Inn
Cedarburg, Wisconsin
53012

Innkeepers: Liz and Brook Brown
Address/Telephone: W61 N520 Washington Avenue; (414)
    375–0208 or 375–3035
Rooms: 9; all with private bath.
Rates: $35 single, $45 double, $55 for rooms with two double beds.
    Includes continental breakfast. Children OK. No smoking.
Open: All year.
Facilities & Activities: Stagecoach Pub, candy store, book shop. Sit-
    uated in the heart of historic Cedarburg, within walking dis-
    tance of Cedar Creek Settlement, the old Woolen Mill, Stone
    Mill Winery, antique, craft, and specialty shops. Ozaukee Pio-
    neer Village, Ozaukee Covered Bridge (the last covered bridge
    in Wisconsin) nearby.

Stagecoach drivers slept on the basement's dirt floor in
bunks made of stone rubble and straw. The chimney that
took the flue for the driver's potbellied stove still stands.

The stagecoach-stop charm carries over to guest rooms
that are decorated with period antiques. "We wanted to keep
the inn authentic," Liz said. "This is a restoration-minded
community."

That's an understatement. The Stagecoach Inn is in the heart of the historic Cedar Creek Settlement, which was anchored by the now-restored Wittenburg Woolen Mills. (The mill provided wool uniforms for soldiers during the Civil War.)

More than 150 rare "cream city" brick and stone buildings stand throughout town, many dating back to the mid-1800s.

Everything at the inn is cozy and cheery, with many special touches. Liz drew the ☞ pretty stencils on the walls and reconditioned the original pine-wood plank floors. Her ☞ antique four-poster and brass beds are covered with Laura Ashley comforters.

The Stagecoach Pub is located on the inn's first floor. I had an imported beer from a massive antique oak cooler at a one-hundred-year-old bar. The tin ceiling adds to the frontier charm. Liz serves breakfast here, too, at antique tavern tables. She offers hot croissants, juice, cereal, coffee, and herbal teas, and she'll recommend a good spot for dinner in the historic town. You can play games and cards here at night, in a warm coffeehouse atmosphere. Late-night sweet tooths and bookworms can find a candy shop and fine bookstore on the first floor.

Look for these inn "originals": the heavy front door dates from 1853; the intricate woodwork on the door and window frames, as well as the crown molding above the front door, is made of single pieces of wood carved to look multi-layered; and the handsome cherry staircase banister is authentic.

How to get there: From Chicago, take I–94 to I–43, just north of Milwaukee, and get off at the Cedarburg exit. This road changes to Wisconsin 57; take it into town (where it becomes Washington Avenue). The inn is located on the right side of the street.

B: *Liz and Brook discovered some original hand stenciling on the walls along the third-story stairway. Be sure to take a look.*

The Washington House Inn
Cedarburg, Wisconsin
53012

Innkeeper: Judy Drefahl
Address/Telephone: W62 N573 Washington Avenue; (414) 375–3550
Rooms: 20, with 1 suite; all with private bath.
Rates: $49 to $89. Includes continental breakfast. Special packages available. Children OK. Wheelchair access.
Open: All year.
Facilities & Activities: Situated in the heart of historic Cedarburg, just 3 blocks from Cedar Creek Settlement: the old Woolen Mill, Stone Mill Winery, antique, craft, and specialty shops. Ozaukee Pioneer Village, Ozaukee Covered Bridge (the last covered bridge in Wisconsin) nearby.

Cedarburg is an historic woolen mill town, with many rare "cream city" brick and stone buildings dating from the mid-1800s. In fact, the downtown area alone boasts more historic structures than any city west of Philadelphia!

One of these is The Washington House Inn, a country-Victorian "cream city" brick building completed in 1886. The tall front doors and authentic frontier ambience made me feel as though I had walked into a scene from the old "Gunsmoke" series. A long lobby sprinkled with Victorian furnishings, with rich parquet floors, brass chandeliers, and a marble fireplace is the perfect setting for "Miss Kitty" to make her entrance.

I looked at the original hotel register that recorded visitors during the months of 1895. How did anyone ever have the time to write in that fancy scroll? I also noticed an unusual display: a 🖝 "wedding brick" discovered during recent restoration with the date "1886" and the names of the happy couple scratched on it.

The guest rooms are named for leading citizens of historic Cedarburg. The country-Victorian decorations are absolutely charming, with floral wallpapers, fancy armoires, cozy down quilts, fresh flowers, and more. I really like the leaded-glass transom windows of some rooms.

In the newly restored rooms, there's more of a plain country feeling, but there's nothing plain about the décor. The 🖝 exposed brick walls and beamed ceilings are spectacular.

It's fun to eat breakfast in a dining room that boasts white pressed-tin ceilings, oak tables and chairs, and tall windows that wash the room in light. Judy's 🖝 home-baked breads, cakes, and rolls are made from recipes found in an authentic turn-of-the-century Cedarburg cookbook. Cereal, fresh fruit, and beverages also are offered.

One of Judy's favorite times of the day is the afternoon social hour in the dining room, with an opportunity to share with guests her love of this historic town. A manteled fireplace with Victorian sofas and chairs just off the main dining area makes things more cozy.

How to get there: From Chicago, take I–94 to I–43, just north of Milwaukee, and get off at the Cedarburg exit. This road eventually changes to Wisconsin 57; follow it into town (where it becomes Washington Street). At Center Street, turn left and park in the lot behind the hotel.

B: *It's just a short walk from the inn to all the fabulous antique and specialty shops at the old woolen mills in historic Cedar Creek Settlement.*

Siebken's
Elkhart Lake, Wisconsin
53020

Innkeepers: Doug and Pam Siebken
Address/Telephone: 284 South Lake Street; (414) 876–2600
Rooms: 53 rooms, 33 with private bath; 1 lake cottage.
Rates: $58 to $60 single, $52 to $68 double. Two- to four-night minimum during Road America race weekends. Children and pets OK.
Open: June through September; May and October weekends only.
Facilities & Activities: Opera House bar on premises. Antique store and gift shop on premises. Water sports, boat rentals, golf course within walking distance; horseback riding, antiquing, go-carting. Road America, internationally famous Indy-style and stock-car racing.

Siebken's really hops during Road America weekends, when internationally famous race-car drivers come to relax in the old Opera House bar after spending an unnerving day speeding down the straightaway.

Doug's family has run this turn-of-the-century summer lodge, situated just across the street from Elkhart Lake, since 1916. It's filled with country antiques, wicker furniture—and friendly critters.

I was greeted at the door by the inn's three dogs: Chelsea, an old English sheepdog, and Bailey and Branigan, both Irish wolfhounds. Their gruff barking is just a friendly welcome. After I became part of the inn "family," I was often called upon to gently stroke these lugs behind their ears while they tapped their paws in delight.

A ☛ large enclosed sun porch on the first floor, one of my favorite spots, reminds me of beach houses on Cape Cod. The TV/game room is another favorite, especially when I visit in the fall during the major-league baseball playoffs.

Pam's antique-filled dining rooms serve ☛ large portions of Wisconsin-style homemade foods. My roast duck on a bed of wild rice virtually filled a platter-sized dish. The rest of the meal, including fresh vegetables, broccoli soup, a large salad, and homebaked bread and rolls, was overwhelming. Of course, I made room for the dessert platter: a choice of chocolate or raspberry torte or ice cream.

Rooms in the main building and annex are eclectically styled, comfortable, and airy. My room was quiet and cozy, with a bouncy spring bed covered with a brightly colored quilt. Summer guests can use ceiling fans to cool their rooms; hallway radiators provide heat for chilly Wisconsin nights; fluffy comforters and wool blankets further ward off chills.

There's a small bar in the main house, but the real fun is at the ☛ Opera House bar across the courtyard, where locals often come to down a few. And see if you can get Doug to roll out the piano and sing some of his wacky tunes.

How to get there: Siebken's is about 60 miles north of Milwaukee. Take I–43 to Wisconsin Highway 57 (Plymouth exit). Continue north past Plymouth; then turn left on County Trunk J and right on 67 to Elkhart Lake.

The Griffin Inn
Ellison Bay, Wisconsin
54210

Innkeepers: Joyce and Paul Crittenden
Address/Telephone: 11976 Mink River Road; (414) 854–4306
Rooms: 10, with 2½ shared baths; 4 cottages behind inn.
Rates: Summer, $37.50 to $59; winter, packages only, $90 per person double occupancy. Includes 3-course country breakfast with main inn rooms; continental breakfast with cottages. Five-course dinners served only in winter. Children OK. Pets in cottages only. No credit cards.
Open: April through October daily; December through March weekends only.
Facilities & Activities: Free bikes to guests, sports court and volleyball on grounds. Fishing, boating, and swimming within walking distance. Golf, horseback riding, tennis, art galleries, potters, antique shops, restaurants, and the Peninsula Players theater group within short drive.

Here's a little bit of New England on the rugged Door County peninsula. Joyce and Paul's charming white clapboard inn, built in 1921, rests among nine quiet acres that include an apple orchard and a lovely gazebo.

I like the cozy country feeling of the main-floor library

as well as the sitting room, with its large stone fireplace surrounded by high-back Queen Anne–style chairs and sofas. A crooked cornstalk broom hanging next to the hearth adds more country whimsy.

Ten quaint rooms line the hallway of the second floor. They're eclectically decorated in antique and country styles; most of them feature ☞ handmade quilts on the beds.

The rich wood tones of the dining room are set off by many attractive antiques. A cast-iron wood-burning stove in the corner keeps winter's cross-country skiers nice and toasty. Meals are served on ☞ long bench-style tables.

"Since everyone eats together, it's like staying at a friend's house," Paul said. "Communication and sharing are an important part of the experience."

Joyce offers a ☞ huge country breakfast, prepared in her kitchen daily. Treats include fresh muffins, potato pancakes, zucchini and carrot breads, pan omelets and quiches, coffeecake, and tea. There are many good restaurants in the area. I like the C and C Supper Club in Fish Creek, especially for its scallops.

Nighttime meals (served only during winter) are five-course feasts, often featuring specially prepared chicken and fish delights, with a good assortment of fancy vegetables, soup and salad, and dessert.

In summer, the inn provides bicycles (no charge) to explore the beauty of "The Door's" rugged countryside or to ride to the many art galleries and specialty shops that line the streets of the tiny lakeshore villages that dot the peninsula.

How to get there: From Milwaukee, take I–43 to Wisconsin 42. Go north on 42 to Ellison Bay and turn east on Mink River Road. The inn is about two blocks up the road.

Eagle Harbor Inn
Ephraim, Wisconsin
54211

Innkeepers: Dick and Celeste Wegman
Address/Telephone: Route 42 (mailing address: P.O. Box 72B);
   (414) 854–2121
Rooms: 9, all with private bath; 11 cottages.
Rates: $46 to $65. Includes continental breakfast. Two-night mini-
   mum on advance reservations; 3-night minimum in July, Au-
   gust, first 2 weekends in October, holiday weekends. No
   children under 15.
Open: April to November.
Facilities & Activities: Outdoor basketball court on the property.
   Hiking, cross-country skiing at Peninsula State Park just south
   of the inn. Famous Wilson's Ice Cream Shop up the road. Art
   galleries, craft stores, and specialty shops in harbor towns.
   Nearby restaurants serving heralded Door County fish boils.
   Charter fishing, water sports. Seasonal Door County apple and
   cherry festivals.

    Eagle Harbor Inn is a charming white clapboard build-
ing near the bay shore of fabulous Door County in perhaps
the ☛ most charming and picturesque town this peninsula
has to offer.

266

Celeste and Dick, two friendly former Chicagoans, are veterans of big-city corporate wars. Now they've retreated to the beauty of "The Door" to get away from that hurried lifestyle.

Nine cozy guest rooms are in the main house; during summer, there are also seven housekeeping and four do-it-yourself sleeping cottages, which do not have breakfast privileges.

I found the guest rooms warm and intimate, yet unusually roomy. "We found many of the antiques [in guest rooms] on persistent trips to area antique haunts," Celeste said. ☛ Chests of inlaid wood, dressing tables, tall headboards, and other treasures are some of their finds.

Pegged floors made of pine run along the first floor. The front parlor, with its comfy sofa, is a good place for the 5 P.M. wine break, a tradition at the inn. In back, the quaint ☛ fireplace room is littered with collectibles: antique pewter mugs on the mantel, branding irons, and baskets of colorful yarn. An old Grundig console stereo looks exactly like the one my Mom had.

At breakfast, I feasted on Celeste's ☛ homemade country-style treats. First came a cinnamon-topped baked grapefruit (a favorite of mine), then fresh croissants, chocolate-chip coffee-cake (another irresistible), and blueberry muffins—with fresh fruit juice and a tall glass of milk.

For dinner, I headed over to the White Gull Inn at nearby Fish Creek for a local specialty—the famous Door County fish boil, where whitefish is boiled in a huge flaming cauldron. Al Johnson's Swedish Restaurant in Sister Bay, a short ride away, serves tasty food, but the real attraction is the ☛ goats grazing on top of the grass-thatched roof of the building.

How to get there: Take Wisconsin 42 north from Sturgeon Bay and continue to Ephraim. The Eagle Harbor Inn driveway is on the right side of the road.

ᗺ

B: *Chances are you'll consider Celeste and Dick good friends of yours by the time you leave for home. I know I did.*

White Gull Inn
Fish Creek, Wisconsin
54212

Innkeepers: Andy and Jan Coulson
Address/Telephone: 4225 Main Street, P.O. Box 159-C; (414) 868–3517
Rooms: 10 at inn; 5 with private bath. Cottages and buildings for multiple couples also available.
Rates: Inn rooms: May through October, $46 with shared bath; $54 to $64 with private bath; November through April, $58 to $76. From Nov. 1 to May 1 includes breakfast. Two-night minimum on weekends, 3-night minimum on holidays. Children OK. No credit cards.
Open: All year.
Facilities & Activities: Large dining room featuring famous Door County fish boil on Wednesday, Friday, Saturday, and Sunday nights. Situated in the heart of historic Fish Creek, walk to art galleries, specialty, and antique shops. State parks and golfing nearby.

Russ Ostrand, the inn's "Master Boiler," is a bear of a man. He sits perched on a small chair in the dining room, pumping his concertina and singing "oom-pah" songs to guests as they devour his latest ☞ fish boil—whitefish, potatoes, and a secret combination of herbs and spices boiled outside in a huge cauldron with flames darting toward the sky. Served with hot loaves of bread, homemade coleslaw, and mugs of ice cold beer, it's a Door County institution. A tasty extra is home-baked cherry cobbler for dessert.

I like the casual atmosphere of the White Gull Inn; it makes me feel right at home. The landmark 1896 white clapboard inn also looks "New England picture perfect."

Andy said that the 🖙 inn originally sat on the other side of Green Bay, eighteen miles away, in Marinette, Wisconsin. During a frigid Door County winter around the turn of the century, it was dragged on a crudely fashioned log sled by draft horses across the frozen waters to its present location. Sort of a Victorian mobile home.

The guest rooms are small and cozy, comfortably furnished with country-Victorian antiques that create an intimate, romantic retreat. I love the iron-rail beds that Andy has painted a cheery white. There are also high ceilings and plank floors covered with braided scatter rugs.

The inn lobby has a large fireplace often ablaze to take the chill off a typically nippy Door County morning. Besides Russ's famous fish boils, the dining room also serves all-American staples like turkey-dumpling soup, baked beans, glazed baked ham, and lots more.

How to get there: From Milwaukee, take Wisconsin 43 north. Near Manitowoc, take Wisconsin 42 north past Sturgeon Bay into Door County. In Fish Creek, turn left at the stop sign at the bottom of a hill along the twisting road and proceed about three blocks to the inn.

⏳

B: *Don't miss the fish boil, especially you first-timers. It's not just a dinner; it's a real happening.*

The Heidel House
Green Lake, Wisconsin
54941

Innkeeper: Margaret York
Address/Telephone: Illinois Avenue, P.O. Box 9; (414) 294-3344
Rooms: 82, plus estate buildings; all with private bath.
Rates: (Vary seasonally) $44 to $151 for rooms in lodge or special
   buildings. $70 to $141 for Pump House. Children and pets OK.
   Wheelchair access.
Open: All year.
Facilities & Activities: Full-service dining rooms. Heated indoor
   swimming pool, sauna. Piano bar, Rathskeller bar with live en-
   tertainment. Water sports in lake,  private parties on the
   inn's yacht, beach cookouts, and shore dinners. Charter fish-
   ing. Horseback riding, 3 golf courses nearby. Winter cross-
   country skiing, ice fishing, and nearby snowmobiling. Dinner
   theater nearby. Specialty shops in town.

Driving along the winding, tree-lined roadway leading to
The Heidel House is like touring a tiny country village. I
passed many buildings done in various styles, from restored
nineteenth-century stable-and-tack houses to a lakeside
lodge retreat.
   But stay at the tiny  Pump House. It's a small brick

building at the top of a hill that formerly stored huge water tanks used for irrigating the gardens and indoor "water closets" at the historic estate.

Now this charming structure is a delightful, private retreat. I loved climbing the wrought-iron spiral staircase leading to a cozy loft bedroom. The big brass bed is reflected in a mirrored wall.

Downstairs, more antique furniture gives the house a country-getaway ambience, and a stained-glass window in the little kitchen adds touches of warm colors.

In the romantic Viennese Room of the main lodge building (just a short walk away), an aura of formal elegance takes over, with romantic candlelight dinners served in a room overlooking the lake. More than thirty entrées made it difficult for me to make up my mind. I finally settled on tasty country-fried chicken, while my wife chose veal Oscar. We also devoured the home-baked carrot-and-raisin rolls, an inn specialty.

You can walk upstairs to the less formal Fondue Chalet and dip fresh goodies in Swiss fashion.

I found that the local Goose Blind restaurant is a great place in town for terrific pizza and beer. It's also the village's "hot spot."

How to get there: Take Wisconsin 23 to Business 23; then continue to South Street and turn left. At Lake Street, make a right and continue to Illinois Avenue, where you go left again. A short drive on Illinois leads to the stone pillars that mark The Heidel House entrance on the right.

B: *Golfer's note: Nearby Lawsonia is a fabulous course designed in the style of traditional Scottish links, with incredible elevated greens, and a new nine that features a hole with an 80-foot-deep stone quarry from mid-fairway to green!*

Oakwood Lodge
Green Lake, Wisconsin
54941

Innkeeper: Marcia Klepinger
Address/Telephone: 365 Lake Street; (414) 294–6580
Rooms: 10; 6 with private bath.
Rates: $37 to $45 double occupancy; subtract $5 for single occupancy; 10 percent off daily rates for weekly occupancy. Room rates include breakfast, Oct. 1 through April 30. Two-night minimum May 1 through Sept. 30; 3-night minimum on holiday weekends. Children OK.
Open: All year.
Facilities & Activities: Water sports and activities. Will arrange weekend golf and charter-fishing packages. Three golf courses nearby; horseback riding; specialty shops in town; dinner theater.

The huge white cottage with the arched second-floor balcony jumped out at me as I approached the bend in a back country road. It was surrounded by tall trees, perched lakeside in a perfect getaway setting.

I discovered that this is one of only three buildings that remain of the original massive Oakwood Hotel complex built in the 1860s. Now it's a charming inn with "the 🖝 best view of the Green Lake," according to Marcia.

We sat outside on her 🖝 back-porch dining terrace, just a stone's throw from the lake. Marcia suggested that I try one of her breakfast specialties: blueberry pancakes. She needn't have said any more. There were also hearty helpings of her homemade breads and rolls, and cakes and sweet rolls for morning sweet tooths. What a fabulous way to enjoy the day's first meal—lakeside al fresco.

Marcia has fashioned ten charming rooms in this historic building; 🖝 my favorites are four upstairs facing the lake. I like to just sit and watch all the colorful sails bob along the waters. Some of the rooms have high walnut headboards and brass beds. And she's constantly adding to the inn's antique collection.

Marcia doesn't serve dinner, but the romantic Viennese dining room of The Heidel House resort is a one-minute drive down the road. Marcia also recommends Norton's, a nearby seafood restaurant right on the lake—a local favorite. The Goose Blind is good for scrumptious pizza and beer.

How to get there: Travel Wisconsin 23 west to Business 23 and then turn left on South Street. Take South to Lake Street and turn right. Oakwood Lodge is at the intersection (bend of the road) of Lake Street and Illinois Avenue.

Wisconsin House
Stage Coach Inn
Hazel Green, Wisconsin
53811

Innkeepers: Betha and John Mueller
Address/Telephone: 2105 East Main Street; (608) 854–2233
Rooms: 5; 2 with private bath.
Rates: $35 to $55, with second night $5 less. Includes full country
   breakfast. Well-behaved children only. No credit cards. No
   smoking in bedrooms.
Open: All year.
Facilities & Activities: Nearby: biking, canoeing, historical and riv-
   erboat museums in Galena, Illinois; skiing, antique, and spe-
   cialty shops in Dubuque, Iowa.

   This 1846 stagecoach inn served travelers on the Mil-
waukee-to-Galena, Illinois, stage. An ☞ old tin horn from
one of those historic stagecoaches sits in the upstairs hallway. And there's a copy of the original stagecoach handbill
on the wall in the parlor.
   John, a tinsmith, ☞ makes the stencils for patterns
adorning the walls and plank floors and entertains visitors
with his Swiss heritage–style yodeling. Betha collects an-

tique cookie cutters and maple-syrup molds and sometimes sings some of her Norwegian heritage folk tunes.

The inn is handsomely decorated with all kinds of antiques and collectibles, the passion of more than thirty years' antiquing by the innkeepers. My favorite is a ☛ 16-foot-long breakfast dining table found at the nearby New Diggings Methodist Church. "We were lucky enough to find these balloon-back chairs, the type made in Galena in the 1840s," John added.

Upstairs, the guest rooms are furnished with country antiques, including some with canopy beds, high-back chairs, bright curtains, and more. All are named for noteworthy inn visitors, including one for U. S. Grant, a frequenter of the Wisconsin House.

"We like to keep on schedule, so breakfast is served at 8 A.M. sharp," Betha said. It consists of ☛ family-style fare, with meat, eggs, French toast, home-baked muffins, toast, cheese, and potatoes. Specially prepared gourmet dinners are offered by reservation only on Saturday; some of the choices include Yankee pot roast, torsk (broiled codfish), beef barbecued ribs, and more—all made from authentic country inn recipes. (Here's a secret: Betha and John surprise guests with Swiss folk songs and yodeling after their hearty meals.)

How to get there: Take U.S. 20 west from Galena to Highway 80 north into Wisconsin and continue to the town of Hazel Green. In town, the name of the road changes to North Percival. Turn right on Fairplay and go to East Main Street. The inn is on the corner.

B: *John and Betha were childhood sweethearts, growing up on neighboring Wisconsin farms. It still shows.*

The American Club
Kohler, Wisconsin
53044

Innkeeper: Susan Porter Green
Address/Telephone: Highland Drive; (414) 457–8000, toll free in Wisconsin (800) 472–8414, toll free in northern and central Illinois, Iowa, Michigan, and Minnesota (800) 458–2562
Rooms: 110; 2 suites; all with private bath.
Rates: $69 to $139 single, $84 to $159 double, $114 to $134 suites. Each child over 10, $10 extra; children 10 and younger free. Two-night minimum on weekends from July 1 through Labor Day weekend, Memorial Day weekend, and December 30–31. Wheelchair access.
Open: All year.
Facilities & Activities: Six restaurants and full-service dining rooms. Renowned for extravagant buffets and special-event and holiday feasts; large Sunday brunch. Ballroom. Sports Core, a world-class health club. River Wildlife, 800 acres of private woods for hiking, horseback riding, hunting, fishing, trap shooting, canoeing. Cross-country skiing and ice skating. Nearby: antiquing, lake charter fishing, Kettle Moraine State Forest, Road America (auto racing).

Just four miles from the sometimes turbulent waters of Lake Michigan, amid tall pines, patches of white birch, scrubbed farmhouses, and black soil, is one of Wisconsin's best-kept secrets. It's The American Club, a uniquely gracious guest house.

I found an uncommonly European ambience at this elegant inn. With its Tudor-style appointments of gleaming shiny brass, custom-crafted oak furniture, crystal chandeliers, and quality antique furnishings, The American Club ☞ looks like a finely manicured baronial estate.

Built in 1918 as a temporary home for immigrant workers of the Kohler Company (a plumbing manufacturer still located across the street), the "boarding house" served as a meeting place where English and citizenship classes were taught—a genuine "American Club."

My room boasted handsome oak paneling and furniture. ☞ Handmade European comforters with four fluffy pillows adorned each bed, adding a cozy touch.

The rooms also serve as a showcase for Kohler Company bathroom fixtures. Mine had an expansive whirlpool bath; that's where I enjoyed champagne and a shrimp cocktail.

Some have four-poster brass canopies over huge marble-lined whirlpool baths. Special suites contain a ☞ sauna-like environmental enclosure with a pushbutton choice of weather—from bright sun and gentle breezes to misty rain showers.

The inn's showcase restaurant is The Immigrant, where I dined on a gourmet meal of smoked Irish salmon. The wine list was impressive, too. For dessert, I walked to the Greenhouse, in the courtyard. This ☞ antique English solarium is a perfect spot for chocolate torte and other Viennese delights.

How to get there: From Chicago, take I–94 north and continue north on I–43, just outside of Milwaukee. Exit on Wisconsin 23 west (exit 53B). Take 23 to County Trunk Y and continue south into Kohler. The inn is on the right.

From the west, take I–94 south to Wisconsin 21 and go east to U.S. 41. Go south on 41 to Wisconsin 23; then head east into Kohler.

B: *I love River Wildlife's charming backwoods cabin—just sitting in front of the huge stone hearth sipping an exotic drink. The restaurant here even serves buffalo steaks.*

The Collins House
Madison, Wisconsin
53703

Innkeepers: Barb and Mike Pratzel
Address/Telephone: 704 East Gorham Street; (608) 255–4230
Rooms: 4 suites; 2 with sitting rooms. All with private bath.
Rates: $55 to $75. Includes light breakfast on weekdays, full breakfast on weekends and holidays. Children and pets OK.
Open: All year.
Facilities & Activities: Inn located on shoreline, with neighboring beach. Madison is state capital: art museums, galleries, theater, ethnic restaurants, specialty shops. University of Wisconsin main campus here, with major arts, sports, and entertainment activities.

Barb had just finished her latest baking binge as I stepped in the door. "It's a compulsion," she joked. Lucky for me and other guests who reap the considerable benefits of her "compulsion." I literally devoured delicious chocolate marzipan bars that were still warm from the oven.

This landmark turn-of-the-century inn features the ☞ distinctive architecture of the Prairie School made famous by Frank Lloyd Wright. And it hugs Lake Mendota, boasting striking views of its glistening waters.

I loved the open interiors and natural woods, all characteristic of Wright's designs of simple lines and open spaces. Mike was stoking a fire in the living room graced with ☛ striking mahogany woodwork while we tried to decide which classic movie to watch from their video library. (I wonder if Barb caught her baking bent from Mike; his family owned a large bakery in the St. Louis area.)

The guest rooms are very spacious and are decorated with period furniture. Some have ☛ bay windows that overlook the shoreline of the white-capped lake; others boast leaded glass that peers out at the historic "Old Market Place" neighborhood.

I stayed in the largest suite, the Claude and Stark, named after the house's architects. The arched entryway is a nice touch, and its separate sitting room comes complete with a claret-colored fainting couch.

Barb's home-baked breads and scrumptious pastries, juice, and coffee are the breakfast fare; on weekends and holidays, she serves a full breakfast of eggs, bacon, and more.

For dinner, I drove to the nearby Fess Hotel restaurant located in an historic Victorian building with high ceilings and long hallways. The food was excellent; my roast duckling with brown sauce and Montmorency cherries was delicious. Other tempting dishes were fancy *crêpes aux fruits de mer* and hearty Midwestern fare like Iowa pork chops.

How to get there: In Madison, proceed to the state capitol plaza and go east on East Washington Street to North Blount Street; then turn left. The inn is at the intersection of Blount and East Gorham streets.

Mansion Hill Inn
Madison, Wisconsin
53703

Innkeeper: Michael McInnis, manager
Address/Telephone: 424 North Pinckney Street; (608) 255–3999
Rooms: 10; all with private bath, including 3 suites.
Rates: $70 to $170 double occupancy. Includes continental breakfast. Two-night minimum on holidays and football weekends. No children under 12. Wheelchair access.
Open: All year.
Facilities & Activities: The Mansion Hill Historic District invites touring, especially among floral displays of nearby Period Garden Park. Madison is state capital; many fine ethnic restaurants, specialty shops, art galleries, recitals, theaters, nightclubs. Also University of Wisconsin main campus nearby. Swimming, fishing, boating in surrounding lakes.

What an extraordinary inn! I knew it would be special as soon as a tuxedo-clad manservant opened a tall door, graced with elegantly stenciled glass, to officially greet me.

This 1858 building is an architectural showplace. Its fine construction materials include ☛ white sandstone from the cliffs of the Mississippi, Carrara marble from Italy, and ornamental cast iron from Sweden. The original owner imported old-world artisans to do all the construction work. It shows.

Nearly two million dollars has been spent to restore the mansion to its former magnificence. I love the handsome arched windows and French doors that let the sunlight spill in. Hand-carved white marble fireplaces blaze with warmth, and a 🖝 spectacular spiral staircase winds four floors up to the belvedere, which provides a panoramic view of the city.

All the rooms are exquisitely furnished in beautiful antiques—some of the finest I have ever seen. I was lucky to stay in the McDonnell Room, which evokes a bold Empire atmosphere. I felt like royalty in these surroundings: arched windows, French doors, a large crystal chandelier, and an incredible 🖝 10-foot-tall tester (canopy) bed that one might find in the sleeping quarters of the Prince of Wales.

It also had an oval whirlpool tub, where I soaked in the swirling hot waters with a set of tub-side stereo headphones clamped on my ears.

Another extraordinary room has 🖝 floor-to-ceiling bookcases with a hidden door opening into an incredible bathroom with arched windows, classical Greek Revival columns, and a huge marble tub.

Afternoon tea is "veddy English." I sampled scones and delicate fruit pastries served by tuxedo-clad butlers, who always seem to be around ready to serve you. You can also dine on gourmet meals, which are specially arranged on request. Why, the innkeeper will even order you a pizza and deliver it to your room.

How to get there: From Milwaukee, take I–94 west to Madison. Exit west on Wisconsin 30 to Wisconsin 113. Go south to Johnson; then west to Baldwin. Turn south on Baldwin to East Washington, and then turn west toward the capitol building. At Pinckney Street, turn north. The inn is on the corner of Pinckney and Gilman.

B: *"Too much is not enough" is the inn maxim.*

Marybrooke Inn
Oshkosh, Wisconsin
54901

Innkeepers: Mary and Brooke Rolston
Address/Telephone: 705 West New York Avenue; (414) 426–4761
Rooms: 4; with 2 shared baths.
Rates: $40 single, $45 double. Includes full breakfast. Children
   over 12 welcome. No credit cards. No smoking.
Open: All year.
Facilities & Activities: Near Experimental Aircraft Association Mu-
   seum and spectacular annual airshow that draws almost half a
   million people. Also near Payne Art Center and Arboretum,
   OshKosh clothing outlet store, Oshkosh Symphony and Uni-
   versity theater, swimming, golf, tennis, riverboat cruises.

Mary and Brooke were high on a scaffold applying a coat
of Williamsburg-blue paint to the exterior of their inn. "I like
the color," I shouted up.

"Wanna grab a brush and climb up here?" they replied.

This lovely turn-of-the-century home is located on a residential street just a mile from Lake Winnebago. Both innkeepers contributed to the interior decorating. Mary did
cross-stitching—including the likeness of the inn logo hang-

ing in the entryway—and handmade the comforters and quilts that adorn guest-room beds. Brooke also made one of the quilts and the hooked rug hanging on the sitting room wall.

The sitting room not only is a comfortable resting spot, but also its antique armoire contains a wealth of area information: go (activity) guides, restaurant dinner menus, and much more.

I told Mary how much I admired the fancy lace fitted over a window in the dining room. "I picked that up in Amsterdam," she said. She also has a collection of bells from all over the world.

The upstairs guest rooms are furnished with well-appointed Wisconsin antiques, rich country prints, and handmade comforters; on chilly nights, electric blankets are a welcome modern amenity.

Mary's breakfast is a tasty delight, with cheese omelets, sausage and egg casseroles, home-baked banana and date breads, muffins, and beverages. The innkeepers can recommend a good restaurant to match your dinner tastes.

What a way to start the day!

How to get there: From Milwaukee, take U.S. 41 north to Oshkosh and exit at U.S. 41 Business, which goes south to New York Avenue. Turn right; the inn's at the intersection of New York and Cherry.

☼

B: *You're in for a real treat when Mary serves up her special baked-apple pancakes for a morning surprise.*

Tiffany Inn
Oshkosh, Wisconsin
54901

Innkeeper: Linda Anderson
Address/Telephone: 206 Algoma Boulevard; (414) 426–1000
Rooms: 12, with 5 suites; all with private bath.
Rates: $40 to $80. Includes continental breakfast. No children.
  Wheelchair access.
Open: All year.
Facilities & Activities: Guest enjoy large living and dining rooms,
  library. Inn has access to 2 private clubs, including a wildlife
  preserve. Near the Experimental Aircraft Association museum,
  where mid-summer air show draws nearly half a million spec-
  tators each year. Close to OshKosh clothing outlet store. Riverboat cruises on Lake Winnebago in paddle-wheeler.

  Exquisite charm! That's the best way to describe the
Tiffany Inn, an elegant Victorian home graced with manicured grounds, tall trees, and a wonderfully colorful flower
garden for summer guests.
  Linda told me that the 1906 home has had quite a
checkered history, including a stint as a fraternity house for
the local university. What's amazing is that the ☞ beautiful

leaded windows withstood the ravages of wild toga parties. ("An act of God, no doubt about it," Linda said with a chuckle.)

Both the main mansion and the carriage house have rooms named for their decorating themes. The Plantation Suite boasts antebellum-style furnishings, with a ☞ pre–Civil War piano converted into a writing desk, and a walnut dresser set. It has a sitting room and an especially nice walk-in shower.

Sea Mist is fashioned like the office of a ship's captain. Linda said the ☞ ship's wheel displayed here is the "largest ever found in the state." There's also a brass diving helmet and other nautical artifacts.

The Gandy Dancer is another charmer, its railroad theme highlighted by a large pewter locomotive.

An especially attractive room in the carriage house is the Parsonage. Front windows look out at the signed Tiffany window gracing the Episcopal church across the street. It's subtly illuminated at night, producing a warm, ethereal feeling. Windows out back look over the old Presbyterian church, another architecturally attractive structure.

The inn also boasts beautiful woodwork, a manteled fireplace surrounded by high-back chairs (a great place for serious book reading on a cold winter night), beamed ceilings, an old-fashioned chrome stove, and Tiffany-style lamps. The list is almost endless.

Linda serves a continental breakfast of fresh fruit, croissants, pastries, juice, and beverages. She will deliver the meal to your room if you're staying in the main house.

How to get there: Approach Oshkosh either from the south (Chicago) or north (Green Bay) on Highway 41. Exit on Ninth Avenue and turn east. Count five stoplights, including the one at Highway 41, and you'll come to South Main Street. Turn left and go across the Fox River bridge to the fourth stoplight. That's Algoma Boulevard. Turn west two blocks to the inn at Algoma and Division.

☒

B: *By special inn arrangement, you can dine at a wildlife preserve, where deer, Canada geese, and other kinds of critters might press their noses up against the restaurant windows lined with dinner tables.*

52 Stafford
Plymouth, Wisconsin
53073

Innkeeper: Cary O'Dwanny
Address/Telephone: P.O. Box 565, 52 Stafford Street; (414) 893–0552
Rooms: 20; all with private bath.
Rates: $49 to $65. Includes continental breakfast. Two-night minimums on Road America race weekends. Children OK. Wheelchair access.
Open: All year.
Facilities & Activities: Irish folk singer/entertainment in bar. Nearby: Road America in Elkhart Lake, state parks with hiking and nature trails, cross-country skiing (in season), Old Wade historic site, swimming and fishing at local lakes, charter fishing on Lake Michigan.

Cary has created a little bit o' Ireland in the middle of cheese country: 52 Stafford, an "authentic" Irish country house complete with imported European appointments, classy guest rooms, and Guinness Stout on tap.

"I wanted the feeling of casual elegance," Cary told me as we shared a pint of bitters, "where you could feel at home in blue jeans or a tuxedo.

"I also decided to use only the finest materials when decorating the inn," he said, pointing out some examples. First-floor 🖙 hardwoods are all solid cherry, with crown moldings and solid brass chandeliers (weighing eighty pounds apiece!) adding classical touches.

He 🖙 handpicked the yarn colors for the handmade floral carpet imported from England that graces the inn. Much of the leaded glass comes from West Germany. 🖙 Chinese silk adorns lobby wing chairs.

There are also marble-topped tables and flower stands done in handsome Italian marble. And the hand-embossed, hand-painted green wall coverings were made in California.

The bar is imposing. It's solid cherry, stretching almost to the ceiling. Green and white tiles cover the footrest. Then there's beautiful 🖙 hand-sandblasted etched glass, with deep relief designs of harps and wreaths done by a local craftsman. Cary turned the lights down low. The glass gave off a lilting greenish glow.

All rooms are individually decorated. Mine had a handsome English four-poster bed and "fox hunt" wall prints, tall shuttered windows, crown ceiling moldings, and an elegant brass chandelier.

Another special inn feature is a first-floor antique leaded-glass window—*above* a fireplace. It has 🖙 more than four hundred jewels and beads in it, with a flue that must swing to the left, around the window.

Cary's continental breakfast includes homemade pastries and coffeecakes, juice, and beverages. He'll recommend full-service restaurants a short drive away; one of my favorites is the dining room at the American Club's Sports Core in Kohler, which serves up delicious chicken or beef *fajitas* among its selections.

How to get there: From Milwaukee, take I–43 north, switching to Wisconsin 57 just past Grafton. At Wisconsin 23, turn west and drive into Plymouth. At Stafford Street, turn south. The inn is on the right side of the street.

⧗

B: 52 *Stafford's St. Patrick's Day celebration lasts five full days, with a semiannual St. Pat's bash in August.*

Jamieson House
Poynette, Wisconsin
53955

Innkeepers: Jim and Carole Gacek
Address/Telephone: 407 North Franklin Avenue; (608) 635–4100
Rooms: 10, with 7 suites; 9 with private bath.
Rates: $73.50 double, $84 suites, $105 deluxe suites. Includes continental-plus breakfast. Dinner in formal dining rooms nightly except Monday, Tuesday; in Rumors, restaurant on premises, nightly except Sunday and major holidays. Children not recommended. Well-behaved pets allowed. This is largely a no-smoking inn.
Open: All year.
Facilities & Activities: Six miles from Lake Wisconsin and boating, fishing, swimming. Great antiquing, with local guide map in each inn room. Nearby is MacKenzie Environmental Center, with 6 self-guiding trails, conservation workshops, arboretum, and pheasant state game farm. Madison, the state capital, is only a 25-minute drive away: art galleries, museums, specialty shops.

My wife and I arrived here at dinner time. The 1879 Victorian home was awash in soft golden lights; that foreshadowed the romantic evening about to begin.

Jim, tuxedo-clad, personally greeted us, as he did each table of diners who had come to experience a sumptuous six-course Victorian feast. Three small dining rooms, elegantly furnished with antiques, high brass chandeliers, and porcelain and sterling tableware, set an intimate mood—so did the ☛ single tall candle that flickered on every table and the soothing madrigal music in the background.

Jim softly recited the evening's special menu choices. We started with wonderful watercress-leek soup, oysters Rockefeller, and champagne sorbet to clean the palate.

Our main course was a succulent chicken *béarnaise* with delicate *pommes de terre dauphine* (potato puffs), followed by an endive salad.

After we finished the salad course, a waitress led us into the ☛ Garden Room—a long enclosed porch done up in rattan and wrought-iron tables—for dessert. We ogled the entire tray of goodies but came to our senses and had a light hazelnut cake.

Then it was downstairs to Rumors, where we enjoyed a nightcap in the Art Deco–style lounge that also serves light dinner fare.

Our room was across the street in an 1883 Victorian house that belonged to Jamieson's son. All the rooms and suites are spacious; ours had a carved walnut headboard on the bed, marble-topped dressers, and a red velvet couch. Some rooms feature a ☛ sybaritic touch—sunken whirlpool baths surrounded by mirrors, with private bar and wood-burning stove.

The next morning, it was back to the Garden Room for a breakfast of Carole's delicious oatmeal pancakes and fresh fruit. We left very happy and hungry—to return again.

How to get there: From Chicago or Milwaukee, take I–90/94 past Madison to the Poynette/County CS exit. Follow that into town, where it turns into Main Street. Continue to Hudson; turn right and follow to the end of block. Park on the left, next to the inn.

B: *I never expected to find quality gourmet dining in a small town that's tucked away in the middle of dairy-farm country.*

Renaissance Inn
Sister Bay, Wisconsin
54234

Innkeepers: John and JoDee Faller
Address/Telephone: 414 Maple Drive; (414) 854–5107
Rooms: 6; all with private bath.
Rates: $50 single, $55 double, $70 for Room #3, triple occupancy.
   Includes 5-course breakfast. Two-night minimum on week-
   ends. Special winter packages that include all meals. Children
   14 or older OK if accompanied by parents. Wheelchair access.
Open: Closed November and December and from March 15 to third
   week of April.
Facilities & Activities: Within walking distance of numerous art
   galleries, antique, craft, and specialty shops. Charter fishing,
   swimming, golfing nearby.

   John is a professional chef who has run kitchens for fine
hotels in Minnesota and Wisconsin. So when he and JoDee
opened the inn during the summer of 1983, they decided
that their restaurant would be something really intimate and
special.

   A ☛ Cajun seafood restaurant at the tip of northeastern

290

Wisconsin certainly is different. (He started serving these delicious dishes long before the current Creole craze.) Exquisite service and masterful seafood creations are provided in softly lit dining rooms—a romantically intimate notion.

JoDee has fashioned the main dining room into a showplace of quiet country elegance, from the simple pink-and-white table linens and fresh flowers to the soothing classical music that washes over the room. I like the ceramic lighthouses that cast candlelight over each table; they were made by a local craftsman in nearby Gills Rock, where he operates a great stoneware studio.

John's menu treats include Blackened Sea Bass, cooked in a cast-iron skillet and dredged in spices—true Cajun style. Louisiana Style Barbecued Shrimp features jumbo prawns marinated in tangy herbs and spices.

Of course, "regular fare" includes oysters, clams, steamed crab legs, and the catch of the day. There's charred prime rib for meat eaters.

The turn-of-the-century inn is tucked into a residential side street off a road that stretches the length of beautiful Door County peninsula, a Midwestern Cape Cod. It's had a colorful history: butcher shop, boarding house—even a bait-and-tackle shop for all the nearby fishing.

Six small guest rooms occupy the second floor, and JoDee has adorned them with antique European and American furniture and a smattering of Renaissance-era art reproductions. There's a high-back reading chair and TV in a tiny parlor.

Mornings at the inn make my mouth water. A fruit plate is followed by JoDee's delicious quiches, vegetables and potatoes, a selection of her freshly home-baked goodies, and juice and coffee.

How to get there: From Milwaukee, take Wisconsin 42 north to Maple Drive; then go west one block to the inn.

B: *The Door County peninsula is an absolute wonderland of natural beauty, colorful harbor towns, and creative craftspeople.*

Bay Shore Inn
Sturgeon Bay, Wisconsin
54235

Innkeepers: John "Duke" Hanson and Paul Mathias
Address/Telephone: 4205 North Bay Shore Drive; (414) 743–4551
Rooms: 29 in main lodge, with 1 suite; rooms also available in beach and ranch terraces, A-frame chalets, and 1 cottage; all with private bath.
Rates: Main lodge $39 to $49 single, $49 to $69 double, $45 to $75 suite; A-frames $53 to $95 double; cottage $43 to $90. (Rates change three times during season.) Two-night minimum on weekends. Children welcome. Some rooms can accommodate wheelchair guests, but the inn has no special wheelchair facilities.
Open: Mother's Day through third weekend in October.
Facilities & Activities: Rowboats, sailboat rides on 22-foot sloop, mini-fish sailboats and instruction, canoes, and pontoons. Tennis court, basketball, croquet, horseshoes. Nature trails on 20 acres. Children's playground and safe beach. Bikes. Fishing. State parks and maritime museum nearby.

The Bayshore Inn is a lot like a favorite uncle's country cottage: friendly, warm, and homey.

Paul, the inn's chef, said that the land is part of a mid-

1800s homestead begun by an immigrant sailing captain, Jacob Hanson, who settled here on Door County's rugged western shore—amid tall trees, bays, and bluffs—because it reminded him of home.

His wife, Matilda, began serving food to summer vacationers, using cherished Swedish and Norwegian recipes. (Paul still uses them to create the inn's renowned butter-fried chicken.) An historic ☛ apple orchard out back, along with a vegetable farm, continues to supply the inn with garden delights.

The rustic main lodge was built in 1921. I love the ☛ massive stone fireplace that stretches to the ceiling; it's a favorite gathering spot when the weather turns crisp. Nine small upstairs rooms are cozy and cute, with early-American wallpaper, lacy table runners and wicker furniture.

Paul is so proud of the ☛ Bay Shore Inn's historic recipes that he publishes its own recipe book. In The Garden Seat, you'll taste some of this hearty food. For breakfast, try some fresh tangy lingonberries served on Swedish pancakes. Hot, home-cooked oatmeal is a good stick-to-your-ribs choice. There are also lots of homemade breads, jellies, and special sweets like cinnamon-swirl loaf and Elizabeth's Swedish Ginger Cookies. (Elizabeth is Matilda's daughter.)

Dinner offers wholesome country fare: baked stuffed pork chops, roast fresh chicken, and a hearty chicken-and-dumpling soup—an inn specialty.

You shouldn't miss Paul's ☛ Door County fish boil, held during weeknights in July and August and on Saturday evenings in June, September, and October. This reservation-only feast of whitefish, potatoes, and vegetables is boiled in a huge, fiery cauldron outside the dining room on the beach. It's great fun to watch the flames lick the sky.

How to get there: In Sturgeon Bay, take the Route 42/57 bypass to Gordon Road. Turn west and continue to Bay Shore Drive (3rd Avenue). Then turn north until you reach the inn, located on the shoreline.

B: *A great family-oriented country inn. You'll never run out of fun things to do.*

White Lace Inn
Sturgeon Bay, Wisconsin
54235

Innkeepers: Dennis and Bonnie Statz
Address/Telephone: 16 North Fifth Avenue; (414) 743–1105
Rooms: 11 in 2 houses; all with private bath.
Rates: $52 to $69. Includes continental breakfast. Special winter
packages. Children not recommended. Wheelchair access.
Open: All year.
Facilities & Activities: Five blocks to bay shore. Close to specialty
and antique shops, restaurants, Door County Museum, Miller
Art Center. Also swimming, tennis, and horseback riding
nearby. Short drive to Whitefish Dunes and Potawatomi state
parks, Peninsula Players Summer Theater, Birch Creek Music
Festival. Cross-country skiing and ice skating in winter.

Bonnie and Dennis call their inn "a romantic fireside
getaway." I can't think of a better place to spend a cozy weekend for two.

The Main House was built for a local lawyer in 1903;
what's surprising is the extensive hand-carved oak woodwork
throughout the house for a man of such modest means.
Stepping into the entryway, I was surrounded by ☛ magnificent hand-carved oak paneling.

Bonnie, who has a degree in interior design, has created a warm feeling in the guest rooms, mixing ☛ Laura Ashley wallpaper and fabrics with imposing yet comfortable antique furnishings—rich Oriental rugs, high-back walnut beds, and canopy beds. ☛ Fluffy down pillows, handmade comforters, and quilts brighten large beds, and lacy curtains adorn tall windows.

The rooms in the 1880 Garden House have their own fireplaces and are furnished in a myriad of styles ranging from simple yet elegant country pieces to bold, oversized Empire furniture.

The fireplace in the sitting room of the Main House is always crackling with warmth during cool weather. Dennis said to be prepared for hot and heavy games of Trivial Pursuit. "Or just come down to enjoy the company," he added.

Bonnie's handmade muffins are the breakfast treat, served with juice and coffee. I love eating in front of a fire early in the morning; it's a great time to swap Door County stories. For dinner, the innkeepers will recommend a restaurant that suits your tastes.

How to get there: From Milwaukee, take Wisconsin 42 north and exit at Business 42/51 into Sturgeon Bay; cross the bridge into downtown and you'll be on Michigan Street. Follow Michigan to Fifth Avenue and turn left. White Lace Inn is on the right side of the street.

Or you can take the Business 42/51 bypass across the new bridge to Michigan Street. Turn left on Michigan; go to Fifth Avenue and take a right on Fifth to the inn.

Rosenberry Inn
Wausau, Wisconsin
54401

Innkeepers: Jerold, Patricia, and Doug Artz
Address/Telephone: 511 Franklin Street; (715) 842–5733
Rooms: 8; all with private bath.
Rates: $40 single, $45 double. Includes continental breakfast. Children OK.
Open: All year.
Facilities & Activities: Walking distance to downtown Wausau and the Mall, Washington Square shopping complex, antique shops, boutiques, restaurants, and the renowned Leigh Yawkey Woodson Art Museum. A short drive to the Dells of Eau Claire, with nature trails, rock climbing, rappelling, fishing, and canoeing. Five miles away from Rib Mountain for winter skiing, with many additional cross-country ski trails nearby.

I have just arrived at the Rosenberry Inn on an early weekend morning. Inside on the guest-book stand rests a cowbell to alert the innkeepers of new arrivals.

It's library quiet in the house. I just know I'll wake the entire place if I ring that bell, and I don't want a guilty conscience—especially on a Sunday morning.

Oh, what the heck. *Cllaaannnngggggg!*

A smiling Jerry came down the stairs. "Well, well—we've been waiting for you." Let's say that I was relieved.

Jerry, Pat, and Doug worked endlessly to rescue this wonderful house from ruin and restore it to its early-1900s splendor. There's rich woodwork everywhere. ☞ Leaded and stained glass cast prisms of light on the stairwell. Antique photographs and prints add to the bygone-era feeling.

"We've named all the guest rooms after relatives we cherish," Pat said. All the rooms are graced with Victorian antiques and some country primitives; four have fireplaces.

In the rose-colored Agnes room, I like the iron-rail beds and the working fireplace—good to take away the winter chill after a day of skiing at Rib Mountain nearby. Leona has ☞ antique Victorian bedspreads, homemade comforters, and a fireplace that transforms the room into a cozy retreat.

My favorite is John, with its pressed-tin ceiling, fireplace, and ☞ collection of *bierhaus* steins.

Pat created the charming apple-design stencils on the walls of the third-floor card room. It's also filled with cheery country crafts.

I like eating breakfast (juice, Pat's home-baked banana bread, muffins, and coffee) up in the old attic, now cheerily decorated with ☞ wall stencils of farm animals, along with antique tables and chairs. The White Horse Inn is a good dinner bet; it's just a short drive downtown. Choices include steaks, pan-fried chicken with fettuccine, and additional nightly specials.

How to get there: From Milwaukee, take I–94 west to U.S. 51 and head north until you reach Wausau. At Highway 52, go east to Franklin Street and turn left to the inn.

Westby House
Westby, Wisconsin
54667

Innkeepers: Elizabeth Benjamin and Phillip and Annette Park
Address/Telephone: 200 West State Street; (608) 634–4112
Rooms: 3, with 1 suite; 1 private bath, and 1 shared bath.
Rates: $38 to $52. Includes continental breakfast. Children OK.
Open: All year.
Facilities & Activities: Full-service restaurant. Short walk to specialty stores and antique shops. In Wisconsin Amish country, with quaint back-road exploring. Winter cross-country skiing, major ski-jump park and training site. Town celebrates many Norwegian holidays.

This charming Queen Anne–style inn, located in a fun Norwegian community, is a Westby landmark. The eighteen-room mansion, built in the 1890s, has all the usual special Victorian touches: a ☞ tall tower, stained-glass windows, gingerbread finery, and elegant interior woodwork.

I saw a 1915 photograph of the house in the hallway. Doesn't look as though it's changed much since then. Lucky for me—and you, too.

The elegant chandeliers with cranberry-colored shades

cast a rose-tinted glow. The 🖛 antique Amish quilts hanging on walls make an attractive backdrop.

To reach the second-floor guest rooms, I walked up a long staircase. I came to a small sitting room that displays more handmade Amish quilts and other collectibles for sale. My favorite was a blue star-point quilt that begged me to take it home.

The old butler's pantry is between the sitting room and the guest-room hallway. It's fun to imagine servants scurrying about up here, preparing breakfast for the turn-of-the-century household.

The guest rooms are small-town charming. The spacious Anniversary Suite has a large brass bed, lacy curtains on windows, and a Victorian fainting couch and chair; it's my favorite.

There are two white iron-rail beds in the Greenbriar Room. And the Squire Room has cheery country accents like eyelet lace curtains, and more.

Downstairs, the busy Victorian dining room draws people from all over town for its delicious, hearty food. I sat in front of a manteled fireplace, at an antique table complete with bentwood chairs, and devoured my lunch: a hot crab-meat sandwich with tomato slices and jack cheese. Dinner also looked pretty inviting, with choices like a nine-ounce center-cut pork chop smothered in sour cream gravy, and ham steak served with Dijon mustard and homemade applesauce.

I suggest that you try the 🖛 *torsk,* an inn specialty. It's eight ounces of Norwegian cod baked in lemon butter and served with egg noodles.

How to get there: From LaCrosse, take U.S. 14/61 southeast into Westby. The inn is located right at the corner of 14/61 and West State Street.

B: *Westby's Olympic-style ski jump draws top athletes to its winter competitions every year. It's a great time to enjoy the Westby House hospitality.*

Wolf River Lodge
White Lake, Wisconsin
54491

Innkeeper: James Peters, manager
Address/Telephone: White Lake; (715) 882–2182 or 882–3982
Rooms: 9, with 1 suite; 1 room with private bath.
Rates: $78.50 double occupancy. Includes breakfast and dinner.
  Most reservations are made through week-long or weekend
  package rates: winter ski season (Christmas season to mid-
  March), $125 per person/3 days, 2 nights; spring, summer,
  fall, $115/3 days, 2 nights; packages include 3 meals Saturday,
  2 meals Sunday. Children welcome.
Open: Mid-April to October 1; Christmas to March 1.
Facilities & Activities: Full-service dining room, bar, wine cellar,
  parlor and game rooms, outdoor hot tub. Located on Wolf
  River, with world-class white-water rapids during high-water
  periods. River is always runnable, April through October. Excellent trout fishing May and June. Ideal terrain for cross-
  country skiing.

I enjoy things that are different. That's why I like the
Wolf River Lodge.
Where else could I find ☞ world-class white-water rap-
ids, kayak instruction, and a trout-fishing and fly-casting

school ... in a spot where eagle and osprey soar overhead and roadsides are smothered by early summer wildflowers?

This rustic lodge is a center for river rafting on the Wolf River. In the majestic Nicolet National Forest country, frothing white-water rapids tumble over boulders and ledges, dropping twelve feet per mile for twenty-five miles! The crystal-clear water is often icy cold.

The log lodge is surrounded by tall trees and teeming wilderness. A large dining room is very rustic, with exposed logs, long oak dining and tavern tables, and solid fare.

A cozy sitting room with a crazy-quilt arrangement of chairs and sofas is a favorite guest gathering spot—the ☞ large stone fireplace is the reason. Some relax here after a long day of cross-country skiing; others just watch the glow of the fire.

I browsed through piles of books sitting on a large coffee table. Naturally, lots of them give tips on white-water rafting, canoeing, and kayaking. My favorite was a surfing handbook.

The guest rooms are small but cozy, with pine furniture and country finery. I like the ☞ brightly colored quilts and braided rugs that add color to the rustic charm.

Dinners are simple but delicious. Breakfast means a morning treat: the lodge's renowned crêpes. Most evening meals feature delectable trout, delicious roast duck, and thick, juicy steaks.

How to get there: From Milwaukee, take I–43 north to Green Bay; then take U.S. 41/141 north to Wisconsin 64. Head west to White Lake. Turn north on Wisconsin 55 and then watch for the Wolf River Lodge signs that direct you there.

Indexes

Alphabetical Index to Inns

Inns with Full-Service Restaurants

Bed and Breakfast Inns
(Serve Breakfast Only)

Island Inns

Riverside Inns

Inns near Lakes

Inns with Swimming Pools

Inns near Downhill or Cross-Country Skiing

Children Welcome

Pets Welcome

Historic Hotels

Historic-Town Inns

Rustic Inns

Romantic Inns